ROME

ROME

The First Book of Foundations

Michel Serres

(translated by Randolph Burks)

Bloomsbury Academic
An imprint of Bloomsbury Publishing Plc

B L O O M S B U R Y
LONDON • NEW DELHI • NEW YORK • SYDNEY

Bloomsbury Academic
An imprint of Bloomsbury Publishing Plc

50 Bedford Square	1385 Broadway
London	New York
WC1B 3DP	NY 10018
UK	USA

www.bloomsbury.com

BLOOMSBURY and the Diana logo are trademarks of Bloomsbury Publishing Plc

First published in English 2015

Originally published in French as *Rome: Le livre des fondations* © Société Editions Grasset et Fasquelle, Paris 1983

All rights reserved and controlled by Société Editions Grasset et Fasquelle

English language translation © Bloomsbury Publishing Plc

British Library Cataloguing-in-Publication Data
A catalogue record for this book is available from the British Library.

ISBN: HB: 978-1-47259-015-2
ePDF: 978-1-47259-017-6
ePub: 978-1-47259-016-9

Library of Congress Cataloging-in-Publication Data
A catalog record for this book is available from the Library of Congress.

Typeset by Fakenham Prepress Solutions, Fakenham, Norfolk NR21 8NN
Printed and bound in Great Britain

With the present book and, if my life isn't too hard, with some others to follow, I express my gratitude to the community of historians that welcomed me thirteen years ago when the pressure group then in power expelled me from my former paradise: philosophy. Thereby making my life hard.

With this same book, I thank René Girard, who, in similar circumstances, welcomed me, a quasi-refugee, into the hospitable America and who then taught me the true ideas developed here.

CONTENTS

The shaking that grips me upon starting a book on history isn't from fear; I'm not afraid. And yet, here, terror reigns, murder, blood and tears, constant iniquity. I know that we never encounter any social system that's just; I've rarely known, living or dead, any powerful man who was good. The shaking gripping me is not from fear; it is, if I may, from logic. It would be an exercise in futility if a philosophy formed from its instauration by the rigorous and precise concepts of the sciences of the object brought its practices into the unstable cloud of time. It either wouldn't understand, or it would be formed with shaky outlines. History is fuzzy and vague, but it was precisely the sciences of the object that prepared me to think this shakiness with exactitude. So here I am on the terrain of terror, for the first time, finally ready, despite my anxiety. This century we have new tools. Here they are.

MICHEL SERRES

THE GREATNESS OF THE ROMANS: THE FABLE OF THE TERMITES

Sowing: geographical sites aren't subject to simple reasons. Islands, ports or coves, straits, coastal outlines, plains, valleys and relief are distributed without any apparent order. The Mediterranean seacoast is capricious; its recesses can't be predicted.

The ancient cities are sown sporadically along said coast (Tyre, Ephesus, Agrigentum, Pergamon, Alexandria) and not far from the coast (Troy or Sparta) in a long and not very wide band, according to geographical circumstance. At the outset, I'll give myself the sowing of the ancient cities in space and, for the moment, outside time. I'll assume ignorance at this moment of how things are with time. Antiquity shows us a set of cities that's fairly dense by the sea, disordered like the Sporades in the sea, and sparser as one gets farther away from the sea. Hittite or Semite cities, Etruscan or Ionian, Sicilian, Greek, Massiliote cities. The ancient city was for a long time a concept; it was a type and even an ideal; it's time to see it simply as a set.

Let's take a colony of termites, whose apparently Brownian motion at this moment will seem, long after, to have been ordered for the construction of a termite hill. This latter is a gigantic work in relation to the size of the individuals; it's a fairly regular work in relation to the disorder of their comings and goings.

Each termite, or almost, is carrying a ball of clay, let's say. It doesn't take it anywhere; it puts it down in the space considered. Said space is nothing but the set of the placed balls. The termites withdraw and return to the clay pit. The balls placed here are distributed sporadically. They form a sowing.

The ancient cities are thus sown in or by the geography.

Their set is a non-standardized multiplicity. Each city is very different, and we don't know very well where this set ends. Near the Parthians, the Germans, Mauritania, Dacia? It's of no matter.

It happens, it can happen, through some circumstance of some kind that two termites might put their clay balls down in the same vicinity, perhaps in the same place. This has an effect; one ball looks to be two times taller and bigger. The same circumstance can even happen, even more rarely, to three termites or four.

The termites leave and come back loaded with new clay balls. They don't take them anywhere; they put them down. They are going to place them, by preference, on the first taller, bigger ball. The effect of the latter is one of attraction.

Our reason dreams of reconciling Democritus and Newton, of weaving together stochastic sowing and the law of harmony, dark chance and clear necessity, order and dissemination.

The second wave of termites puts their balls down just anywhere, but a fairly reasonable number of them form double, triple and sometimes quadruple balls. The set is now made up of monads, but a subset of dyads appears, as well as a subset of triads, even less powerful, and so on.

The waves of termites never stop. They go in search of balls and come back to deposit them. The density of clay grows in this expanse; the probability of the appearance of double, triple and quadruple balls grows as well. The piles grow all the more by virtue of the fact that they are already voluminous: the attraction effect. As the waves bring in what they carry, large centres, like poles, form; sub-centres form, an entire constellation of dwarf, medium and supergiant balls.

The model, I repeat, is Democritean. It forms by set and by elements. Each individual, the carrying termite or rolled ball, seems to follow its own whim, is subject to crashes, encounters and in relation to the global work of the termite hill seems to fluctuate randomly. Local Brownian motion in a world subject to some strong global law. But the model, again, is quasi-Newtonian since a large ball seems to attract the carriers and has more chance of growing than a more exiguous ball. The model, in total, is a cloud, in the sense I have given this word in the past, but this cloud sown in a space has a tendency to organize itself under the impetus of said Newtonian law. Like mayonnaise when it sets.[1]

It can therefore happen that at a given moment a giant ball might attract a set of already large balls and that in total, this well might suddenly suck in all the workers: then the termite hill begins.

I'm sure that here and there, around, a few individuals will always continue to deposit balls on the ground while the Tower of Babel is being raised. These termites are the guardians of the possible. They sow the time of hope while laws and the repetitive are being solidified by the crystal next to them.

The ancient cities are disseminated, non-standardized, along the shores of the Mediterranean Sea. One sole law: they fight each other. One sole law of order: hatred. One sole rule of attraction: slaughter. Destruction, absorption. Rome levels Alba; it brings an entire population inside its walls. It also knows how to put the totality of the defeated to the sword. Geography orders the sowing; it's the Democritean order, the cloud that never stops, that has perhaps never begun, that – I have to hope – will never stop. Secondly, there is only need for one law, that law without origin, the hatred which never stops, always there, unforgettable, perhaps – alas – ineradicable. Rome, therefore, destroys Alba and grows.

One ball widens; this was called war or conquest, simple slaughter, collective butchery, sanctioned, sanctified by the texts of history; the ball absorbs its neighbour, and these enlargements fluctuate across time. Here is the cloud of small cities, and the subcloud that manufactures an empire, and the subcloud as well of great confederations, with quick or long lives; notice the parallel with what I just called dyad, triad, tetrade and so on as long as you please, pentade. The attraction, the power varies with the volume. This power is indeed a capacity to attract, to absorb, yes, to subsume the multiple. So the earth known to us is a constellated sky of balls – dwarf, medium, large, supergiant – within a tenuous scattering of very small towns. The fluctuations of this field create the time of history. One might say the history of the heavens.

Let's now consider a ball, a single one, a city, and the place where it was put down. It is small, it dies, devoured; Alba has just passed away, Alba disappears into the dust. Another one was narrow; it grows, lasts, stable, independent for a certain time, confederated, sometimes a satellite, the centre from which violence comes changing; it died, one day, medium-sized. Veii disappeared, with its inimitable language and culture; all of Etruria collapses. A hundred thousand small cities were seen, a thousand medium-sized cities were seen, each time distributed in a different and unstable manner; there are a hundred now; while the thousand others strive to last, nothing can stop the hundred that grow to power; they spread their violence over a part of the accessible space and quickly enough encounter their equivalent, face to face. The game of hegemony continues.

You see something like a fairly irregular cascade with fairly labile thresholds form, like a slack ladder of fuzzy subsets. The poorly defined roundness, variable, of the city-ball assures its attraction over a fairly indecisive space, moulding as well to the constraints of the locale, climate, geography, the singular expanse for each of the sites, as far as the ridges of the network of mutual impediment. Exchanges might also pass along the network. They don't change very much in the matter, for they very quickly define an analogous type of mutual impediment. The state of the fluctuating network appears to be complex; however it follows a simple law that's invariant across several avatars; economy is the continuation of war by other means. In the global network or the distribution of the set of cities, we can successively read the sub-networks of the large ones and the super-giant ones, etc. At the end of the cascade or the series of thresholds of size, we can conceive a unique threshold – this one decisive – beyond which there is no longer, in the network, any mutual impediment for whoever crosses it. The ball has taken on too much roundness for it to encounter any single volume in the game space that could impede it. The Latin ball absorbs Greece and no longer encounters anything but the immense African power. So Carthage must be destroyed. With this latter reduced to dust, everything changed dramatically, and the termite hill is founded. It will no longer have to do with anything except the frontier marches of the game space: Parthians, Celts, Barbarians, Huns, Turks, Goths and the others. Nothing resists the attraction of its volume any longer. The ball has become that in comparison with which no other ball has any weight.

If the time from a small state to a state that's almost as small can be very long, so long that it seems to define a state of equilibrium, it can clearly be brief, lightning fast, once past said size threshold; it can also be almost nil from the giant state to exclusively occupying the expanse considered here. Suddenly, unexpectedly, the termite hill is there; everyone is working in it. Almost unpredictable, yes, since space was saturated with noises, with singular, very disordered Brownian motions, in any case non-coordinated ones. Neither predictable from the initial state, nor completely readable through the retrograde movement of the true. Abruptly, as though by miracle, form emerges from the unformed; it rises quickly now, simple, total, it has recruited everything. Suddenly, the Roman Empire is founded. Suddenly: in the almost nil time where everything changes dramatically after the threshold. Suddenly: this time isn't quite long enough for the observer, as though dazzled by what seems a miracle to him, to grasp the solidification of the dissemination of origin. You might think Aphrodite, standing, born from the waves. Myth always says a bit more about things, from the good side of reason: the first Venus was quite exact.

To understand the formation of the master of the world Rome, we've only needed the on the whole natural circumstances called geographical: the shore of our sea and its occupation by disseminated cities. A non-standardized multiplicity, a cloud. As well as the martial rule of hatred – a simple and monotonic law – in its ordinary work. I admit that this rule can take on other appearances, like that of exchange; we shall have to think about that. We haven't needed anything other than Democritean distribution and an order said to be rational. We haven't needed anything other than their mixture. Another reason appears, ancient and new. Reason is not a law imposing itself on the illegal; it is not an order to which disorder must submit; that reason is pure hatred. Its true name is hatred and its final production is the monstrous, glaring bright god of hatred. Pure reason, pure hatred. Here is the work that the unity of redundancy and the non-standardized multiplicity have in common. I said in *Genesis* that their first encounter produced time. Reason is in this encounter and in this work, and unity can disappear into the cloud, as the multiple risks stiffening in repetition. The reason I'm invoking, ancient and new, is therefore triple: it is harmony, it is noise, it is their amalgam, their alloy, their moiré fusion, their crossing or cross-breeding, their musical temperament. A certain rationalism of old enjoyed eliminating, filtering out the multiple and confusion; it held a little less than a third of what it called the truth.

The multiple, crazy growth and the formation of form above this numerous bushing-out are formally described in the chain of *Genesis*. It's only a question here of an application.

You see a thousand slack seaweeds at the bottom of the water. Some grow quickly and immediately die, right from the infancy of their time. Others rise to adolescence, while still others grow and die children. The grown-up ones die young too. And all of a sudden one of them, sometimes, abruptly grows crazily and recruits everything. The essential thing to me seems to be for the diaspora or distribution all around the recruiting tower to endure. The essential thing to me seems to be for the tower to lose its crown, for the termite hill to lose.

The following text is, save a few exceptions, a continuous and free reading of Livy's first book. A few references are placed, when needed, at the beginning of the relevant section without resorting to footnotes for fear of rendering the sequence of words ugly from the numbers.[2]

PART ONE

THE BLACK AND THE WHITE: THE COVERING OVER

I BLACK BOX: THE TRAMPLED MULTIPLICITY

Livy 1.7

Romulus and Remus, abandoned Alban twins, suck at the dry breast of the she-wolf [*louve*]; I say dry because the Latin for she-wolf, *lupa*, indicates a whore, a brothel whore [*une putain de lupanar*]. False sons of a whore, true sons of a vestal and Mars, legendary, sons of violence and rape, sons of the god of war and a chaste and savage priestess, Romulus and Remus are also grandchildren of enemy brothers. Murder among brothers didn't begin today.

So Romulus kills Remus, and he founds Rome.

I want to recount that foundation; I want to know what it signifies; I want to understand this gesture and, perhaps, the city. I'm going to do it naively; I arrive at the Tiber's banks without ideas, without methods, without arms, alone.

Romulus kills Remus, and Rome was founded.

But before. Before this history and at about the same spot, a legend is recounted. One twin, Romulus, has just executed his twin, right here, and he is sacrificing. To Hercules in particular. Hercules had passed through there. Heracles, the twin of Iphicles, had killed Cacus there.[1] As though a murder always preceded a murder. As though one foundation weren't sufficient to truly begin. As though an origin required its origin.

No doubt we will never know if there's a single word of truth in all this, truth in the sense of naive history; no doubt we will never know whether myth, softly, came down to earth, the earth of phenomena. Did Livy know? Livy is hesitant; he recounts cautiously; he reports traditions. Do we know, after two millennia of study? So many people claim to be free of myth, all the while telling nothing but myths. But suddenly everything changes. From the beginning, from Aeneas' departure after the capture of Troy, it has been a question of Rome, of its founders and their long genealogy, and now here abruptly is a legend, here is a narrative within a narrative, well defined, like a cartouche in a painting, like a legend at the bottom of a map. It has been a question of men, Aeneas, Latinus, Romulus, and now here is a god, Hercules. It was an urban place; and now here is a pasture, meadow grass for cattle. Latin was being spoken, and now Greek is being spoken: Geryon, Cacus, Evander. Suddenly the proper names are Hellenic, and the atmosphere is divine.

Gods come before kings. A hero becomes a god in the spot where the twin becomes a king. Hercules mounts an altar, Romulus a throne. Romulus killed Remus, Hercules killed Cacus. Romulus risked his life in the battle to the death in the midst of the mob. Hercules risked his life in the crowd of shepherds from the vicinity, all come to help Cacus. Hercules was recognized to be a god, a son of a god by Evander; Romulus seeks recognition, he seeks legitimacy. The legend intervenes in the middle of the legendary narrative with a change of language, a change of register, tone, with a change of scale, state, space and time; you might say a metalanguage. A legend, in the map sense, is always written in a metalanguage. What is written in Latin is perhaps latent: hidden, coded, to be deciphered. This idea about Latin is not mine, it's traditional. And what if what was put in Greek was clear? And what if the Greek legend illuminated the Latin shadow? And what if history, difficult, found its philosophy here? Yes, legend indeed means: how to read what is to be read.

Well defined, cut out, standing out in the middle of said history, the legend, perhaps, deciphers its mechanisms. We have so often explained legend by history that we will be excused for risking the converse for once. We will be excused in thinking that the Herculean legend here resembles the *Homeric Hymn to Hermes* on many points. I'm in the habit of trusting Hermes. He is the god of codes and secrets.

Remus has just died, whether killed by his brother in the vicinity of the walls, on the other side of their outline, or whether struck down in the middle of the crowd, of the mob, passionately debating the subject of vultures. A dead man torn to pieces in the middle of the vultures.

Romulus, remaining alone, is sacrificing. But he is sacrificing to Hercules, among other Alban rites. Hercules comes into the Latin narrative as foreign. Foreign due to his Greekness, due to his warrior function during the reign of the first king. He has just dispatched Geryon during a triple combat and stolen his cattle, wonderfully beautiful. Tired, he rests in the thick grass. But while he is sleeping, Cacus, a shepherd from thereabouts, wants to steal his cattle and hide them in his cave. Livy seems unaware of Cacus' three heads, but that's of no importance. The latter, profiting from the night, leads the most beautiful of the animals into his cave, dragging them by the tail; in this way their tracks are only turned toward the outside. At dawn, Hercules, awake, looking for his cattle, is fooled by the stratagem: confused and uncertain, he prepares to leave the disquieting place. Right then, the remaining cattle of the herd low, and the cattle hidden in the cave low in response. Hercules returns, wields his club and beats Cacus to death. Evander, arriving, pardons this murder; the king recognizes the god and promises him a temple. End of the episode.

The tracks deceived Hercules, and the lowing undeceived him. The voices of the cattle brought him back along the path along which he was heading in the wrong direction. He sees the direction of the tracks, and he hears their absent origin.[2] He reads a text that makes him uncertain and confused; he hears sounds that bring him back to the place the tracks had chased him away from.

During that distant epoch a Greek, an émigré from the Peloponnesus, Evander, was governing the country through his personal influence. He was revered for his miraculous knowledge of writing and as the son of Carmenta, a goddess with the gift of prophecy. The cattle leave tracks before Evander's stylus; they low at dawn before Carmenta's cries. Evander is mortal, even though governing and wise, even though son of the prophetess who signifies; Hercules is going to enlarge the number of the gods. Evander knows letters; Hercules reads tracks. Evander speaks, interrogates; Hercules remains silent at first; he hears the voice of the cattle. Hercules' reading precedes Evander's; the god knows how to read a meaning that man did not put there. The hooves of the cattle, in the mud and dust, mark and preserve a meaning. It's a question of meaning [*sens*] and of direction [*sens*] in space. The cattle in the cave, Cacus' black box, let it be known that they are no longer there through the vestiges left behind, let it be known that they are there through sounds. The origin of meaning is there, and it is absent there. It is black: it is, it isn't. Well before Evander's writing, that of man, of the good man, of the historical man, accomplished because he writes, Hercules' sacred cattle left tracks and marks in space; before Evander's language, the brute cattle raise their voices. The first stamp on the soft ground, primary lowing in the thin air after the dawn, before man, by the animal, prehistory. Already meaning has happened; it comes straight out of the black box. Already nonsense blocks it, and forbids it from returning to the source.[3] Already voice calls back to meaning; it brings back to the origin: into the cave full of shadow where Cacus is murdered. From that shadowy mouth sequences surge up resembling the scarifications on the ground; from that source of mute shadow our memory wells. The animals' writing is already false; it doesn't say anything yet, and yet, already, it deceives. The animals' voices bring back to the origin and bring back to murder. To Hercules' murder of Cacus. Evander, writing, I mean the human, the historical, are never deceived: they set up an altar, a temple, at the murder site, the greatest of altars even, the Altar Maxima. And this was the first sacrifice, where the cattle were killed in Hercules' stead.

Taking auguries, before our first gesture, before the first word, before the first plough track in the space, in the soil of Rome, taking auguries, before men act, consists in recognizing sounds and tracks in places where we think only our tracks and sounds signify. It's to recognize with humility that there is meaning in the world before Evander writes there, before Carmenta cries out there. Before voice and writing, the cattle leave hoof tracks in the mud and dust; they low in the cave. Before men in cities, there are vulture flights. There is noise in the world before we raise our voices there, before the crowd makes its grumbling cries. Lightning writes its forked inclination in the sky; birds trace their flight there, in direction and meaning. There is meaning in space before the meaning that signifies. Taking auguries is believing in a world without men; inaugurating is paying homage to the real as such. Of course we can't say anything reasonable about it yet, but we can't do anything without drawing liberally from this original meaning. Inauguration is this prehistory.

What's incomprehensible is that this meaning, one day, became comprehensible. The physicist is an augur who succeeded.

The brute animal marks the ground with a *sens*: the direction that goes to the cave and the one that leaves it. When part of the herd lows, the lost part lows in response across the stone walls; the air, in the morning, is traversed with meaning. There is meaning, in the mud and wind, before a man comes from the Peloponnesus to create letters and repeat the cries of his mother; there is meaning in space, there is direction, there is the coming and the going, the downstream and upstream tracks, the flights of the Aventine and those of the Palatine; this meaning is inaugural. Only later do the brothers slit each other's throats. The world is there, full of vultures and animals at pasture before the murder, before human relations. There is first the *sens* of objects. Even the Albula goes toward the sea and can't go back to its source.

I don't know, Livy says, where going back to the origin or the foundation of Rome is going to lead me. I don't trust historians, lost written archives or oral traditions. The quellenforschung never ceases, goes back to Valerius Antias, to Claudius Quadrigarius, or to Fabius Pictor, to Cincius Alimentus and so on. Cattle hooves after cattle hooves, we never leave texts, and we turn our backs to the black origin. The written text brings me into the plain; the oral tradition calls me to the hill. The historian is Hercules and his thousand labours, his confusion and uncertainty. You who read me, don't think that the tracks all and always go in this direction; listen in the morning to the cattle lowing in the blackness. A disquieting search for sources or a quest for the original foundation.

The legend doesn't only tell of the hesitation, a little fearful, of the labourer; it seems to give something like an uncertain and confused theory of knowledge. At the sight of the false tracks, Hercules has mixed feelings; his mind is confused. He is disquieted, he gets ready to flee. What then is history? What is its beginning? What is a foundation? It's the place where Hercules himself, a fearless hero, is afraid. He wants to leave the place where history starts. A hero of labour or better, a hero of cleaning and purification, a hero who purges filth in the Augean Stables, and who purges the world of monsters, a classical god of active thought and reasonable transformations of the real, Hercules sleeps here, Hercules here is a little drunk; he is confused, uncertain and anxious – oh, paradox – Hercules is going to flee. At the origins of history, he reveals that pure thought slumbers, mixes a bit with the pathetic. Perhaps he reveals historical reason; he shakes. The shaking that seizes him isn't from fear, perhaps, he stumbles before the new labour of history. After having vanquished parasites, he precedes the foundation. His labours have prepared him; he changes labours, he changes reasons.

The tracks of the hooves take readers away from the black cave. And the voices of the cattle bring them back. But on this day, for the first time, an ox's throat was slit on the altar. This was the first sacrifice to Hercules; this was perhaps the first sacrifice. The voices of the cattle bring back to the black cavern. The voice of the victim, hidden, a shadowy mouth, calls to the origin, faked in the tracks turned in the wrong direction. There Hercules was caught red-handed at murder. There the shepherds, those herdsmen that the dying Cacus called out to for help, there the neighbouring shepherds and friends of the murdered, there those silent herdsmen, gathering around the stranger, were getting agitated. Who cried out?

Since the tracks deceive, let's put our trust in the voices. Let's listen. Who then cried out? The cattle, most certainly, and not only when the herd was going away. They lowed while leaving the meadow, they lowed in the cave, they lowed under the sacrificial knife. Who cried out? Cacus? Yes, Cacus, under Hercules' club, called out for help. The shepherds thereabouts arrive. Who cried out? Hercules? Undoubtedly. In the middle of Cacus' avengers, he must have called out for help since Evander arrives. Evander cried out louder than everyone; his hail covered over the voices. The voice of the sacred covers over the confused noises of murder. The master said 'silence' to the noise. What noise? The cries of Cacus, the murmuring of the crowd of shepherds, the calls of Heracles and the low chorus of the cattle. Who cried out in the black cavern? Everyone. That is the noise that comes out of the black box.

The cattle hear the cattle, Hercules hears the cattle, the shepherds hear Cacus, Evander hears Hercules. Everyone hears everyone cry out. Transmitters and receptors all. Rome listens to Evander, over its entire history.

There Romulus killed Remus. Remus must have cried out in the middle of the crowd, *turba*, and its clamour. The clamour of the mob covered over Remus' voice, and the voice of history covered over the clamour of the lynchers.[4]

History hears everyone call out: the historian, most often, only hears one voice.[5]

There Evander arrives. He notices Hercules' mien and size. And he hails him as a god, son of a god. So everything changes; an ox is sacrificed, the mute substitute. Brute animal, mute animal. Mute? No. For cattle low. A signal. We are no longer far from the origin. The tracks of written history flee in a different direction. Let's try to listen to the voices. The low lowing, deprived of meaning, hoarse, raw, of the cattle bawling on the altar when they are bled, when their throats are cut. Who cried out, who still cries out? The cattle on the altar. Let's go back along the false tracks. This cry has no meaning, yet it calls me. Evander arrives, and he encounters a murderer, a common assassin over a simple affair of cattle. This can be seen everywhere, from the Far West to Gascony. Evander speaks, and he hails a god. Who changes the direction or meaning of the tracks? The historian arrives, he sees the murder. Yet he writes that Romulus is a god.

Who is silent now? The priest's knife thrusts the lowing into the ox's throat. Throat slit, it is silent. Hercules crushes Cacus beneath the weight of his club. Cacus, murdered, is silent. Evander divinizes Heracles. Ascended onto the altar, transformed into a statue, Hercules is silent. The crowd of shepherds, frightened by what it was about to do – it was about to dispatch a god who's the son of a god – the crowd, having collected itself, is silent. Evander invents writing. He writes, history is written, he is silent. Livy is silent, we no longer hear him. Who is silent? Everyone.

The entire myth is silent. It says the generation of narrative after Geryon's murder. Yet Geryon means voice. What happens after voice has been killed?

Evander, the writer, arrives in order to divinize the murderer of voice.

Evander arrives, and he changes the tracks. Writing arrives and changes the tracks. Written history writes in the wrong direction. Who dragged the cattle by the tail? Cacus? He's dead and silent. The shepherds? Silent. The cattle? Listen to them; they low, they call. Who dragged the boustrophedon by the tail? Evander. Evander who transforms the murderer into a god, who discredits Cacus. Or who transforms the one who was within an inch of being dispatched by the shepherds into a god. The boustrophedon, the path of the ox ploughing from right to left and from left to right, writes in the right direction and the wrong direction. Evander, a Greek, writes in a single direction. He changes writing like a good semiconductor; he forgets one of the two directions; he transforms the alternating into direct. So listen to the ox; he bawls the other direction of the boustrophedon. We must then go back along the steps of the cattle, enter into the black cave where Cacus lies. It's pitch black in there. The victim ox is silenced, a knife at the throat; Cacus is mute, dead and put at fault. Remus is beneath Cacus, Cacus is beneath the ox, lowing since the dawn.

From this black cave, the black box of origins, origins that are present, absent and concealed beneath the writing of this Latin which signifies concealed, from this black box, meaning, writing, tracks, raw lowing, sound, voice, history, origin shoot out, burst forth, in every direction [sens]. The detailed account of time and its conditions.

Who then changed the tracks? The cattle? Certainly, these are their own steps, these are their hooves. Cacus? Assuredly, he dragged the cattle by the tail. Evander? Yes, it was he who lied in naming a common murderer a god. Hercules? He crossed the river so as to erase the tracks. In other words, who lied? Everyone. In what sense [sens]? In every sense [sens].

Questions to the voices: who cried out? Everyone. Who heard? Everyone. Who is silent now? Everyone. Questions to the tracks now: who changed the tracks? Everyone. Who lied by reversing the direction into the wrong direction, or meaning into nonsense?[6] Everyone.

Three Horatii fight against three Curiatii. Two Horatii fall. Three Curiatii surround Horace. A star. Hercules and the three Geryons, Hercules and the three Cacuses. Hercules and the shepherds. Remus and the mob. Combinatory: Remus dies, Hercules is a god, Horatius is a hero. The star of the one dying and of the threatening multiple, the relation of the one to the multiple is the definition of representation.

Horatius fled. But how would I know this? By the tracks of his steps, by the tracks of his running, by the marks of his sandals. In what direction do they go? Turned toward the outside, they shoot forth from the mêlée, from the mob, from the black cave of the Curiatii's violence. Boustrophedon. They come back. And Corneille understood, Corneille who separated the two directions, defeat and victory, with the sublime point of: 'that he die'.[7] The old Horatius suddenly cries out the sublime point of lynching. Sublime: below the boundary, the threshold that prevents from seeing there. If I follow the tracks of Horatius' steps, his story is written in boustrophedon, according to the march of the oxen, in one direction, then in another. Horatius first drew the Curiatii backwards; now, like Hercules, he turns around and goes back, at the victims' call. He was Cacus, and now he is Hercules. He was the victim. Now he is the murderer. He kills. He kills. He kills. This lightning bolt that bifurcates and turns back on itself, that makes you an ox, a shepherd, a god, a murdered victim or a hero drunk with fury is the quite ordinary boustrophedon of history. Originary history ought to be read in the originary writing: the boustrophedon, following the steps of ploughing oxen, runs from left to right, then from right to left; the writer is a ploughman; they don't transport the stylus or the ploughshare to the other end of the field or page in order to always pick up again in the same direction. In one direction, Horatius, a coward, merits scorn, in the other direction, Horatius, a hero, becomes another founder of Rome. The story of Horatius has preserved the boustrophedon for us, but – oh, paradox – the legend of the cattle forgets it.[8] Evander conceals the murder of Cacus perpetrated by Hercules from us. Evander transforms the violence of the shepherds ready to lynch Hercules into the sacred. Evander erases one direction of the boustrophedon. But the legend lets it be understood that the cattle go in the other direction as well, and we restore the boustrophedon: I mean that the bad Cacus can also be named the good Evus and that the prestigious Evander can be called Cacander. The semiconductor only retains the direction or the counter-direction. The direction of history first and foremost calls for its counter-direction. Hercules, robber and robbed, god and murderer, robber and victim, Cacus, robber and victim, Horatius, cowardly and courageous, Romulus, murderer and king of glory. The direction of history is as integral; history doesn't make a choice; it doesn't moralize. It is complete.

I'm recounting Romulus in the language of history; I'm recounting Hercules and Cacus in the language of legend; I can recount Horatius and the Curiatii in that of tragedy; I'll move on to fable.

Horatius runs, he comes back. How do we know? He must have left tracks and marks on the ground. Each step, each turned foot seems a confession of fear, is a presumption of flight and cowardice, 'what did you wish that he should do?' The other way around, each mark is a presumption of murder; it goes toward a Curiatii corpse. Unequal at three against one, the combat is unequal in the other direction at one against one; the three wounded Albans were losing blood; that can be read in the dust. A criminal at each halt, Horatius is a hero for the global trajectory. A coward, upstream; downstream: a murderer in the fragment, virtuous, in the sum.

I promised to move on to fable. We are at the entrance of Cacus' cave; what happens in the black box? What happens in the black box of origins? What happens in the black box of the *turba* in which Remus succumbs? What happens in the black box of the Curiatii's violence? What happens for Horatius to flee? Fable: what happens in the lion's den?[9] As king, he summoned everyone by edict. All the wildlife from the distant horizon come; they enter the den. What happens in the black cave? We don't know; those who enter don't come back out. The fox, at the entrance of the shadowy mouth, says: I don't really know what takes place inside, but I do notice that all the tracks are turned in a single direction. The monster in the shadowy mouth eats all who enter. But I've seen, says La Fontaine, a second cave, where the tracks went in both directions. The lion, grown old, receives a bite, a chomp, a clawing, a horn blow from his subjects; to top it off he receives a kick from the donkey. The wildlife leave the bright cave in which the senile lion is nothing more than a victim, in which the lion is nothing more than a scapegoat. Black box of the murderer, white box of the victim. The boustrophedon goes to and fro; the box contains both directions. Cacus is a thief; he is Hercules' victim; Hercules is a murderer; Cacus is a poor shepherd defended by the shepherds of the vicinity; Hercules was very nearly lynched by them. Everything comes from that black box, the cave with the cattle, the den full of wildlife, the mêlée, the black mob of the three Curiatii around the young Horatius, and whoever is in the box can be black or white. Box: the mêlée of the collective.

And me, who am I then, and what then am I doing there, deciphering codes and decoding the tracks, decorating the ones, condemning the others on simple presumptions, deciding the just and the unjust? Deciding that one can't decide? Who am I? The fox. Smart as a fox, keen nose, pointed ears, sharp eyes, suspicious, who am I? A police detective. What do I do? Policing. Horror.

The philosophy of straight reason, of deduction, of the universal, philosophy, ancient and classical, only served the king. The king and the priest, the two faces of the sovereign. The philosophy of combat, struggle, and the work of the negative only serves the soldier, military man, militant, who undergoes death in order to accomplish the work of history. The philosophy of suspicion, of the interpreter and the fragment, of dust and the magnifying glass, is that of the spy, the detective, the inspector, the police. Horror. The records are there, written, at the disposal of the secular arm, on whichever side it falls. We no longer do anything but history, we no longer do anything but interpretation, we are no more than police detectives. Horror. We no longer do anything but seek out the guilty.

Ever since Remus, Cacus, Curiatius and Camilla have rested in peace, there has been prescription. Justice is founded on it. If prescription never existed, vengeance would rage, inextinguishably. And the blind and sticky emotion would return. The philosophy of history must be founded on prescription.

The inscription, the writing, the tracks tell of the victim and the murderer, the one and the other, neither one nor the other, the one or the other, depending. Animal or god, hero or shepherd. But they above all flatter and place the police champions at the pinnacle, for example he who is better still than he who is even better than inspector Dupin, he who is more intelligent, sharper, more circumspect or prudent than any comparable inspector Dupin could ever be conceived to be. We are, alas, reduced to a philosophy which plagiarizes the detective novel.

Justice is founded on prescription. After a period of time, no one will hunt the guilty parties down any more. The sons of the guilty are not guilty. The sons of the victims are not victims.

Morality is founded on prescription. What hell would a life be without forgetting or pardon?

Rome is founded on a murder, and this murder refers to another murder. He who digs the foundation finds a head at the Capitol, a body, a skeleton, a mass grave. He finds Cacus beneath Remus. And so on. He who enters into a foundation enters a tomb; Rome is the city of tombs. I say, I wish, I pray, I decide: there is prescription. There is prescription, whatever the tracks may be, whatever the inscription on the tomb. The battle, perhaps, will not start up again for Rome, perhaps it will not flare up around the tomb; it blazes, in any case, for the interpretation of the inscription. Peace. May the philosophy of history be founded on prescription. May history itself be founded on prescription. May we one day live a prescribed history.

Prior to every track condemning or proving innocent, prescription was written. Peace.

Peace be to Hercules, to Horatius and to king Romulus, peace be to their historian and peace be to me, his narrator. Peace be to my sentences without guilty parties or causes, peace be to my lamentation. If I had to found Rome today, utopian, I would prescribe its history.

This is perhaps how Hercules acted. This is how he became a god, perhaps. Who stole the cattle? Cacus. Cacus, really? Is stealing stolen cattle stealing? Hercules killed Geryon first. He takes his cattle, of a surprising beauty. Livy: on the shore of the Tiber, in the place where he had swum across the river while driving his livestock ahead of him, tired from the road, Hercules laid down in the thick grass and went to sleep, weighed down by food and wine, while his herd grazed. Did he kill? Did he steal? Why? How? I couldn't say. The one sleeping there, drunk in the thick grass, knew how not to leave any tracks. He went across the river by swimming; the cattle crossed the Tiber; the trail is erased. Cacus is only poorly half-clever; he turns the direction around; he plays at counter-direction, but he remains in direction and sequence; he remains, alas, in the work of the negative. Hercules swims; he erases his tracks; he leaves writing; he frees himself from history; he is going to enlarge the number of gods. If we crossed, by slow strokes, the river of forgetting, we would be gods, shepherds of fat herds, sleeping from wine in the soft grass. The Tiber, at that time, was called Albula, white river.

Manifestly this legend, inserted into the middle of the historical narrative, is written in Greek. The legend is Greek due to its content and its proper names. The cattle imprint their hooves on the ground there according to the boustrophedon. Do they leave their tracks in one direction – Cacus, Evander – and in the counter-direction – Evus, Cacander – good and bad exchanged? No. These cattle don't plough. There are only two directions in the Horatius narrative; the warrior is a plough ox; here, in the succulent grass, the cattle graze, tranquil and beautiful, and the curve they leave is much more beautiful. We are leaving the boustrophedon. We are leaving direction and counter-direction. We are leaving good and bad, victim and murderer, robber and robbed, we are leaving the beam of the double balance, we are leaving dualism and its excluded middle; to every question the answer is: everyone. To every question concerning each person, the answer is that he has played every role. Each of them is at once murderer, victim, powerless witness to the thing, fair, liar, silent and unaware, good and bad, medium, mixed, grey or mediocre, man, hero, shepherd, king, coward, ox and god, just like me and you. This means that the cattle, grazing in the thick grass, go just anywhere; they don't go, subject to the swing plough, diligently from left to right and back again, as in morality or politics; they wander, that's all; they go everywhere in space; their tracks form a crazily complicated graph; this drawing, quickly enough, must fill the entire plain, the whole of its surface as well as the little local details. The meadow, under the pasturage, is no longer anything but the tracks from their steps.

Manifestly, this legend is written in Greek. The cattle, who leave the boustrophedon behind them when they plough, here leave a meadow dense with ichnographic signs. *Ichnos*, in Greek, is the mark of the step, the track of the foot. The boustrophedon is a curve with two directions; ichnography has every direction; it's the finished drawing left on the ground by the herd when it wanders, in which each brute beast, drawn by the tuft, flower and odour, bothered, pushed, bitten by the flies, maddened by a shadow or going about licking another's neck, wanders without knowing where or why. Imagine the ground of the meadow under the pastorage after a day of the herd's wandering. Imagine the ground of Rome after a millennium of trampling by the Romans. Imagine the earth of the forum after the pounding of the feet of the mob. And now, decipher that ichnography. This is the final painting of the Herculean meadow, this is the initial painting of Rome; these paintings have prescribed every direction or meaning. There is prescription of every direction or meaning before the inscription of a single direction or meaning. In the beginning is the ichnography. That is to say, the integral, that is to say, the sum, the summary, the totality, the stock, the well, the set of meanings or directions. The possible, capacity. Each defined direction or meaning is only a scenography, that is to say, a profile seen from a certain site. From here, the narrative says that Cacus is bad, that Evander is the good man; from elsewhere, the narrative will say Evus and Cacander; from elsewhere still, it will have other and still other profiles; this is how things are with the meaning or direction of history: scenes. Scenes, therefore sites from which to see the representation. But the initial painting, but the original legend, but the legend that permits reading the foundation narrative, in beginning sets up the ichnography. Here is first and foremost the total painting of the possible. History ensues from it better than from one source. The black box is the ichnography itself.

The legend of the meadow with the cattle generalizes the painting of the Noisy Beauty.[10] The cave and the meadow resound with noise and fury; the trampled ground becomes the painting itself, totally dense with tracks, a mixed chaos of every form, size and colour. They are both ichnographic: the foot, living and delightful, which signs *The Unknown Masterpiece* at the bottom, proliferates, invades the expanse. What is true for the master's canvas, in Balzac's style, is true for the Herculean legend. A master of the work, there, a master of history, here, head, capital, well, horn of plenty.[11] All the painter's production comes from this, all of Rome's chanson de geste came from this. Ichnography contains the possible. Pay close attention to the possible appearance of the geometral when the footprints, when the marks intersect.[12] Pay close attention to the story of Horatius and to his route that turns back; pay close attention to the fox's speech in front of the lion's den. Sometimes the tracks indicate one direction; sometimes they designate another; sometimes – rarely – they index the space of directions, the open possibility of their number. But before the geometral, the detective activity stops. History opens amid these virtual bouquets.

At the beginning of Rome's history, even before its beginning, the legend of Hercules, placed there in a meticulously separated cartouche, shines softly, like a star; it twinkles in every direction; one might think a starred rosette, a compass, a compass rose. One might think that the entire history is equipped with a compass. The history carries its legend within itself, not only the way a map is marked with its code, but the way a ship, about to set sail back in the day, fixed this sensitive little machine in its topside. Sensitive: able to, upon a minimal prompting, orient itself in any direction [*sens*]. Balanced, vibrant, metastable. It is going to incline, it is going to indicate some direction. It is fixed, as I said, it is already oriented: Cacus is bad, Hercules is a god, Evander is good. I dream that it becomes unfixed; I dream of another legend, one in which Cacander would be bad, in which Hercules would be lynched, Evus would be good; I dream of a completely different legend, in a completely different direction: that being the case, toward what horizon would the vessel Rome depart? Say, what if this was true? What if there existed a delicate machine, difficult to see, which it would suffice to tamper with a bit in order to change the direction of history? And what if myth, from the origins of the world to our time, had obscurely played this role?

I'll begin again. I'll return to Horatius. What happens at the place Horatius leaves and flees, his feet turned toward the outside? Is it a cave, is it a den, is it a black box, all the more black due to the direction that escapes from it? When the Romans come out of the sanctuary woods, these black woods would not function as a sanctuary if one could go and seek upstream where these Romans came from. The woods block the origin, the way the white river blocks the tracks of the herd. The woods are a black box. The forest where by chance the king of Alba Silvius was born seems to me to be a black woods of the same kind. He was born there, let's say, juridically. Let's not search upstream of said box. So the origin is the point beyond which there is some interest in not tracing back. The origin is the black box toward which no one turns around. The cattle enter it backwards, dragged by their tails. The longer the sequence, the more shadowy is the mouth. The more Cain flees his prison, the blacker the tomb is: so black that the eye of God is necessary, at least, to see there. I'll begin again: so what happens at the place Horatius leaves and flees, like a common ox?

What then was he doing against three? Response: he was dying. Indeed, a sublime response, sublime, that is to say, below the threshold of perception, subliminal. Below vision, quasi-invisible, below listening, unheard. The old Horatius cries out, Corneille cries out, the cattle low; we are brought back to the black box by their calls. The cattle, pitiful, are beautiful; the tragic voice, pitiful, is sublime. The lowing pants below direction or meaning; the sublime is almost blind. These cries make us turn around. *Boum vox Herculem convertit*. Hercules turns around; he goes back the way he came; he converts. The cattle turn around, lowing. *Desiderium*. Voice of regret, call, last cry of desire, adieu. Two thousand years after the cattle, the old Corneille cries out. *Convertit vox*. Three hundred years after, I turn around. A voice from the depths of the ages has responded. It always answers the same thing. Yes, Horatius was dying against three, in the middle of the three Curiatii. Three, why three? A group was joining together as a body against Horatius, a group, the first crowd, the first mob, the simplest multiplicity. Horatius in the middle of the three Curiatii is the simplest form of the schema: Remus in the middle of the mob, Hercules in the middle of the shepherds of the vicinity. If he had died against the three, Horatius would have been the founder of Alba. Not of Rome, Alba. The Curiatii, unanimous, would have created the unanimity of the Albans. The crowd or army of Alba around the three Curiatii, the group of Curiatii around the young Horatius, Horatius with his eyes closed in the black box of the collective in the process of forming – that wasn't serving the purpose of Rome. Horatius flees so as not to found Alba. He flees his own lynching. He flees the black mêlée he was the subject of. Subject, that is to say, thrown to the ground, trampled underfoot, lying under the crowd and the group. He flees the position of subject. He flees knowledge. So he enters into the subliminal, in proximity to the sublime. The old Horatius crying out 'that he die' cries out the subject. Corneille subliminally cries out the archaic subject at the same time that Descartes announces the modern subject.

A tragedy is always required in order to give science free rein. Horatius flees knowledge. His sandals, going in the counter-direction, flee the fatal philosophy of the subject. The victim subject flees in order to vanquish.

A ruse of reason, a ruse, a detour. He flees before knowledge. He flees before all knowledge; he doubts hyperbolically. He ignores in order to know better.[13] He obeys in order to command.

The subject flees its state of being a subject; the subject flees its own knowledge. If it remained here more than an instant it would see nothing but a brief flash during which it would know the black box: the heavens are open.

He's called back by his father. He's called back by the old Horatius, after a thousand-year flight. He's called back by Corneille. He's called back by Polyeuctus. He's called back by Descartes.

He's called back by shame, by disgrace.

Convertit. He turns around, abruptly.

He converts. Here he has a conversion. He descended by procession; he went back up by conversion. Suddenly, abruptly, he turns around.

He had left tragedy for some reason. He comes back into tragedy.

And he sees. Tragedy is no longer there. He returns to knowledge. It's no longer the same.

Horatius, converted, no longer sees the black mêlée of the Curiatii, no longer sees the black box he came out of, from which he was reborn, the black box of origin; the Curiatii undid their concourse, untangled their consensus; they no longer form a group, or an army, or a collective, or Alba; the black of their mêlée's interior has vanished.[14]

There, on the duelling grounds, before his open eyes, the unfortunate Curiatii fall off one by one; there, along the path of ignorance, they of themselves divide the difficulty into as many parts as necessary to best resolve it. Horatius coming back up the path encounters the objects there, lying before him, simple obstacles. He kills them. The object of knowledge is put to death.

He was inside the tragedy, enclosed in the black box. He flees.

The tragedy is behind his back. He turns around. The tragedy has vanished; there is nothing left but analysis.

Hercules, reading the tracks, turns his back to the black cave. Horatius, fleeing the Curiatii, turns his back to his lynching. And Descartes turned his back. At the call of the cattle inside the black, everyone turns around, and the cave opens. It is no longer black. Hercules, rushing up, kills Cacus the thief; we will forget Hercules the thief, Evander the liar, Cacus put to death, and the hero about to die. We will forget the integral of the facts, that possible that suddenly shows Hercules to be robber and robbed, murderer and god, cheater and peaceful, shows Cacus as well to be robber and robbed, guilty party and victim, cheater and not very clever, that shows that Hercules is probably no different from Cacus; we will forget the box of the possible, Pandora's box, so as to substitute for it a meagre analytical sequence, one of the possible narratives, meagre and false, false and abstract, abstract and unfaithful to the state of things. Horatius, like Hercules, turns around, and no longer sees the Curiatii's collective box; he will never see Alba again; he sees the individual, analytical, unfurled string of his brothers-in-law, who he kills one by one, in a chain, analytically. Descartes divides the difficulty; he resolves it; he follows the order; he kills the difficulty; he doesn't always see it.

Perhaps Bergson is right. Analysis comes to us from turning around toward the upstream of time. The retrograde movement of the true places the truth along uniform chains.

Today we are acquainted with numerous natural examples of originary processes that only develop by sawing the branch on which they managed to take place. They only develop by erasing their conditions; they only have successors through the destruction of their predecessors. The more originary they are, the more they're turned toward what follows them, the more they turn their backs to the set that presupposes them, to the sequences that condition them. A given element appears that only multiplies by destroying the world that made it appear. Alba must be destroyed for Rome to be founded.

So we are successors; we can go back up to this world, but under the conditions of the series that indicates it as being upstream, it can't emerge; it's impossible or contradictory. A series indicates a cave; it is enveloped in a black box; we are barely beginning to bring a bit of light there.

Without my grandfather, a peasant from Gascony, without his good humour, his health, his simple philosophy, I wouldn't be here, pondering more than a thousand miles from his grave. It's clear that the conditions of life here would cause him to die in less than a week. He wouldn't survive the world he helped make possible. Alba wouldn't have survived Rome.

Hercules stole those admirable cattle from Geryon, the three-bodied monster; he killed Geryon in a fight with three episodes; Horatius must be imagined to be Herculean. This proper name must be translated from Greek: Hercules killed voice, sound, cry, speech; he stifled song; he extinguished the wave of clamour from before language. Nothing will make us recall this Herculean labour any more; we will not turn around this time. Hercules, afterwards, went the way that erases tracks. He can sleep, serene, in the thick grass, drunk with prescription; history has vanished for him, both oral and written. Hercules sleeps in utopia. How would prescription be said for the voice?

These two Herculean actions are limit actions: the erasing of voices, the suppression of marks. In the geometral, they are extremal elements, null elements. All the possible is invaginated in the uncertain meadow, become a white palimpsest. All tracks, no track; all calls, no voice.

White is composed of the totality of colours; the noisy beauty is perhaps Alban; her foot is posed, the first step in the ballet of Alba.

Horatius turned around, Horatius converted, no longer sees the Curiatii's black mêlée, vanished, the way he underwent it before fleeing; he sees, analytical, a chain of entirely simple and easy reasons. Behind the cowardly warrior's back, the black synthesis is still in the box. Facing the valorous converted soldier, analysis unfolds its sequence. I leave the places where full synthesis is behind my back. I turn around and no longer see anything but this easy linear series. Can it be said that the series comes out of the black box? Can it be said that it's the box's equivalent? How can the predecessor vanish to this degree into a successor that no longer says, that no longer does, and that no longer is the same thing? If I reconstruct the synthesis, after operation, the result is no longer the same. The synthesis of the dead Curiatii is not the merging on me of the menacing Albans. A pile of corpses is not an enraged crowd. I'm speaking, through image, of knowledge.

I am, here and now, plunged in a present I scarcely understand, a black box as black as the mêlée the warrior escapes from. I see poorly here; everything is mixed [se mêle]; I only hear sound and fury; no fluctuation can truly be distinguished from any other; no fluctuation thereby announces that it is, that it will be, of consequence. That being the case, I have only to flee. And flight is easy for me since time sweeps me along. I leave the present I don't understand. But called back by some voice, by an ox, by a sublime old man, I turn around, I convert. And I see come towards me the linear generation of one of these till recently mixed [mêlées] fluctuations, now the head of the series, for the others, vanished, didn't have any successors. At the moment of my conversion, I am of course plunged in another present in which the same mixture resumes. It is understood that only the tracks of sequences that descend from the past are recognized there. Only what belongs to this retrograde movement is now recognized to be true. And yet, most often, these are only fluctuations like the others. From the moving mêlée of the present, while my back is turned, entirely occupied with fleeing, a sheaf of simple and easy lines comes out, lines – analytical by reasons and consequences – that will have the same relationship to the vanished present as do the piled corpses of the Curiatii to the intersection of their moving swords over my terrified head. Either I am overwhelmed by complexity, or I dominate simplicity. Either I'm the victim, or I kill, a murderer. This dilemma of death can be refused.

The analytical theory of knowledge is related to the chronicles of the recurrent movement of history. Exact knowledge and historical knowledge are related to each other in this way. This relationship concerns time. This relationship concerns death. It concerns destruction.

It concerns the time we are the masters of. Is it time that, taking into account the site I observe from, undoes the boxes into simple series? Is there one time that opens the boxes and another that closes them – since I'm always immersed in such a black box? Is this due to the observer's site?

It concerns a time we are masters of: when Horatius' sword cuts Curiatius' throat. We are often masters of what philosophy piously calls the work of the negative. We remain persuaded that this slaughter is true work, or that the work must be slaughter. But then who told us so?

I convert. A second time I turn around. With a new effort, I come back to the procession. I no longer see the analytical sequences come to me. I listen. I only hear the voices of the cattle, old Horatius' cry, and Cacus' call, and the agitation of the enraged shepherds around the murderous Hercules. I no longer know how to distinguish who is who. The ox lowed, Cacus cried out, Hercules calls out, Evander prays. From one same mouth comes murmuring, yelling, moaning, threat. I hear someone – animal, shepherd, king, god – I hear the indeterminate white noise; I want to think this synthesis, this mixture directly; I don't want to draw a sword. Or Horatius' sabre, or Hercules' club, or the sacrificial knife, or the deft tool going through the exact joints of the animal. Analysis destroys; knowledge here is still the work of the negative, like history.

Let's stop the cries, the calls, the moans, the sobs. Let's listen, free of threat, to the noises behind us.

What comes out of the black box. The lowing of the cattle, *mugitusque boum*. Then Cacus' calls for help to the shepherds. Lastly the agitation of the same shepherds around Hercules. What comes out of the black box? Noise. Voices, cries, calls, like a hubbub. I have already spoken of this noise, sound and fury, indistinct cries, the only information, perhaps, available upon leaving the social black box. Its meaningless noise, the call for help, the cry of a living being near death, the particles of agitation of a crowd that's disseminated or in a ring around a hole. But here, the lost ox calls out; it lows with regret, with desire. The cattle cry out to the cattle, the same mimetic voice. Noise or meaning depending on the observer; I only hear noise; I believe it to be with desire, but what do the cattle say amongst themselves? And what does the disordered mob say? Might a collective subject be required to understand this collective noise? The ox lows, the next victim at the altar raised for Hercules. In the end, the cattle are from then on going to die; they die substituting for the immemorial violence, for the current violence. They low with regret, during their separation; they low at the moment of sacrifice, the knife in their throats. Cacus attacked, Cacus beaten to death, Cacus the victim cries out. Hercules cries out, besieged, surrounded, attacked by the shepherds; he cries out, calls out; Evander arrives, who saves him by declaring him sacred. What comes out of the black box is the victimary voice, its pitiful call. I do say victimary. The ox, on the altar, takes Hercules' place; Hercules, in the middle of the shepherds, took Cacus' place. Each one, in turn, takes everyone's place, and that's the original meaning of the word 'victim'. The victim is the substitute, the replacement; the victim is vicar; the victimary place is a vicarious place. Who calls out, who cries out, what noise comes out of the black box? It's hard for me to distinguish; one call stands in for another; one cry is emitted instead of another; yes, the noise is confused. The noise made by the crowd is confused; it says the set of possible substitutions. Everyone and the first comer.

If you read the schemas of structural analysis be sure to notice that its play is made possible by the possibility of putting one element in the place of another element and vice versa. Language itself says that this exchange is victimary. So don't only read the irreversible tracks; listen to the noise, the calls and cries of those who go in place. Turn around; have a conversion.

Let's begin again: Hercules is a robber, Hercules is robbed; he is a murderer, he is going to be murdered; he is deified. He takes on every value: base man, hero, god. Cacus is a robber, Cacus is robbed; just as much robber and robbed as the hero himself; confident in his strength just as much as him; Cacus is murdered; Cacus was slandered by the base name attached to him; he is perhaps accused in order to justify Hercules and his apotheosis; Cacus is a quasi-Hercules, Hercules is a super-Cacus. Evander the supermale, the just and learned man, cheats and lies. What comes out of the black box is a thousand-voiced language, what comes out of the black box has a thousand substitutive meanings [sens]. The track comes and goes in every direction [sens]; the word says everything, it softly noises; it is perhaps Carmenta's word. The prophetess' voice says one thing for another thing, says this instead of that; it signifies by substituting. The truth is never anything but a stability amid substitutions; it is only an invariant amid their changing.

Even more, even better, in every point, here, is a brute animal, a man, a shepherd or herdsman, a courageous hero, a coward, a demi-god, a god. The meanings, the values bush out. What comes out of the black box is indeed a geometral of legend, but we need to look more closely. Each one takes on many values, and it's because he takes them on that he is substitutable. Each one is substitutable, while leaving the truth of history intact. But it so happens that certain ones are, if I may, more substitutable than others: Hercules really has every value – robber, robbed, under prescription, cowardly and courageous, uncertain and certain, base murderer and half lynched, a man, for all that, but, finally, a god. Cacus is dead; he isn't a god. Evander is king; he isn't a god. Hercules alone is a joker.[15] The others are quasi-jokers; they aren't completely substitutable. Is it necessary to be a joker to become a god? Hercules alone is a white element; the others are on the way to becoming so. What comes out of the black box? White or semi-white elements.

A god is a true joker. The more god he is, the more joker he is. Look at Jupiter: he becomes a swan, he's a bull, he's that golden rain that beats on Danaë's threshold. The divine is totally substitutable, totally vicarious, totally vicar and victim. Seen from here, Jupiter is a bull, from there, he's a swan; perceived from the doors of the girl Danaë, he's ample and abundant golden rain. Jupiter is the geometral of substitutions; he is the ichnography of the monstrous. The god is not one monster; he's every possible monster; he sums the scenographies of monsters. He is, thus, a white element, white like the sum of colours. And this is why a mythical narrative so often has every value; it puts jokers or white elements into play. And this is why it always overhangs the set of explanations, all of them linear and analytical, all of them inclined. Myth understands history; no history explains myth. History is an analytical series issuing, like the cattle, from the black box with white elements. The *Iliad* is a possible sequence of the infinite games of the Olympic gods; the history of Rome ensues from legend, legend in fact, not myth, since Hercules is the only divine joker in it. Legend is a myth that's been slightly inclined. I mean a geometral that's been slightly scenographied. I mean a compass that's slightly fixed. It inclines toward the downstream; it descends a little slope.

We are no longer very far from the origins. The black box is Pandora's box; anything can come out of it. Myth is rich with everything substitutable; legend includes much of it. Thus Livy, Roman, is closer to history than Homer, Hellenic, but not much closer. Who can flatter himself with being its neighbour?

A first digression, please. The perfect myth, telling the divine, mixes white elements. It draws a geometral by means of jokers. It obtains then every meaning; it is a sum; it is, if I may use the word, pansemic. So any meaning of history is already understood by it. Theorem: we will always be able to understand history by means of theologies.

Silver and gold, paper money are general equivalents. A sum, a sum of money is a white element. With it you can get a bull, a lake full of swans, make a rain of gold flow on Danaë's propylaea, tempt, it seems, the gods themselves. A narrative told by means of such jokers is, once again, a geometral. So any meaning of any history is already understood by it. Theorem: we will always be able to understand history by means of economy.

Conclusion: economy and theology are equivalent explanations of history. Equivalent: I mean omnivalent.

We will sacrifice, in the same temple, to Jupiter and to Quirinus.

But, the geometral is obtained by substitution, by the set of victimary substitutions. Omnivalence is obtained by violence.

We will sacrifice, on the same altar, to Jupiter, to Mars, to Quirinus. Theology, violence and economy are on the same line, or rather, they occupy the same space, I mean: all of space.

A second digression, the last. At the end of the *Theodicy*, Leibniz does a little Roman history. Sextus Tarquinius complains about his destiny. The Prince who ends the book of foundation is in the great pyramid of the possible. The high priest is led to the origin; dazzled to the point of feeling faint, he contemplates under the point of the pyramid, where the real resides, the immense base of the substitutable, combined possibles. He contemplates novels and legends; he contemplates, divinely, myth. What Leibniz calls divine understanding – well, stock, the global reservoir of possible worlds – is there, simply miniaturized in the legendary cartouche. The high priest traces back to the places of the first kings, he traces the series of tracks back up to the black cave, ox after ox, king after king; he comes to the meadow where Romulus was preceded by Hercules. He sees Sextus Tarquinius driven out, killed in Gabii whose master he had been, who wanted to be king of Rome, who wanted history to take another direction; so he returns to the well of meaning, to the capital, to the head, to the source, to the pyramid.

Leibniz draws, he schematizes the narrative. The book of history is indeed the Leibnizian pyramid: the geometral base of the one is the strange legend of the other.

Rome is founded on legend just as the pyramid is founded on its base and the real on the possible. I no longer see the difference between the two narratives, the historical legend and the philosophical tale.

In the real point, Sextus Tarquinius dies, without any possible substitution. Like Cacus. Like Remus. Like Turnus. And so on.

You are an ox; you are going to be stolen; you are going to be dragged by the tail, and you will end your days sacrificed on the Altar Maxima. You are an ox, and you are a herdsman; you are the bad herdsmen Cacus, a thief, a trickster, flushed out by the police detective, beaten to death by Hercules' club, a victim, proven innocent by your call and by the arrival of the other shepherds. You are an ox, you are a herdsman, good and bad, a thief and a sacrificed one, a lyncher and coming to aid. You are a king, a scholar, a writer; you are a good man, the first man of written history; you lie; you saw a strapping, murderous man inside the horrible violence of the shepherds; you were afraid, and you hailed a common ruffian soldier as a god. You are an ox; you are the shepherd, good and bad; you are the king, bad but good; you are a god, a robbed robber, brutal and murderous, but suddenly a victim right in the middle of the agitated shepherds. You are an animal; you are a man; you are a king and you are a shepherd; you are learned and ignorant, good and bad; you are everything, and you pass on to every place. The geometral of possible sites is in you. The inexpiable knot of every value. You are all this at the same time, me too and all of us. And the possible is the pure present before time makes a chain of it.

But the ox dies on the altar, throat slit, but Cacus dies under the club, vanished, but Hercules, in the middle of the shepherds, is going to die; perhaps the king hails him as a god in order to save his head. As Remus did not do. The ox is not a king; the shepherd is not a god, but all of them can be victims. The victim is the element of substitution. The neutral element. The white element, the one that can bear every value.

The black box is full of white elements.

Thus myth is algebraic.

I'm using 'white' in the sense it has in games and in light. White is the sum of colours; it can be broken down into the spectrum of the rainbow. Thus the white token can settle on any value. You are an animal, a shepherd, a king and a god; you are white; you are good and bad, robber and robbed, murderer and murdered; you are white. You are victim, substitute or one substituted for; you are white.

When you aren't white, a determination appears, a mark or a sign. Determination is negative; if you are king, here and now, you aren't an ox or a shepherd or a hero. Indetermination is positive. White is the indeterminate, the limit of the underdetermined, the whole of the positive. You are white – yes, yes, yes – you are every possible world. Leibniz had possible worlds be visited in a pyramid; the pyramid is fire, the fire is white light.

In the beginning is the black box, ignorance, our zero of information. In the beginning is the white, every possible world. In the beginning is the victim, this relation of substitution, and this death, between us.

Livy is at the origins; he writes, with his good hand, the book of foundations. Before Rome, there's dead Alba, a sacrificed white virgin.

Let's leave the herd to graze in the thick grass. The cattle come and go; they wander and aimlessly roam, numerous. The boustrophedon is stupidly dualist: the good are good and the bad bad, or the bad are good, and the good are bad. In this simple and crude case philosophy, the fox in front of the den, is critique, it is judge; or it is post-critique, that is, military or detective. Court and combat require two parties. The philosophy of suspicion plays detective. The cattle, going into the sweet grass, leave a complicated curve under their hooves, all folded over itself, like a protein, implicated, duplicated, replicated, traversed, crossed, striated, mixed, many-coloured, tiger-striped, streaked, damasked, moiré, loaded like a heraldic shield or a labyrinth, multiplied. Before such a multiplicity, the fox detective is hardly of any use to us, nor is suspicion or the dual.

This is the striated multiplicity, here a neighbour of the white Albula, dedifferentiated.

A question, a worry, a dream: what if the compass, true geometral, or compass rose, placed there, was not only passive but active; what if it was a rudder? What if the legend was a machine for infinitely copying the legend? Hercules kills Cacus, Romulus kills Remus … and Brutus kills Caesar … a nightmare. Dream: what if the legend contained a productive agency, a Herculean force, an agency of replication, the printer of the cattle's hooves, and an agency of control, I mean the king-writer, Evander, who judges who is god and who murderer?[16] What if the legend was a geometral machine automatically indexing all the history to follow? And what if all of history, mechanically, crazily, repeated the legend, slightly inclined in one direction? I'm dreaming, of course; I'm doing nothing but dreaming. What if that abominable horror, that long river of blood and tears, had been programmed, in the middle of the cartouche, in that appalling self-replicating automatic machine? And what if, on the contrary, I was lucid, and it was this that was our nightmare? And it was this that was our illusion of history? And what if we – hallelujah – had the freedom to fix the rudder anew, to change course on the rose of the legend, what if we could rewrite the program, another time in a completely different direction, renaissance?

2 CITY OF ALBA: THE WHITE MULTIPLICITY

Before. Before the foundation, the inauguration takes place. Auguries must be taken before the city can commence. Beforehand, the sites – Aventine, Palatine – from which the twins are going to observe must be selected. Before the inaugural site, prehistoric or archaic places, forests or the fig tree Ruminalus, vast wild solitudes, can be seen. Before the foundation of Rome, before Romulus kills Remus in this place, Hercules passes through the site, and he dispatches Cacus. Before the foundation of Rome, the foundation of Alba Longa takes place, by Ascanius, the son of Aeneas. Before the foundation of Alba Longa, the foundation of Lavinium takes place, named after Aeneas' wife, the daughter of Latinus. Before the foundation of Lavinium, two establishments take place, both of them named Troy. The one at the end of the Adriatic, where Antenor lands, the other in the territory of Laurentum, where Aeneas' tribulations at sea end. Before these two cantons of Troy, the capture of Troy takes place elsewhere, the destruction of the Asian city by the Greeks.

The origin refers to another origin, the beginning demands a beginning, the instauration wants auguries, the foundation requires preliminaries; it seems a ray of light that, caught between two almost parallel mirrors, goes on reproducing image before image; everything flees in the infinite sequence. *Iam primum omnium*, first of all, this is nevertheless how the book of foundation opens. The book entitled *Ab urba condita* begins, once the 'first of all' is announced, begins, as I was saying, with *Troia capta*, the captured city. A lightning-fast short circuit, from the first opening, between the origin and the capture. The book of the foundation of the city begins with the destruction of the city. The first Rome is the child of the razed Troy. The foundation of Troy would have to be meditated upon, recounted, rediscovered. Yet another condition. A book of foundation assuredly would have to be rewritten, not only from before Livy, but even from before the *Aeneid*, from before the *Iliad* and the *Odyssey*. This latter would require a new one: so from what fabled city destroyed in the midst of what forgotten horrors did what escapees come, desperate, to found Troy, the beautiful city? The search for conditions never ceases to discover conditions; it gets lost, before, or turns back on itself. The foundation lets another foundation be seen, upstream. The first short circuit, from which the book ensues, *condita-capta*, brings face to face the foundation and the capture, the origin of Rome and the end of Troy, the condition and the concept. The concept demands a condition; the condition demands a concept. The capture requires a foundation; the foundation requires a capture.

The time of history is seeking its zero point. It seems inaccessible; it's an accumulation point: another point is always intercalated, iteratively, before. One city demands another city, one history requires another; we don't really know how time flows. I have often visited sources, of the Vienne, of the Garonne, of the Albula; I always saw that the source point was the mouth for a head of hair setting out for bogs or the edges of glaciers. I'll soon forget Rome and Troy, Alba and Lavinium so as to directly pose the question of time, of the processual and sources. Later. First we must pass through the hell of history without time, ours.

But look at the repetitions that wind around each other already. Romulus and Remus, twins, are of the blood of Numitor and his competitor and rival brother, Amulius. Trace back from brothers to brothers and from rival twins to rival twins, and it will have to be that, *primum omnium*, from the origin, from the flight from destroyed Troy, they are two, *duobus, Aeneae Antenorique*, Aeneas, the founder, and Antenor, his antonym. Set out from Troy, the two antonyms found in all two Troys. Nothing changes, and everything repeats itself. Already the nightmare of the same has begun, the nightmare of the same and the other. Has it truly stopped? Already two laws are opposed and superposed, the law of war and the law of hospitality, *ius belli et ius hospitii*; we shall soon see that the narrative of foundations, from the Sabines to the Tarquins, is wound up in their dismal repetition: *hostes hospites*, hostility, hospitality, the ancient parasite law. One might think that the simplest and stupidest operators that the most popular philosophy has put in place to prevent us from thinking time when we think history are already there, like plaster dogs face to face, at the entrance of the propylaea of our culture.[1]

The origin is repeated; this repetition covers over space. With every origin resaid, we leave a site. Before the walls of Rome were dug, the space between Aventine and Palatine. Before that space, Alba. Alba is not on the hills of the city. Before Romulus and Remus, Hercules and Cacus.

Hercules came from elsewhere; he was ravaging Europe, destroying those who ravaged. Before Alba and Lavinium, the two Italic Troys, before these latter, Asia. The same operators cover over space and make us thereby believe that time is at stake. Before landing among the Aborigines, Aeneas came from elsewhere, from the wine-dark sea, from unhappy love affairs in Africa, from a Far Eastern coast where a battle was inexpiable; let's try to forget. Let's try to forget the origin by multiplying its images toward an inaccessible vanishing point; our successors will grow tired of explaining it. Antiquity never ceased lamenting the horrors of the Trojan War, just as we never cease to lament the day of Hiroshima; if we want to create history, let's forget that once and for all, but everything comes from there. Ancient history comes from the end of Troy, just as our new history comes from the end of Hiroshima; let's not forget it.

Time has not begun, yet; it has not yet been thought. The places are there, only the places. To trace back to the origin is to leave one site for another site, going from the City to Alba, from Alba Longa to Lavinium, from this latter to the Italian Troys, then to the Troy of Asia Minor; it's also to leave the site of men for the space of gods, to trace back Aeneas' lineage to his mother Aphrodite, to go from the murderous twins to the murderer Hercules, a twin as well; it's to leave the pedestrian prose narrative, Livy, for the poetic narrative, Virgil. Before the history, before the so-called history, the *Aeneid*. Each image detaches from a place. The place of the gods, behind, and the place of War.

Before thinking time, let's try to think places. The search for the origin covers places the way the cattle cover the meadow with their tracks. We have read the places of the cities sown around the sea. Does the origin go through every city? Is each one of them originary? Here the places of total war seem to coincide with the places of the gods. The repeated images of Aeneas with Antenor, Amulius with Numitor, Romulus and Remus, Horatius and Curiatius, symmetrical images of monotonic rivals, are transported by the glow that comes from the burning of Troy, by the light come from Olympus, that is, from a hearth in which violence and the sacred mix.

So before Rome, Alba swarmed off from Lavinium. The very first king of Alba, after the founder Ascanius, was named Silvius, from his sylvan origin: some circumstance had him be born in a forest. The long genealogy of the Alban kings will repeat this origin: Aeneas Silvius, Latinus Silvius … Tiberinus Silvius. Rhea Silvia, the mother of the twins, a vestal, is of this lineage. Just as the cattle come out of the cave, a black box, just as the murderer, the thief, the herdsmen, the quasi-king and the demi-god come out of it, the kings come out of the black woods.

Now, to be able to populate his city, Romulus opens a place of sanctuary between two sacred woods. Violence calls a truce in this sacred place. There, obscure people find refuge, a mob without distinction of individuals who are avid, for whatever reason, for new things. It is translated into French that they wanted *se refaire une blancheur* [to make themselves white again]. They will not be asked about their origin. They come from the woods and that is enough. The forest obscures their origin, hides and covers it. The sacred covers it over. The sanctuary protects it. But everyone knows that it's worthy of the gallows tree. The sacralization of the woods stops the violence and renders blind to the origin; that which was to be demonstrated. The foundation by violence and the sacred never ceases. It is covered over; it is hidden; it can be hidden by conceptual laws and operations. That there is a labyrinth before the origin perhaps proves that we don't want to see this origin.

The kings of Alba come from the forest, just as the Romans come from these woods. I called them sylvan kings; I should have called them savage – it's the same word, but it expresses better. Before Rome, before the history that begins at the foundation of the city, Alba only has savage kings. Rome is civilized, Alba is savage. Rome is of walls, Alba is of woods. History is political, in the literal sense, but prehistory is savage. Historical thought seems linear, as though processual, as though it were following the river of time; savage thought is combinatory. It occupies space with the network of its pseudo-novelties. It invades places. I'm not making anything up; I'm only saying what Livy says. Here are some examples from the royal line. Aeneas, through his son, begets Silvius, who begets Aeneas Silvius; Aeneas, through the daughter of Latinus, begets Silvius, who begets Latinus Silvius; the founder of Alba begets Silvius, who, through his grandson, begets Alba Silvius. Combinatory. The kings are all marked on the right with invariant primitive savagery, by the institutor of the variation; they are marked on the left by the past, places or the future. The future: Romulus Silvius also reigns, and he dies struck down, like the Romulus of Rome in the thunder and lightning of the swamp of Capra. It is indeed a question of prehistory; there isn't really any time; there is space and the combinatory. The kings of Alba have the names of places – Tiber river, Aventine Hill, city of Alba, sylvan forest; they have combination names which mix space, past and future; the combinatory genealogy freezes time hard; history has not begun. Due to the combinatory, savage thought is not historical; this is already said in Livy. It forms a simplex in a network suited to invading places; it does not know time.

The kings of Alba and the Romans come from the woods, savages. Born in the forest, reborn in the forests, they are made of wood. The origin is in that material; the word 'material' itself says, in the Latin language, roughly hewn wood for future construction. Virgilian wood that can be found in forests.

The wooden combinatory, savage, as we say wooden tongue, is of itself placed before time.[2] It is only originary due to its impotence to think time. We are still at this point.

Cacus, half-clever, turns the tracks of the cattle's hooves around; Hercules, a half-god, clever, swims across the river pushing the handsome livestock in front of him; there's no track that the running water doesn't erase. Better: no need to counterfeit or erase the marks; the river, of itself, forgets them. The water doesn't receive them; the water has no memory. The robber will be able to say that he has been robbed; no, the robber who crosses the water is able to say he was robbed; the murderer can pass for victim, the victim for a god: neither seen nor known, Hercules sleeps in the thick grass; now, he reposes in the perpetual present, in the sweet quietude of prescription. He comes out of the river without a past, baptized; he comes out of the river white, the way others come out of the forest or the sanctuary woods whitened.[3] If the Greek myth opens what the Latin narrative closes, must one think that those who are born in these woods or forests have also stolen cattle, killed men and voices before penetrating into the matter of these woods? They repose in the origin, they sleep in prescription. Whitened by the water, blackened by the forests, come out of the prehistoric hyle. The origin is the black box – cave, woods, forest – it is the black matter of these woods, the zero point that always refers upstream, that upstream we are cut off from by the white course of the Albula. Let's forget this once and for all, but everything comes from there.

Tiberinus, a savage king of Alba, drowns in the Albula. What was he going to do in the middle of the eddies? Why was he amid the *turba*?[4] He dies in the white river and leaves it his name. I repeat: he dies in the Albula; he leaves a track there; he gives it his name. This is very new. The white Albula changes into the Tiber; the Tiber is no longer white. Hercules crosses and leaves the river of forgetfulness as it is. Hercules swims across, living, surviving; the Tiber remains the Tiber. Tiberinus dies from crossing, and the Albula loses its whiteness. This death was necessary, this king in the middle of the troubled waters, of the *turba*, to leave a track, even on the river of water that generally erases it. This drowning has erased the power of erasing, all the white river's power of forgetting.

To understand, one must again speak Greek. Albula, white like forgetfulness, would be like the Latin name for the Lethe. That's the river of hell that drowns the memories of the dead who cross it. Yet when the savage king of Alba dies in the middle of the waters, he takes the power of forgetfulness away from those waters; the river will never again be white; it will never again be Albula. If the Lethe ceased to be the Lethe, it would become Aletheia, the truth. History has just begun. Amid the pure processual, time descending the thalweg of forgetfulness, this is the first memory. Here, on the white sheet of flowing, the first truth of history gets screwed down. The truth: the savage king is dead, drowned, in the middle of the undistinguished multiple. He died in the first turbulence.

The Tiber remembers the one the Albula would have caused to be forgotten: the king Tiberinus Silvius suffocating beneath the flood of the multiplicity without memory.

In truth, a king is never anything but the one to whom similar adventures happen.

Before the beginning of history, the white river erases tracks;[5] the pure processual is laminar; time is not coded. Time has just been marked by the first turbulence, by the first circumstance. It has preserved this first trace, that of a dead king, that of a drowned king, or of a king who was king from having perished drowned amid the multiplicity without memory. This is the first truth.

The truth. It is what remains, on the white waters of forgetfulness, of the drowning in the turbulence of a savage king of Alba.

Alba is not an image, nor is the Albula a comparison. The city and the river, and, we shall see, the dictator, the population and the hills, together define an abstract preliminary, a conceptual form of a stunning exactitude. We will never know whether it's a question of a historical narrative; we will never decide whether the myth prevails or not over the real narrative, but we can draw the precision and rigour of this abstract form without shaky outlines. Before a certain history can be written, the writer gives himself the white. Before a certain time can be determined, the indeterminate is met with. Alba precedes Rome: indetermination precedes the determinate.

Alba is the virgin wax, the tabula rasa before codes, before signs and meaning. It is the white of preliminary indecision, chaste, like Rhea Silva, vestal, virgin and mother, white and violated, incised and firstly torn to pieces. I have just, by means of Alba, understood the situation of origin of the holy virgin and mother. Chaste, white, undecided; incised, marked, maternal. Thus the white, undecided, indeterminate, shows a static and dynamic situation of equilibrium, of stable, unstable, metastable equilibrium, from which determinate thalwegs have issued forth, running the valleys to the seas, thalwegs more and more dug out. If you climb back up to the very high plateau where the sources are placed, their digging is less and less deep, to the point of illegibility. It's a situation that's, let's say, natural, a geographical given, a state of space, at the same time as a very simple abstraction.

This situation is expressly drawn: since Lavinium was overpopulated, flourishing and rich in those days, Ascanius left it; he left Lavinium to his mother or stepmother. He founded a new city himself at the foot of the Alban Hills, which was called Alba Longa because its position was stretched out straight along a ridgeline. Alba is below a mountain; it is on a mountain; it is positioned on a pass. It is called long from stretching along a bit; it's named Alba from being high and low at the same time. High on its hill, source; low at the foot of the mountain, source again. For a source is at the same time an origin and a collection, spring and well. The waters come from it; the waters must definitely come to it. But above all Alba is white because it's in equilibrium on the summit of the pass. The pass is low, it's even the lowest low point of all the points in the Alban Hills; the pass is high, it's even the highest point of all those on the ridgeline it dominates from its position. Alba is high and low, the highest and the lowest, stretched out along its saddle; Alba is the site where the highest sites are equal or rather identical to the lowest sites. It is indeed the site of indecision, the site of indetermination: the saddle point.

The Albula is no longer there, in the places where the Tiber now flows; it has changed site. Yet an Albula still exists; it has regained its true place. At the upper end of the Upper Engadine, on the highest watershed in Europe, on the highly situated plateau at the foot of the high Alps, I mean low enough to collect the supplies brought to it, lies the source of the Albula. It's the Alban site translated into space, but hardly translated, since Livy himself defines it thus. Go there and see the thalwegs before they draw or determine themselves. Follow the fluctuations a little of a few water drops scattered in the vicinity of the source site: if this flow deviates a little, a very little, infinitesimally little, due to the random encounter of an obstacle poised there – a small pebble, a small lacunar stone, a dove's small foot resting a moment – it will steer very surely toward the Black Sea, due east, whereas without the slender finger of circumstance it would have pursued its course toward the North Sea, due north, the Inn, or the Rhine, whereas due to the foot of another dove, due to the resting of another small poised stone, it would have fled due south, toward the Mediterranean Sea, via the Rhone. Tell me now, in the very vicinity of the stone, a bit upstream from its situation, where this handful of indistinct water is going to throw itself in the gigantic choice of the compass rose over immense distances. Almost zero cause, stupefying effects. This is the stable, unstable, metastable situation of white indetermination. The white waters of the Albula dance. The valleys, afterward, already a little lower, write the European topography. On high is the plateau, white pass.

Before writing on history, it would be wise to reflect on the existence of plateaus with zero causality. At the upper end of the Upper Engadine, anyone can, by eye or foot, trace the places where the fluxes are white. The water there isn't in a thalweg; no chreod is dug out there; any old gentle breeze will push the waters any which way. They laugh in the zero cause; they vibrate in the possible. Before being fluxions, they are fluctuations. The indeterminate has no direction; it has all of them.

I don't believe that these waters chiefly owe their happiness to their high situation. All the waters of the world are collection waters; they already come from higher up. On a very level topographical feature, below glacial latitudes, pockets or lakes can be seen, sometimes connected, sometimes linked over a long space; they haven't achieved their river destiny. They are below the threshold of percolation, isolated; they don't flow. I'm tempted to say that they are distributed in space, that they haven't yet entered into time. Their flux is white. The world serves me as a model. I do believe that anywhere, everywhere plateaus with zero or almost zero causality exist, that they mix with the very strongly determinate valleys; I believe that we perceive them poorly, so much is our reason only alert to inclined sequences, so much is it blind to the white plains. Reason is like Rome destroying the city of Alba; reason, strong like Horatius, murders the white Curiatii. There exist, in time, in the time of everyone as well as in the time of history, fields of white circumstances mixed with decided series; the possible, sown into the determinate, accompanies us, everywhere dense in time. Without these temporal plateaus mixed with the valleys, there would be no hope, no future, no change, always useless repetition, without these zero-cause planes, there would be no history, there would be nothing but laws, reason, the predictable, death. History follows the martial law of death often enough for us to understand how much we hate Alba, how little we understand it.

Alba crumbles into dust; it accompanies us. We drag its shadow behind us; the reason of history is posterior to its event; we push Alba in front of us, without seeing it. Alba precedes Rome, the way the possible is before the realized; Rome destroys Alba, the way force kills freedom. Rome would not exist without Alba, without the matrical indetermination in which the sword will trace the thalwegs of history.

Alba is in Rome the way the possible is in power.

The drawing of the thalweg is not a bad law. The river digs out the already dug out valley; the lowest line recruits the streams; they become its tributaries. None of them have ever followed but lower than themselves; none have ever obeyed but this law of falling. I have elsewhere sought what flows by the steepest slope, violence or money. Great power drains; that is how it grows.

At the end of the *Considerations*, Montesquieu discovers the law: it's also the end of Rome. The empire, he says, 'ends like the Rhine, which is no more than a stream when it disappears into the ocean'. Choking, he puts down his pen. The last line of the book doesn't say what the book says. A river descends, it descends all the time; it doesn't first of all climb so as to then only follow the slope. It doesn't grow to greatness so as to deliver itself over to decline: it grows to greatness at the same time as it decreases in height; the Rhine is immense and low toward its delta. Now Montesquieu would have to begin his book again. He's so tired; that's been obvious for more than twenty pages. He's so lazy, as we know how to be in the region of the Garonne. No, he will not take it up again. Why didn't he see the Garonne flow? No river climbs before going down again. Why would Rome have grown so as to then fall? It has always flowed along the descent, like the Tiber or the Albula, flowed along violence or money or the I-don't-know-what that recruits. Yes, Rome's dying was never-ending; nothing was situated lower than it. Even those who occupy Rome fall into the well of Rome and, Roman, continue what they believed they had destroyed. It's the Rome said to be growing that invents this low digging out. The question is always to find the valley. To find the determination, the inevitable decision.

For the moment we're at the plateaus of the origin where decision precisely vanishes. Alba, prior, is of an indeterminate whiteness.

By dying in the middle of the river, the drowned king first codes the white; the sacrificed king left a first determination on the prior indeterminate. A first truth, a first memory, on the flowing forgetfulness. By the rape of a savage vestal, Mars codes the white again. Rhea Silvia, chaste, is undecided or incised, violence leaves a scarification there.[6] Rhea flows like the Albula; she flows in the Hellenic language.

Rome, Plutarch said it well, Rome – always in Greek, we must speak Greek again in order to understand what the Latin is concealing – Rome, in Greek, means force. Alba precedes Rome, and Rome destroys Alba. Before decision is indecision, and force codes the white. This is an origin: force determines the primary indeterminate. It codes it. It codes it in Latin. It conceals it; it makes it latent.

What is writing a history? Livy answers: it's coding an indeterminate white space; it's determining it by force. And so concealing it.

A force impels toward a thalweg what is in equilibrium on the high plateau, on the high pass of the white waters. So the thing falls, flows.

I repeat: is this myth, legend or history? Is this a reconstruction that's advantageous to someone or other, imaginations, truths? Who can flatter themselves that they might ever know? The criteria are lacking, from the outside. I repeat: what is said in Livy's narrative is precise, exact, rigorous, abstractly coherent.

Alba and Rome, for the moment, are abstract forms, and Livy is a theoretician. The tragedians have pillaged him; the moralists have pillaged him; I am discovering little by little that the philosophers of history have spoken less profoundly than he did.

When I draw the geometral of the superabundant myth in which Hercules passes, a herdsman, and becomes a god after a murder, when I decipher the painting in which the cattle, grazing, leave abundant tracks, I understand that to all the questions the answer is always: everyone. I see that each person holds the set of places or that each person, if it can be said, is everyone – robber, robbed, liar, deceived, supplicant, silent, listening, murderer, victim, herdsman, hero, demi-god. Thus white is composed of every colour, thus white light brings the possible hues with it, thus the equilibrium of the high plateau is the capacity of all the low valleys or the zero of opposing forces, thus the matrix or the virginal womb is the capacity of maternities, of possible genealogies; on the wax every text is inscribable, beautiful ones, base ones, lying ones, true ones or ones deprived of meaning. The great black complexity is sometimes equipotent to the white. Each ox recounts a history, heavily imprinted on the virgin dust; each historian ox tells his history or writes it; the herd of all the cattle no doubt leaves on the thick palimpsest of earth a curve that goes through every point; I mean, Livy means that the possible directions can all be followed: either we are totally free or we no longer see anything there. Black state of totality or white state of capacity. As though in the incomprehensible, everything was permitted, as though in freedom, the incomprehensible rejoined the comprehensible. Every possible colour together can suddenly restore the white or clash in the chaos. History lets the proximity of these two multiplicities be seen.

Alba the White is the meeting place, upstream, of the large population that seeks sources. The white place where every point is possibly marked out. The place to which the oxen of history slowly go back up to drink.

Explanation is the invention of a schema, of a hypothesis, of an intelligible principle that applies without exception to the set of occurrences of the thing to be understood. Every time Livy talks about Alba, the same schema returns.

The armed centurions circumvent Mettius: the Alban dictator is at the centre of a circumstance. The young Albans, stripped of their weapons amid the armed Romans, experience a common terror among diverse emotions; they keep silent. When the Roman soldiers go to destroy Alba, the inhabitants will be in mournful silence, in a mute pain. Alba, tacit, is the city of silence. The king of Rome condemns the Alban dictator to death, who doesn't speak, who doesn't respond, who doesn't defend himself, remaining in a white silence: you divided your soul between Fidenae and Rome; you made your army hesitate on the field of battle, so shall your body be divided.

Mettius is put in the middle of horses. His stretched limbs are made fast to two four-horse chariots. Tullus Hostilius has the horses whipped. Eight horses abruptly advance and each in its direction. Mettius' body, a high plateau, is suddenly a flat plain, in the middle of the horses' force. Undecided, indeterminate amid the horses, which pull out in a star. The indecision doesn't last; Mettius, quartered, stretches, distracted. The plateau is not undecidable and white for long; it's going to yield to a tear. No one can guess which members will follow which horses. Mettius, incised, is analysed. It is said that you must not forget to put the knife at an animal's natural joints. Tullus Hostilius, aided by a few charioteers, follows the analytical method. He divides the difficulty into as many parts as the body comprises. Analysis and decision are contained in the primitive *diasparagmos*.

Rome cuts the Alban king into elements; it destroys the city of Alba into its elementary dust.

The vanguard of the cavalry sent from Rome empties Alba Longa of its population. The soldiers of the legions then demolish the city. No tumult, no clamour, no running, no frightful scenes, none of those disorders seen in captured cities when the gates are burst open. A sad silence, Alba suffers silent sorrow. A white silence, Alba vanishes. The Albans there are undecided, indeterminate: either motionless by their thresholds or wandering, vagabonds, through the city; the soul of the people is as white as the space, is as white as their voices. What should we leave here? What should we take with us?

Then the Roman horsemen shout that they have to leave, then the fracas of the houses collapsing rings out, then the dust rises from the outlying quarters, the edges collapsing first, then the fog spreads; it extends everywhere; it penetrates everywhere; it takes up the entire place. Of the houses, not a stone is left standing; of the rocks, only dust is left; only a cloud, Alba, a white cloud. They tore off my hands and pierced my feet; they counted all my bones. Analysis descends to the cloud, to chaos, to the limit, to whiteness. Passes from limbs to dust.

Alba returns to its first whiteness during the erasing; behind the cloud, it sees houses in ashes; it sees its laurels in dust; the *diasparagmos* of its king stopped at his limbs; the analysis of the city descends completely to dust; it returns to dust, to whiteness without elements. Thus atomism is born from the horror of scattered limbs; read Lucretius.

Corneille's young Horatius is unfailing, decided. Our tutors would sometimes have us think about Curiatius' hesitations; we were supposed to, I think, find him to be more human than the other brute beast of competition, but imbued with a bit of inferiority. The winner has short hair and a hard jaw; the loser is more vacillating, he smiles with gentleness. The class prepared little Horatii by crushing a few Curiatii. Curiatius, yes, is undecided, more indeterminate than his adversary. Psychology, as they used to say then, is not the precise place to put indetermination: it is everywhere in Alba.

Curiatius is undecided. The Albans, when the trumpet sounds, are in equilibrium on their thresholds; they wander and roam. When they're stable they are on the edge; when in motion it's a wandering route. *Deficiente consilio*, Curiatius is Alban. The dictator Mettius is also Alban. He wanted peace in time of war; he is now seeking war in time of peace, *ut prius in bello pacem, sic in pace bellum quaerens*. Before the signal for the engagement, he proposed the brothers' single combat; he lost, he wants the engagement. But he wants others to be engaged, Curiatius, first, in his stead, the Veientes and the Fidenates in his soldiers' stead. Undecided, seeming disloyal, his behaviour forms a chiasm; his body, like his soul, between two quadrigea, will be torn apart by the same schema, like the chimera. He bifurcates, anxious. The summit of a pass is at the same time the low point of a high valley and the high point of a low hill. Mettius is on the threshold of the battle, the way his citizens are near their doors: daring neither to remain nor to openly move on, *nec manere nec transire aperte ausus* – it's a question of crossing a river at its confluence, at its branching, at its bifurcation with the Tiber, the river of Hercules and Tiberinus; it's a question of crossing the river that Tullus has just crossed with his Romans, the Anio, the river the Veiens have just crossed, the Tiber; it's a question of cutting across the river, the two rivers, their confluence, while the allies have decided to do so, as well as their adversaries – daring neither to remain on the bank nor to cross it, not knowing who his rival is, the enemy on this bank or the enemy on the other one, no longer knowing the difference between friend and enemy, rival and ally, bank and river, he approaches the mountains unnoticed. He imperceptibly climbs the virtual; he seeks the summit of the pass where difference is erased. Undecided, he tries to gain time to see which way the wind is going to blow so as to incline his forces toward luck and fortune. *Fluctuans animo ... inclinare vires.* He will hurl his forces, finally inclined, from the fluctuation on the mountainous flank of virtuality into the valley of one of the two rivers. He climbs back up to the origin, seeking to regain the stable pass from which he will see two thalwegs, seeking the central point of the chiasm where difference is abolished, therefore regaining the white, a royal Alban.

Tullus, in the critical circumstance of seeing himself uncovered on his Alban flank, vows to create two temples, one to Pallor and the other to Panic. A good reader, good strategist, the Roman king says what he sees. For two spaces divide the classical line; Tullus' soldiers are on the edge of panic; the allied legionnaires of Alba are white phantoms, pale as their leader and their space. To Panic goes the Roman side; to Pallor goes Alba the White. *Pallor* and *Pavor* are assonant like Horatius and Curiatius, or Romulus and Remus, Aeneas or Antenor. Alba is pale: it is a rival, and it doesn't know where the riverbank is; it's the enemy's sister, it's allied on the left flank, it yields at the last moment.[7] It is at the neutral and null point of bifurcations, at the knot of the confluence where no one can know, not even the king, whether the waters of the Anio or the Tiber are in question. I see Curiatius in white armour armed with a bifid lance in equilibrium between two waters, in the city of the pass. Curiatius' soul, a pale and undecided image, is white because everything is white. He is in the white geometral.

'Alba is your origin.' Corneille's Sabine calls Rome and addresses it sharply: 'stop and consider that you are plunging your sword into your mother's womb.' Horatius, converted, did not stop that day. The brothers, the brothers-in-law, the twins fight each other; they haven't stopped since the overflowing Tiber when the riverbanks became erased and the twins, rivals, were saved; this hasn't stopped since the Albula has no longer been the Albula. No, it's not a question of the dismal repetition of history. It's a question of a mother. Can a person have the so rare audacity to kill their mother?

One person fights against another. By dint of fighting, the one is no longer separated from the other; you don't know who is who in the heat of the mêlée that melts differences. It's impossible to intervene; this is known. If I try to knock out the enemy, I might just hit the friend as well. Brothers, twins, assonant names, soon identity will come. The history of the combat goes from difference to the undifferentiated. It goes to the white; it goes from Rome to Alba and from the Tiber to the Albula; it goes from the daughter to the mother. The combat runs to the origin. It repeats it.

There are two combats, and Sabine, a woman, saw this; and Corneille, after Livy, saw it. The brothers' combat, that of Horatius and Curiatius, an abstract, common and conservative operator, the death instinct's dismal equilibrium without any novelty; and that of the daughter against the mother, that is, of the determinate against the indeterminate. The first one, a balance, a statics of the strong and the counter-strong, motionless in its fury, nothing new all around the horizon, is in space; it even occupies the totality of space; only it is seen, only death is seen, nothing new under the sun. But the other one is in time. It is time itself. How does the determinate gush forth from the indeterminate?

Alba is your origin. White is your origin. Your mother's virginal womb is white; it is undecided, not cut up, not determined, underdetermined to the very limits of indetermination. Alba, the white virgin mother, is the matrical space of the Platonic χώρα [chora], the new uterus, the imprint-recipient from which everything has come. White is so indeterminate that it is the geometral of all determinations. You, Rome, you, force, you are plunging the sword that marks into the white womb of your Alban mother. You are beginning to determine that indeterminate space, the way in the past the word Tiber was written on the white waters of the Albula. History is beginning.

All that needs to be done now is to add up to be finally convinced. The Albula erases tracks, and it is coded as Tiber by Tiberinus' death in its waters. The city of Alba is at the saddle-point where the lowest line is identically the highest one. The Alban dictator is quartered; he forms an equilibrated plateau, stretched tight, between the horses. It's because he had wanted peace during war and battle during peace. Yet, in the middle of the battle, not far from the point of bifurcation, suspending all decision, he has his armies climb to the middle of the mountain. The inhabitants of Alba, on the day of the end, a day of wrath, that one, hesitate on their thresholds or wander aimlessly. The undecided whiteness is in the naming; it spreads into space, into the topography, into the bodies, battles, tortures, strategies, the crowd, the souls. There is no mention of Alba where this same trait does not appear: it is essential. Alba, in its space and history, repeats its naming.

It is, on balance, a concept, that of the indeterminate.

The book of foundation is first of all ichnographical. It is written black, it is written white. Everything is written on the legend page, nothing is written on the Alba page. All the possible is in the former, implicated; all the possible is in the latter, virtual. The one is the well, full; the other is the white, virgin. Livy, at the origin, describes the most simple operators, a black jar – full, closed – and a white jar – open, empty.

Decision tears apart and cuts up. Rome, with a stroke of a sword, destroys Alba. Horatius kills Curiatius; Mars, father of Rome, rapes Rhea Silvia, the Alban vestal virgin. Rome decides; Alba, undecided, is torn apart: like its dictator and its priestess. The indeterminate plain inclines; time flows with blood and tears.

The overdetermined [*surdéterminé*] doesn't bring anything more to the determined than superslaughter [*surtuerie*] does to slaughter for those killed by weapons. Power is always stupid and brutish enough to dig up the dead in order to kill them once again. We aren't the first to want to superslaughter, we who are preparing forces likely to destroy the enemy on earth three and seven and thirty-three times. The Romans already knew how to kill Curiatius three times. Hercules already tried to kill Geryon three times, and Cacus, perhaps, three times. Fury, superfury. I'm looking for water basins to cool off the superslaughter. Useless and barbaric overdetermination.

The underdetermined seems richer and more interesting. It's a much more invaluable concept in history. It mixes the possibles with the achieved and makes bifurcations abound. The underdetermined ceaselessly accompanies us; it is the lightness of what is anterior. At the limit, the undetermined is placed at the origin, simply. It is time's upstream. It is white. It is peace. It is capacity. It is the virgin who's going to be mother. It is silence. It is virgin, holy, before the word, the first vestal. This is Alba. An immense tree with an infinity of branches comes out of it, can come out of it.

An immense river with an infinity of branches can gush forth from it.

The Albula flows, laminar. In a white river, a wave [*lame*] follows a wave and precedes a wave;[8] nothing is seen there, nothing is marked there; does the Albula flow? How are things with time?

The savage kings of Alba, on the other hand, weave a combinatorics. It occupies space; it totally freezes time.

The Albula starts flowing; we remark, we observe that it flows at the first mark, at Tiberinus' death. The Albula is prehistorical; it is laminar; no one knows it descends; it erases the tracks. The Tiber is historical; it is coded by death.

The combinatorics drowns in time. As a result, time, coded, flows differently; it flows turbulent.

We only know how to think codes, marks, laws, stabilities, exchanges, substitutions, in brief, combinatorics. We don't really know how to think time, the pure processual.

Livy lodges our historical obligations in the Alban precession: of course we need to think the tracks, but that's easy; deceit, ruse, hatred, passion for combat are there to help us in this. We above all need to try to think the pure processual, the white river that becomes Tiber.

Genesis, pp. 71–2, 'The Chain'

On the white surface of water, Hercules doesn't leave a ripple. On the same surface of water, a fluctuation, a bit of turbulence, one day swallowed up the king of Alba. The same circumstance either has no consequence or forms a line of descendants. The line of descendants runs, it stops; Alba is no more than a destroyed city. In the white womb of the vestal, a rape, punished by death, doesn't leave any line of descendants. Or it leaves such a one that can be said to be the master of the world.

The fluctuation erases itself of itself; it falls back into the well of the possible. It grows, founds the stock of a line, bifurcates, bushes out, grows larger, thunders, falls. A thousand fluctuations fall back in this way onto the white surface of the Albula every day. A single one made it the Tiber. A single one made it historical. A single one produces the Alban history or legend, which comes to a sudden end. Another produces Romulus, the son of a virgin and of rape, and the founding father of the people that would one day be the most powerful in the world.

The white fluctuates, it scintillates under the sun. It is the present.

Rome, the sole object.[9] *I confess to having, like many, scorned Rome. That stupid, crude and rough people neither had nor gave access to what makes our lives worth living: true knowledge, science and philosophy, and the mad mythology that sheds light on the shadow, ecstatically; it never had, except for rare exceptions, access to beauty. Rome suffers, despite its size, because of its weight, from the vicinity of the Greeks, and the Semites as well. I used to read the Greeks and the Bible, my daily bread, and I left Rome to its stones and its old dead might.*

Today, I understand. Mature age favours incarnation. Livy doesn't say what I say he says, me a little Gallic Greek, me a Jew and Greek at the same time, a Christian Hellenized before the dawn, a little exact scholar, long humanized in interpretation. He says, with Virgil: Aeneas saw Troy die; he brings a curious mixture to the Italian coast. For his passage to Carthage and his Semite love affair with Dido don't count for nothing. Dido, a victim, who dies of it. At the very origins of Rome, everything of what we, Greek and Semite, are is there. Before Rome, I was. Before Rome, the conditions of knowledge are there.

Rome doesn't speculate, doesn't talk, never dialogues for the sake of ultimate refinement; Rome fights, Rome prays, it is pious, it humbly accepts the black of meaning in the repeated gesture. It builds, it extends, it preserves. It is not the negative, that work of destruction that, it seems, makes things progress. No, it doesn't progress by means of the no; it progresses in the black. I now see Rome as black, as black as Alba is white. It gives flesh to the word, it builds. Rome incarnates itself; it is construction.

I seem to be touching today, through an experience, on what can be called incarnation. Rome is not of the word like Athens; it is not of the book, of the breath or the written, like Jerusalem. Conversely, it is not of water, like the first, nor of the desert, like the second. Rome is hard and dumb like rock, black like the bowels of a rock, never transparent like the pyramid or tetrahedron of Greek epiphany, never multiplied like Hebraic interpretation over the white space of the desert. Jerusalem is light and supple like a hundred thousand signs; Athens flies around the logos; Rome is heavy. It stutters, stammers, gestures; it never knows. It is of ritual, not of myth. The body holds the staff; it traces the temple and plinths; it doesn't know why. The Jew knows how to write why seven times; the Greek can say it eleven times as much. My Judeo-Greek culture is so light that I can carry it beyond the sea, beyond the desert. It flies like language and writing. It is software.[10] Rome is in its gestures and its body, when the sign stops and becomes stuck in the mud. Rome is hardware. Its hand is as sure as the Greek mouth is rapid or as Jewish complexity bursts into networks. Rome cannot be outside of Rome, as Athens was outside of itself, as Jerusalem has never ceased being. Rome is in Rome entire and always within its walls. Athens is mind, Jerusalem is sign, and Rome is object. Res. Res publica, sometimes. Brutus, brutish, carries a staff made of cornel-wood with him whose inside is gold to offer it to the god Apollo in Delphi. This is the riddle of Rome, and this is its solution.

I believe I understand, but that is nothing; I believe today I am touching this object. I see it being built; I see how it was built. Crude, coarse-grained, rough, stiff in gesture. But I have always known this because I've lived that experience. My father, uncultured as they say, nevertheless bequeathed me all that in me lives on culture, that is, all that lives in me and repels death, whereas the discourse called cultural never taught me anything but a few *pieces of nonsense. If you give me a sign or a word, above all a clear meaning or a diaphanous theory, you give me a content that holds everything in its container, a glass marble or a crystal ball. In an instant, I know; I've only received a minute or a flash. This can be great and beautiful; this doesn't fill my time. Above all, this cannot produce a time, this does not yet make a history. I have received pieces of rock from my father; he was a rock-breaker; I have received from him swathes of clay, he was a ploughman; I have received from him sand and gravel, hard and black. From the neolithic to my death, these things in stock remain to be understood. Of course, it's good to learn what we can understand, but we live on what we haven't yet understood. That's what it is, in the literal sense, to carry symbols with you, those broken rocks, those tesserae. I live bathed in the transparent light that comes to me from the eastern Mediterranean, from Athens, from Jerusalem. Plato shines, Isaiah sparkles. They project light around them. But Livy is black. He throws out no light. He receives it, takes it, envelops it and keeps it. He receives it from Greece, Hercules, Evander; he receives it from Troy, Aeneas; he receives it from the Semite shore, Dido. Never again will he give it back. Rome is not an organon of comprehension; it takes comprehension and imprisons and implicates it. Athens and Jerusalem explicate, endlessly make things explicit to the point where the object becomes desert. A torrent of light comes from them. The tracks, in Rome, are turned in the counter-direction. They come from the black cave where the white cattle, the shepherd Cacus, the man Evander and the god Hercules are. The tracks enter, if the narrative is Greek. In Greek, there is only, in the black cave, what one has put there. They come out, in Latin, and no one knows what is in there. No one understands anything by means of Livy; we have to understand Livy. If I hear the voice of Saint John crying out in the desert, if I hear the fearsome voice of the writer prophets of Israel, if I hear the logos of Heraclitus, I hear, more than meaning, the source, the condition, the emergence of meaning itself; in Rome I only hear the voice of cattle answering the voice of cattle. One turns around upon hearing John or Hosea or Amos; one turns around upon hearing Heraclitus or Parmenides – who would turn around at the cattle's baritone? At this low lowing, beneath meaning. One turns around to go toward the mountain of light – what good is it to turn around toward a black cave? Greekness, just like Odysseus, comes out of the cave toward the light, comes out of the dark cave where blinded monsters, wounded, live. Rome brings us back there, Rome calls us back there. I have heard the voice of the cattle, by chance. I know the difference between a marble of light and a rock from my father. This black cave in which light, meaning and the tracks are imprisoned is the very inside of this rock. That's even what being an object, a thing of the world is, and it's the flesh of incarnation, a captured, seized light, locked inside the walls.*

Livy is there; a thing and a cave, Rome is to be understood, whereas Athens and Jerusalem have, for four millennia, created understanding, like beacons. Rome became an object; Athens and Jerusalem are subjects. Rome is as dumb as an ox; it accepts being black as the tomb where Cacus' triple body lies; it isn't a subject. It is a tomb of stone. We had understood nothing by only ever immersing our bodies in light. Perhaps we hated the black; perhaps we had the duty and right to do so; perhaps we hated the object; perhaps we hated the world. Idealism detests incarnation. We are accustomed to having the tracks of meaning go in one direction and one direction only, and to their being oriented, yes, toward the Orient, where the sun dawns. We don't know how to, we can't go back over our steps. Drawn, fascinated by the givers of light, we don't carry the clarity into the heart of the black bodies.[11] Like all children, we get impatient with time. The eye takes no time to cross transparency. Rome is rock; it is object; it has time; it makes time and requires time. It folds light into its stone walls, into its partitions, its armour, its ploughs and rituals. It incarnates meaning. Incarnation, for two thousand years, has been the word submerged in the flesh, in the black entrails of the untouched virgin, the white light in the darkness of life. This ancient incarnation – but we would have to change words – this descent of life to the inert, of Hercules to Evander, of god to man, of Evander to Cacus, of scholar to herdsman, of Cacus to Geryon's ox, of the shepherd to the animal, of the ox to the cavern, of the brute living thing to the rock wall, this incarnation or this petrification, ab urbe condita, for two thousand seven hundred and fifty-three years, or for three thousand one hundred and eighty-four years, has been meaning submerged little by little into the black entrails of the cave, into the foundations of the city, into the tomb of rock; you are rock and in this rock meaning is now buried, trapped, latent. Latent, Latin. Rome absorbs the light and doesn't give any out; it gives a rock in its stead, and it will take you millennia to understand. This is how light descends into the petrified world here below; this is how the darkness is powerless to see the light. Rome is above all darkness.

Yet the light is there, from the dawn, and Rome, dark, receives it, doesn't receive it, and absorbs it. Alba is as white as Athens or Jerusalem. Alba came from Aeneas, who came from Troy, from Greece, from Carthage, and Rome destroys it, absorbs it, encloses the white and no long returns it. Alba is the imprint-recipient; Rome is the black force that traces and codes imprints. Rome is the weight of the cattle, their feet or their hooves, knife, plough, sword; it is the black of the sign when the white disappears. Alba the White is subject. Yet, like every subject, it is thrown to the ground, under Rome, crushed, trampled. Rome killed its brother; Rome killed its mother, but then stop persecuting Rome. Alba the White is subject; Rome is object. Rome, the sole object. It builds the object, in the black cave that encloses the voices, in the *founding furrow that encloses the brother's body, in the stone tomb. Nothing emanates from that object except the voices of the cattle. How can we imagine that there is something there to be understood, a stupid, crude and rough people, peasant, that calls to itself only with that low, hoarse and monotonic voice, the voice of the object, the noise of the muffled world?*

Athens by dint of light throws geometry onto the way of the universal. Jerusalem by dint of interpretation throws history into the universal of time. But it is to Rome itself that, two millennia later, physics is judged to belong. The object, finally, delivers up its meaning.

The meaning in the object, the light in the stone, the eye of God in the tomb, the buried victim.

I need geometry to see distinctly where Alba is situated, at the foot of the Alban Hills and on a promontory, in the saddle-point of that pass; I need geometry and the simple science of language to draw the chiasm of Mettius and the distracted star of his diasparagmos; *I need analysis and science to see Alba in the fog of its atomized dust, the final scattered pieces of the city destroyed after the exploded pieces of its dictator, houses in ashes and laurels in dust; so I need Evander, son of Hermes, to see clearly there; so I need Athens to evaluate the Alban indetermination. Livy, bringing history and the Herculean rite, no doubt needed these things as well. I need to know how things are with time and history in order to evaluate the river Albula in its valley of tears; I need Jerusalem for the coding of history on the indeterminate white river. I remain Judeo-Greek, by logos and in time.*

Rome devotes itself to completely different work. It builds the object. Closes the cave, closes the tomb. The black light is trapped in the kiln. We might say that Rome is a trap, a light trap, just as an object is. Athens and Jerusalem are dispensers of light, but Rome absorbs it, imprisons it, locks it in, like an object does. Brutus, an imbecile, mute, leaves for Greece carrying a staff of gold hidden in a staff made of cornel-wood. We have to shed light on Rome via Athens and Jerusalem in order to understand; we have to tell its reason and history. Apollo will open Brutus' staff, and Brutus is, himself, the second of the founders of Rome. We have to shed light on an object via geometry and history to create a physics of it. We have to shed light on Rome-object via geometry-Athens and time-Jerusalem in order to begin to understand a little. In Rome, Galileo. In Rome, the well-named Galileo saw the object, saw the object in its necessary place, for the first time; he saw it in space, number and time, pondere, mensura, numero; *he founded mechanics.*[12] *I'm making the same effort as Galileo; I'm making the effort that's conditional to Galileo's intuition. In Rome, in the third Rome, a scientia condita, Galileo discovers the object. I'm saying that Rome forged it; I'm saying that Rome has been building it since its own foundation. For the object to be there, perceived, and for it to be an object of science, history and geometry aren't enough; geometry must be incarnated, time must plunge into the world, the Albula must not flow white indefinitely. Geometry must become stone before the word becomes flesh. We must therefore try to understand how this object was formed. Two incarnations were necessary, and I'm speaking about the first one, archaic, unknown.*

The object grasped by Galileo requires two worlds, or rather two spaces and one time. The incandescent space of geometry and the black world of opaque mass. Nothing is so easy as understanding the first one; it is only there to understand and be understood; nothing is so easy to understand as the word, it's there to be understood; but nothing is so obscure as the second one; nothing is so difficult to conceive as the body, flesh or stone, to under- stand as the noise that emanates from it; nothing is so difficult as knowing how it receives and envelops the light. It is incomprehensible that it might be comprehensible. Einstein's astonished questioning, the old Cartesian question of union together form modern deliberation, stemming from physics. Beyond the Christian mystery of the incarnation, the question goes back to the foundations of Rome. To the triangle of our three mother cities.

In the middle of the wood where Numa met, he said, Egeria was an opaque grotto from which a perennial spring flowed. The tracks of the king Numa go to the dark grotto, and the direction of the stream that erases the tracks leaves it. We know what was in Cacus' cave, even if he cheated; the Greeks are so talkative that they can't keep a secret. Greek or Jewish texts are always easily explained; they are there to be explained; they are always already explained a thousand times over; the only difficulty we have is that of the bush that's too leafy from too many explanations. We don't know what's in Numa's grotto; no one has ever seen the nymph. Furthermore, Plutarch calls her Tacita, the silent, the poor mute. The Latin texts are latent; the grotto is black; the spring carries us in the wrong direction; the rivulet erases the marks; it only murmurs with a white falling.

Chance had Silvius be born in the forest. From the savage forest come the Alban kings, white combinatorics. From the savage grotto in the middle of the woods comes an unceasing river. From the dark cave comes the voices of the cattle. Three times the black box, the originary upstream.

What comes out of the black box is white noise, the silence of meaning.

Yes, but how is that dark object made?

Isn't the object merely what geometry says it is?

It's easy to think about places where thought already is. It's easy to turn a rich and loose compost. Nothing is simpler than practising philosophy on subjects or in the languages in which philosophy has long been cultivated. I can speak Greek, rethink geometry; it wouldn't be much trouble; I descend the best slope, for geometry is dense with thoughts, present or latent; the language of the Hellenes is that of philosophy itself, in its nascent state. I can also speak French or German, sometimes English; I can still, in these languages, endlessly retrace the tradition of thought; nothing could be easier. Even productive sometimes. I can write in Hebraic signs and produce a deciphering; it's the straight grain of their own genius; I can translate the prophets into Jewish terms of wisdom and history; I am again following the best descent, the simplest thread, the good method. The good soil for cultivating has been turned a thousand times already, cultivation of the plains. Athens and Jerusalem have been writing, speaking, thinking since anyone has thought, spoken or written around the Mediterranean Sea.

In the places where thought has not yet been, it is difficult to think. A bad slope of sterile rock. On subjects or in languages where philosophy has not occurred, *it is necessary* to practise philosophy. It is necessary out of duty, out of research or quest. Out of duty: those bad rocks, abandoned by culture, can return some day. And I'll change images: the same rocks serve for stonings and slings, violence, and for pediments, construction. The barbarian demolishes the edifice in order to bring the stone back to its function as a projectile; wisdom [*sagesse*] builds in order to immobilize the stone, to appease the hatred, for protection. Why then do you think walls, cities and temples exist, when we can sleep under the stars and prostrate ourselves before the horizon? We have never built except to settle the stones down [*assagir*]; without that, they would fly too much between us. The builder's plan hardly counts; the architectonic ideal is only there for representation; the essential thing is for the projectiles to be immobilized. Why, everywhere, ruins? History destroys in order to make the built into a quarry for weapons. We stone people better in ruins and non-active building sites. This we know quite well, we who have lived such a long time on destruction, we who have lived science and knowledge, plastic arts and philosophy, devoted to that destruction. We no longer live anywhere but in the midst of ruins, that is to say, projectiles. Building is nothing but immobilizing them. Peace.

The quest now is to search for veins of gold in the sterile rock, to practise philosophy where it hasn't yet appeared. Running the tremendous risk of the improbable, even if it means failing, rather than walking along in the repetition of the sure and certain. So here it is: what's the situation with Rome, from its foundation, brute force and opaque language? If I speak ancient Latin and if I think Rome I'm not, at the outset, assured of thinking. Nothing there is disposed for that; nothing is prepared. Science never appeared in Rome, neither did geometry or logic, never anything but politics. Certain people, sometimes, made a trade of importing a bit of philosophy into it, physics as well, fairly poorly integrated into the Latins' stony speech. Rome had to wait until it was no longer entirely in Rome and it spoke Greek, and other languages as well, for the importation to succeed in settling in. Rome doesn't invent philosophy, it doesn't invent inventive thought at its source. Never did ancient Rome think by itself. The source and spring of the new never gushed forth there. Nor did it ever think of itself or about itself. The City didn't have a passion, like other cities, to understand itself, to explain itself or to say itself or to search its depths – at the risk of destroying itself – for its spirit, its concept or its motor force; it was never reflexive. Rome remains of rock. It was not a philosopher: neither inventive nor meditative. This is great luck, I think. For we must be one for it, in its place. It's not every day that philosophy finds virgin ground in such a frequented place. If it wants to invent, it finds Rome. If it seeks its pleasure in remaining inside itself, it leaves the City.

Vesta, Hestia, epistemology. Rome constructs the object; how can this be done?

The cult of Vesta, it is said, is of Alban origin. Remus and Romulus are Rhea Silvia's sons, the vestal virgin and Alban savage. Before the founder, his mother.

The mother is virgin, white like Alba, untouched, inviolable, undecided or incised; she is violated, torn up like the dictator Mettius in the middle of the horses. The vestal is chaste; she keeps continual guard of the pure and perpetual fire. The fire is a centre; the earth revolves around the centre; it revolves around the fire. The fire is Vesta and Monad; Vesta is Hestia, Hermes' consort.

The history of religions, right here, discovers the most archaic constellations of the modern philosophy of knowledge and understanding. There is an epistemology of Hermes; there is another more profound one of Hestia. And all the more so as there is a good chance that these are the same word. Hestia is stable; she keeps, a fixed point, to her hearth. Science, episteme, could be formed, in its name, from the same stability: from the same invariances and the same conservations. What then is science? What then is epistemology? Archaically, it's Hestia's chanson de geste, the discourse on Hestia. Hermes' epistemology is modern, decentred, unstable discourse. The epistemology of Hestia or Vesta, more foundational, is the ancient centred discourse. Implied. The foundation of modern knowledge, the foundation of the knowledge of the object, the foundation of the third Rome, during the enlightenment or modern age, rejoins the prefoundation of the first Rome, through Romulus' vestal mother, on the far or on the hither side of the foundation of the second Rome, Christian, still sacrificial, virginal and maternal, once again. Yes, the foundations of our knowledge plunge into the shadow just as far and just as deeply.

The fire contemplated by the vestals is at the centre of a round temple. The fire illuminates. The Greek pyramid's fire makes the tetrahedron transparent; geometry's ideality is diaphanous, epiphany. Athens, I've said, is the source of light; it propagates light; it demands coming out of the cave, out of the black box, into the sun. Athens is of the sun. Vesta's pure fire doesn't cross the solid, the temple, so as to make it pure ideality; on the contrary, it is walled in, enclosed, locked in, in secrecy. The vestal's face is dazzled by fire; it remains under veil. The light can't be unveiled. What can be said about the truth?

If the fire goes out, it must be relit by a play of concave mirrors that make the rays converge on the same unique centre. The temple is round to represent, perhaps, the world or the heavens; it is round to form that convergence. The light, the fire don't shoot out toward the outside, don't diffuse, don't dispense themselves; they are concentrated.[13] Athens and Jerusalem are beacons; Rome is a kiln. The fire and the black light, the black radiation are trapped. The fire and the light are hidden; the vestal is hidden; she hides the sacred objects of the cult. No one else could see them except the pontifex. An open and empty vase and another sealed vase were furtively seen when the Gauls sacked the city and the vestals were fleeing. If the jar opens it's empty, and the black box is closed; we will never know what is in the black box. If the virgin is violated she is no longer vestal.

This cult is of light and confinement, of the closure of the visible in the invisible, of hidden brightness, of the universe that locks its conditions of knowledge inside itself. Of the eye in the tomb. Of knowledge and ignorance.

This cult is of covering over, of knowledge and of the veil. I see there the primary images of epistemology, a very ancient foundation of a certain kind of knowledge.

When a vestal commits an offence, she is whipped by the pontifex behind a veil and in a dark place where she stands naked.

The vestal is under veil, under hymen, under curtain, under the wall and ground.

Open the wall, open the hymen, open the veil: death.

If a vestal, under her veil, encounters a man going to his death he will not go to his death that day. If a vestal, under her veil, encounters a living man, he will go to his death that day. Through the vestal we know the unknown or we don't know the known. Death is placed on life and life placed on death. The vestal is placed on the chiasm of Mettius, Alban. Virgin and mother, already.

The vestal is hidden: in her temple, in her veils, in her litter, underground, or behind her hymen. The vestal is illuminated: day and night in front of the pure and perpetual fire, guard and watcher. She is the nearest to the centre of the earth. She is under the light, living; she is in the shadow of the black wall.

She is white, she is black; she is totally white, she lives totally in the black box.

The relation of violence and this latency must be understood. What is hidden is a light; what is closed off is a brightness. Why this mortal relation to darkness?

It seems to me that I'm approaching the savage foundations, anthropological, of knowledge, of its theory.

Any vestal who unveiled her virginity is buried alive at the Colline Gate. A subterranean chamber is dug in the mound, beneath an access chimney. A bed and a lamp, bread, a vase filled with water, some oil and milk are deposited there. The cortege that is about to cross the forum prepares in silence. The litter carrying the victim is closed; no one can see her; she cannot see; she cannot hear anything, in white silence, strapped with belts; no one can hear her voice, an enclosure of the body in linens and belts, an enclosure of the glance and sounds. The procession advances, mute, deaf, blind, black. Here is the mound and its raised earth where the torture takes place. The priests utter secret prayers there. No one understands; do they understand? And the sky toward which the palms of the hands are raised, does it understand? A meticulous enclosure of the senses amid the open voice.

The spectacle is frightful; it is a dismal day.

The guilty party is extracted from the litter, entirely covered with a veil and put on the ladder descending into the tomb. Everyone withdraws. She descends. The ladder is removed; the crypt is filled with dirt so as to leave the spot level. On the raised earth, the mound at the Colline Gate, no trace remains of the abominable assault.

The chief priest presides at the rite, surrounded by priests, surrounded by the crowd, surrounded by the city. At stake is a lynching. Everyone forms in a circle and rushes at her. You might think it Tarpeia's lynching. We will never know whether Tarpeia delivered up the city; we will never know whether Rhea Silvia enjoyed the god Mars, but we do understand that these three stories are all one. To better hide the lynching of the vestal, the Sabine shields, or the gold bracelets, or the jewelled rings, worn on the left hand, the sinister side, are all more sure and certain coverings than the filled-in ground at the Colline Gate. Tarpeia introduces the enemy into the place; she opens the closed door; she lifts a veil, a hymen, and I know not what; she opens to a knowledge that the hard roof of the shields immediately covers over again. Rhea Silvia was a victim of the god Mars; she calls violence by its name. She receives violence in her, and she will give birth to the enemy brothers, to the victim and the murderer. The king puts her in chains and throws her in prison; no one will hear anything more of her.

Here is the light, a perpetual fire, ineffably pure, come from the sun by mirrors, at the centre. The white light is at the centre like a sun in the universe. The light is white like Alba; the vestal cult is Alban; Hestia is the virgin mother. Yet here is the darkness: it doesn't exclude the light, as John might say; it includes it. It encloses it under a proliferating and multiplied covering, under the hymen and the veil, under the ground and the wall, under the shield, the bracelet, the strap, the litter.

Here is the light, hidden. What are you hiding? Why? In the mortuary rite of Vesta, what is hidden is the murder of an innocent. But the essential thing in all this is to hide. I'm not seeking what is hidden. I'm simply saying: well-organized ignorance covers over knowledge. From the depths of the litter, from the depths of the hole, the tomb, the abyss, the vestal's voice doesn't even reach us. Not even the voices of the cattle. Nothing. Silence. Not even the tracks going in the counter-direction. Nothing. Levelled ground. Not even a ray of light. Nothing. Blackness. A dark place, and the veil in front.

This constitutes an in-itself. The object. The sole object.

Fundament, in a tomb, of the knowledge of foundation.

Plutarch gives us a long shudder of horror; he describes the torture of the deflowered vestal. Livy tells the lynching of Tarpeia. The two texts, parallel, illuminate each other from one language to the other. Living, the vestal Tarpeia is buried under the shields of the Sabines. She opened the gates, the wall, the way Remus had jumped over the hymen, the limit, the edge. The ritual burial of the living victim is a blind lynching that's kept from being seen by a thousand veils, that's only said in silence, that's only touched from afar; Tarpeia's lynching is the ritual burial of the living vestal: the roof of shields becomes precious stone; the stone becomes earth; it is analysed into tiny pieces, the way the houses of Alba became dust and fog. Tarpeia translates τροπαία [tropaia], that is, *pharmakos*, she or he who averts fates, or wards off ills. So the canonic rite and its example or its application illuminate in return the very origins of Rome, I mean of Romulus. The two twins, born of Rhea Silvia, follow their destiny on the banks of the river; the Tiber has overflowed, violent, too full of the dead and weapons, and hides its riverbanks and the rivals. But Silvia won't be spoken of any more; she is vestal, and she is violated; she was even violated by Mars; she was therefore the seat, the victim, the object of violation par excellence. She therefore incurs the prescribed punishment. Livy cautiously says: *vincta in custodiam,* the entire circumstance in two words: enchained, enclosed. Bound by straps, we know. But where is the black box? Under a few shields or under the mound at the Colline Gate? Yes, we have just discovered how the mother of Rome died. Lynched, hidden, tied up, buried alive. She lies under the foundation, under her son Remus' very corpse. Foundation of the foundation, tomb under the tomb.

The first consequence. Mars is at the origin; the flooding river is at the origin; the two twins, their fight to the death is at the origin. All the images of violence are present: the god, the rape, the growth of the flood, the rivalry. Father and brother. Only one is absolutely missing: the mother. She is hidden like a vestal, buried like a vestal, strapped up like a vestal, smothered like a vestal, forgotten like a vestal. All the images of violence surround the lynching and bury it beneath Rome, beneath the foundation of the city. But two words make them be forgotten. The mother is hidden beneath the ground, and she is forgotten in the text.

In this tomb is light; in this blackness is knowledge, that of Alba the White, crushed beneath Rome, a black force. This light trapped in the black body is constitutive of the object. The second consequence, quasi-Egyptian. Thales' Platonic light makes the pyramid transparent and diaphanous; the Roman blindness blackens it, petrifies it, fills it with dirt, objectivizes it. Rome constructs the object.

The light comes out of the tomb: geometry. The tomb encloses the light: object of the world. Perhaps the appearance of another incarnation and another resurrection will be necessary for physics to emerge, for light, one day, to shine through from the depths of the brute object. From the stupid fall of mute bodies a ray of geometry wells up, miraculous. The rock has just been rolled away from the tomb.

The three texts – rite, history or legend – all form one more or less developed text. Plutarch enlarges on the rite. Livy recounts the Tarpeian legend, quickly; he hides the primary Silvia with two words. You might say a cone with its point downwards: three lynchings coming closer and closer together, more and more hidden, all the way down to the originary point. The origin is discovered by extracting this cone from the ground.

Plutarch, *Camillus*, 20.7–8; 21.1–3

The secret of sacred objects buried beneath the vestals themselves, here it is, patent, and such as Plutarch gives it, in passing. Here are two little jars. Is this the testimony of Lucius Albinius, the man with the cart? I believe it because of his name, white light. Light come from Alba perhaps, but light in any case in the darkness of knowledge. Lucius Albinius furtively saw, perhaps. The vestals are fleeing Rome occupied by the Gauls. Overcome with fatigue and following the riverbank, they are carrying precious objects in their breasts. Lucius Albinius has his wife and children get down from the cart and has the vestals climb on. Perhaps he saw, in a flash, in the breasts of the female brethren what must not be seen. It's because he was transporting the immobile, after the vestals had unbolted the closed. Here are two little jars. It's not known whether they were buried or whether they were carried away.

One is open and empty, the other full and sealed. If the jar is open it is empty; if the jar is full it is closed, sealed. When the box is open, it is white; when the black box is open, it is white; it is black, if it is closed. When I turn my back, the phenomenon takes place; I turn around, I think I see it, it vanishes. Or again: here is the object, an object, whatever object it may be, for example this pyramid or this tomb. I open it, and I'm Greek; the incandescent tetrahedron shines with diaphanous geometry, epiphany. No, it is full, it is closed, it remains black, the black box of the opaque thing. Yes, here is an opaque thing, and here is that transparent ideality, an empty jar and a full jar; knowledge is one and the other, but it is above all their union, their inseparability. The physics of the world is the geometry in the things themselves, an empty jar and a full jar, an open jar and a closed jar, a black jar and a white jar, and no one knows why they are together, twins; no one has ever understood their incomprehensible harmony. So unearth the jars, so open one jar, look furtively at the jars in the open breast of a fleeing vestal, the secret rests there, patent, in their union, in their association, in their twinship. Theory is empty, white, and the thing is black, sealed. So open the temple door, open the walls of Rome by paying Tarpeia, open the veil, open the strap, open the hymen, eviscerate the mound at the Colline Gate, and you will find the intact white virgin and the buried black virgin, the fire, the interment, the shadow and the milk, knowledge and ignorance, together. Titus Tatius, king of the Sabines, pays Tarpeia to open the gates for him; he enters, and he covers the body of the vestal herself with her pay. At the moment of knowing, he covers, and he covers with the price he paid to know. Tarpeia is violated, inviolable; she is always beneath shields. As though experience, as though theory itself, as though the energy used to invent and acquire them suddenly darkened the object to be known. As though the conditions of knowledge were accompanied, twins, by dark conditions of ignorance. Whatever the progress of our knowledge may be, the real, as they say, remains veiled. The cult of Vesta reveals and hides the multiplicity of veils and shadows. We tear one veil off, two; this isn't unveiling, it's the old Harlequin of the old Italian comedy who is never done removing his next-to-last livery. Even if he were naked, even if the vestal were violated, even if the jars were seen, the secret remains, patent. The wise man knows, in addition, that he has made no more progress than when he began.

Beneath the institution, or in its foundation, the black box is black. It is closed, sealed by the institution itself, located above. Let the institution disappear and leave the glance free, and the box will be white and empty. We are never certain of seeing the real corpse.

The cult of Vesta doesn't tell of the cave of shadows or of the exit into the great sun of transcendence. It isn't dualist, and it is feminine. It mixes, and it accompanies; it is wise. The dualist posits a space of error, illusion and ignorance, and an open plateau flooded by the sun. Error, truth; the known and the unknown; the unsayable and the said. Knowledge and ideology, the conscious and the unconscious, science and poetry, heaven and hell. His simple world is made up of a black planet and another white planet; it's handy for judging. No one speaks starting from the black planet. Yes, the two jars, precisely. Consequently, if you illuminate the cave, you will get Ariadne's thread, the complete blueprint of the complexity. You will be scholarly; you will be able to act; you will be cured. Victory of the sun over the ignorant shadow. Not so fast.

Dualism is imaginary. It belongs to violence; it belongs to the tribunal, and it belongs to the police. It belongs to those who want to be right. This has nothing to do with the process of knowledge. The cult of Vesta tells of a more concrete gnoseology, a subtler one and more faithful to the state of things than the myth of the Greek cave or the Cretan labyrinth. It says that the black jar always accompanies the white; it says that ignorance never ends. It says that Tarpeia exited outside the walls so as to immediately disappear beneath the shields and bracelets she went in search of. It says, I say, that Lucius Albinius, white light, briefly saw, through the vestal's veil, her opening and virginity the day the walls of Rome were forced open by the Gauls' violence, and that this violation – software, soft – went unnoticed: the secret is magnificently patent and latent at the same time.

Yes, knowledge is patent and latent at once; it is never either one or the other. There is as much shadow in exact or rigorous or experimental or verified knowledge as there is light in all that we call shadow. There are theorems in poems and darkness in intuition. This never ends, and the veils pile up. It took me twenty years to understand Taylor; it was von Koch who made me understand. I'm not in question. If Taylor had really been understood, von Koch would have been from the seventeenth century.[14] It has taken me as long to understand that Vesta helped me to understand, much better than the black box with the Platonic cinema. Clear things take as long to see as things said to be of the shadow, which are sometimes just as clear as the clear things. And, as I have said elsewhere, light in the air diffuses everywhere; it wanders crazily in the atmosphere. No one comes out of a cave abruptly so as to arrive at celestial dazzlement. We always travel in a spectrum of lights and shadows. And when I open a black box, it often happens that it still contains some shadow. And when a veil comes off, the body, far from being naked, is once again veiled. The solution to some given problem suddenly unearths the conditions for ten problems, often more difficult than the preceding one. What researcher doesn't know this? We are all travellers of the chiaroscuro. And this lets us understand why the old rationality used the same images as their enemies: reason illuminates like belief, and unreason darkens like nonbelief. By dint of fighting, they have become twins. The spectrum I'm talking about covers, in fact, the space of all knowledge, from incandescent mathematics, the jar said to be white, to the history of religion, the jar said to be black. The patent secret is, as I've said, in the middle of the two jars; it's in their coexistence. For any piece of knowledge we must always consider its associated ignorance.

No one, I believe, has ever truly assessed the price of ignorance presupposed by, required by, produced by knowledge. Clarity at the price of obscurity. Strictly, a black place where shadow was amassed was formed. An old jar of hypostases. We must examine rather how knowledge functions. Knowledge and its ignorance aren't pots, aren't places.

Knowledge, in its progress, in its process, every day, at every instant, produces shadow. This burner or that lamp gives heat or light in the laboratory, but its entropy increases, inevitably. Science spends; it's not the pure acquisition one might think. By credit and debit, there is an economy of knowing; epistemology has long neglected to keep its books, its balance sheet, its accounts. The best, the most subtle, verified, exact knowledge is not a pure activity, pure, that is to say, free. The rationalists believed this; they would well have liked to make us believe it. Those holding power believe and make others believe that this power is free or gratuitous. Pure doesn't merely mean abstract or disinterested. No, knowledge isn't free. But it's not paid for only by money or energy. Yes, science is expensive, in investments, salaries, purchases, and in the general goods of capital assets and operations. Yes, science is expensive in power. Laboratories exist that consume as much electricity as a large city. In a certain manner, that doesn't count; it doesn't enter into the book I'm opening, into the balance sheet I'm calculating. For everyone has to pay in his own coin. Paying with money or with energy is paying with the coin of others; it's paying in funny money. Knowledge, like everyone, has to pay in domestic coin, in its own currency, in the coin of knowledge; it therefore pays in ignorance. Shadow, therefore, follows light.

The temple of Vesta was equipped with a stercoraceous door [*Porta Stercoraria*], through which the ashes of the pure fire were disposed of. Ashes of knowledge do exist. Knowledge gives off shadow, the way a factory pollutes the surrounding atmosphere. Science pollutes gnoseological space at the same time as it works and produces there and illuminates it. If not, it would be the only pure and free work; rationalism is an angelism. Paying with money or energy is still being free for knowledge qua knowledge. Energy is paid for with entropy; information and negentropy are also paid for, in their own order. Knowledge mixes with ignorance, in all places and times, neverendingly accompanied by it. It's the subtle spectrum of light and shadow or of chiaroscuro. Otherwise there wouldn't be any history. However pure the fire of Vesta may be, it leaves ashes as it burns.

We will, perhaps, one day be able to assess, for a discipline or an encyclopedia cell, the acquired knowledge that's due merely to its being cut up, or the set of artefacts produced by its locality; we will perhaps be able to assess the effects of limitation or blindness induced by the decision to set boundaries, the forces that impel to these boundaries, the relations of force, of hatred, of war and strategy between said disciplines; we will perhaps be able to assess, above all, the results tied to polemics and the dust raised by the squabble preventing us from seeing in it, the results tied to the struggles for power of the petty king at the heart of the locality; we will perhaps one day be able to assess the imitation of the epistemes and their iteration in the cell by the simple power of the petty king – add up then these artefacts and subtract these dark products – refuse, garbage – of the global products of the discipline, what will be left in net profit? Indeed, what will be left of light? Even more, or less: I'm focusing the light on a well-determined spot. The more punctual the light is, the brighter or more violent it is, the more I encircle this spot with a little ring of shadow and blindness. The discrete set of these spots and these rings forms a spectrum of light and shadow. A global effect of dancing fireflies, this is what is left of the ancient lights, what happened to the Greek cave. And I'm not taking into account the destruction of the object being illuminated by a too violent beam.

Knowledge is perhaps not as vast as believed, in view of these shadows.

Perhaps it isn't so difficult to think knowledge; perhaps there is less water there than the raging ocean of publications would lead us to believe. If we set aside shadow, the shadow created by war and the war of shadows, the shadow produced by the light that surrounds us and the lights that are a bit weak, or if we sort out the accepted shadow of the light produced, for a short balance sheet, the remaining light, so beautiful it makes our hearts race, is not as impossible to grasp as it is said to be. It doesn't exceed my life, I think: it makes it.

To write these few lines on the continuous spectrum, I myself have moved along a continuous spectrum. I can, if I want, go farther, go into more refined analysis, go to the most precise aspect of a speciality. I will always find there that black ring around the point of impact, black jar, white jar. I can consequently write a very local epistemology. And the same situation returns for epistemology itself. Either it is ultra-refined, and it only repeats, white and black, what science itself says, or it is broader and loses in precision; it is no longer knowledgeable in its words; it is full, but it is black. The serious one is only a copier; the non-copier is not serious. Beyond this second discourse, generally parasitical, gnoseology or the theory of knowledge finds it to be incomprehensible that the comprehensible might exist, a union or harmony, difficult to think, of the theoretical and the object, of the theorem and the thing. And metaphysics can crown, if you like, or support, for the others, the enterprise quickly said here. We have never, in any case, left the archaic constellations of Hestia, of the priestess of Vesta. A continuous spectrum runs from the most refined views of the most cutting-edge science to the most ancient rites of the history of our religions. I do believe that there is as much light in our laboratories, and as much shadow, as there is beneath the smooth mound of the Colline Gate.

And that there is, in both cases, a skeleton inside.

What remains hidden? The light itself or the deflowered vestal?

Either the truth lifts the veils, pierces through the walls, or it piles shield after shield on the virgin Tarpeia.

We wish the difference might be clearer: that science might cause fewer deaths than religion. That's the only truly decisive criterion. It's the only one I will adhere to from now on.

The history of religion frequently furnishes us with full and dense constellations. It lets us see here knowledge and its strategies, and its incorporated epistemology. We appear to be superficial, we moderns, in sticking to partial, fragmented, lacunary reasons. As though our history had been for us a slow unfolding of these implicated formations.[15] But if we trace back our time, our sporadic and clear reasons would meet in the round temple under the enclosed light of Vesta. We have finally arrived at the prehistory of our knowledge. I'm writing here the prehistory of science. And I'm writing it without the common scorn flowing from knowledge for she who engendered it, without the murder of Alba by Rome.

Here Rome shows the reverse of our practice of reason. It shows us, while hiding it, a blind practice of implication. It behaves as though it knew, at the origin or from all time, that our time or our science endlessly explicates, exploits, analyses, separates, excludes, as though it knew that it was first necessary to prepare the folding and the covering. You will only discover those we have covered over, before you. We dig up and it buries; we open tombs; it closes them; it erases tracks. Rome is the city of tombs.

Rome is the closed site of implications.

Can we finally write history or prehistory without putting our predecessors to death?

I'm no longer talking about myth; I'm no longer talking about rite, and I'm leaving the history of religion and the continuous spectrum of knowledge for a moment. I'm talking, quite particularly, about our theories of knowledge.

All of them belong to light, all of them belong to opening, all of them belong to explication or putting outside. However opposed they may be among themselves, and they are often so to the point of contradiction, to the point of the devastating hatred stemming from their excluding nature, all of them have in common since the modern age, I mean at least since the Renaissance, the movement from shadow to light, decoding and deciphering, detecting, the movement from the riddle to its solution or from the secret to its tearing open. One unveils, one uncovers, one unties, one undoes. Analysis untangles: the knot, complex, is untied into long and simple sequences of running ends, of standing ends.[16] One unfolds, one unfurls, and one unrolls. One explicates or the thing itself evolves: it becomes seen. All the force goes from the inside to the outside, from the black box to its lit-up threshold, from the hidden to the publicly posted, from veil to unveiling, from the constructed, from the entangled to taking apart thread by thread.

This presupposes a point of view; this presupposes passions; this privileges certain people, certain groups and certain actions. This privileges policemen more than thieves, the police more than the private person, the interpreter and not the composer, the professor and not the writer, the parasite and not the producer. Don't mistake me, I'm also for the light. Who isn't for light and science? I'll have to come back to the passion for destruction. I'll have to come back to the groups of parasites become dominant.

Today I'm assuming that a knowledge exists – but perhaps we should call it something else – that demands implication, and envelopment and the veil and the knot. This is also taught and learned from building. A knowledge that demands folding, that requires coding, that piles cipher upon cipher, and knits knot upon knot. Hermes and Hestia are here, together. I no longer see why knowledge would only be that of Penelope at night, she who, in the dark, undoes her weaving. Why wouldn't knowledge also belong to the diurnal weaver who knots the threads under the design of the tapestry, who crosses and envelops? The direct labour of the work shows me every morning that more light is needed to sew than to unsew, or to put up a wall with a plumb bob than to dismantle it into its primary stones. We're seeing the long milky night come to an end, a night in which works were formed by dismantling forms, by destroying them, or fragmenting them, in which books were wound by unwinding other books, the night without risk or fatigue or clarity, in which Penelope unwraps, the analytical night of the interminable discourse of explication. Penelope points us to the works of day and the works of night; this doesn't depend on their nature; this doesn't depend on their content; it depends on their manufacture. Theorem or poem, description or narrative, reason slumbers in parasitical comfort when, analytically, it disaggregates a solid there. I will therefore assume a knowledge that multiplies gestures in a short time in a limited space in order to make information denser until it forms a rarer place that sometimes becomes a black solid. There Penelope envelops, and the tapestry, a knot of knots, an intertwined system, appears. One day the idea, today so common, will appear strange to us, the idea that only analysis or unweaving belongs to the light, whereas most often, if the knot is well-made, it can be undone with your eyes closed. Analysis unwinds and runs along the time of inflation; the books of the analytical night grow bigger and quickly fill space; bad money greedily drives out the good; synthesis does nothing but cross two threads, running or standing; analysis's bringing to light is entropic, and that was only a false light.

Analysis unties, and it is negative. Our knowledge unknots; it remains negative in its elementary operations, in its globality. I'm not talking about its drives or its passions. The theory of knowledge takes up again perhaps, in different places, unrecognizable, the ancient and venerable apophatic theology, negative. In which conjectures were also refuted at length. I wish for the advent of a desmology, a discourse of ties, ligaments, ligatures. The overlapping strands cast shadow on each other, and it's in accepting this shadow and this overlapping that knowledge grows – and can be summed up. I wish that the gnoseological value of the operation of knotting, of folding would be recognized. Diurnal Penelope, she who envelops, knots the threads beneath the canvas, threads that at the same time ensure the hold, the colour, the chiné, the design, and the hard or soft texture of the work. I don't know of any work, hand or language that holds together differently, a secret labour always taken up again. No, knowledge is not only separation, distinction, unfolding merely; no, knowledge is not only of the no, subtracting, dividing, conjecturing, critiquing, dialectics and polemics, debate and combat; no, I mean yes and no, knowledge also folds like a rope; the sequence, the long chain of reasons goes back over itself, loops over itself and interlaces. Alexander, young, in a hurry, virile, cuts the Gordian knot with his sword. This work was brief and simple, violent. I wish we would remember the humble, the forgotten maker of the knot that tied the beam of the plough to the yoke, that combined them, remember the female maker, in fact, as I guess, remember she or he who made the knot under the sword. Knowledge is folded over itself like a rope, like a protein or a tissue; it is invaginated as well and thus becomes dense; it fills with complections; it fills with information; yes, it goes toward knowledge. It goes toward deflation. The work is covering over with layers and leaves, onion or artichoke, fetus, like a succession of automorphisms. Analysis peels the layers off the onion, destroys it, undoes the heart of its complection, dilutes the dense, loosens. The work of complection goes back up entropy, goes back up inflation, condenses, attaches, folds, folds back, knots, associates, ties, constitutes networks of knots, tightens. But this work has no negative, except for the common classical theory that, quite entirely, runs along its negation. The ancient theory of knowledge is on the other slope.

The new one is, consequently, a theory, a work of inclusion. The knot, the fold are inclusive; automorphism and absence of negation are equally so. I believe it's possible to think without excluding.

I have spoken elsewhere of chaos; I have spoken elsewhere of mixed sets;[17] I have also spoken elsewhere of logics of the included third; we are, in this very place, at their productive root. At Rome and at its foundation. At the object, at its construction.

First, woman. Here is the cult of Vesta; here is what Penelope said; I'm returning for a moment to abandoned ground. Folding, stitch, knot, weaving, invaginated implications, women, you put everything in order. I strongly fear that the common and classical theory is conjugated in the masculine, violence, exclusion, destruction. Perhaps the work of the negative is only the brief effort of the male. Here knowledge is feminine; the work is in the feminine. Hestia, Vesta are the goddess or the priestess of the new epistemology.

What is the baker doing when he kneads the dough? Here is an amorphous mass, first; let's imagine it's square-shaped. The baker stretches it, spreads it, then he folds it, folds it over; he stretches it again and folds it over once more; he never stops folding the mass over itself, an exemplary gesture. And if he wishes, the initial square will never be transformed into anything other than the square. This is also called automorphism. Nothing is simpler and more common than this gesture; nothing is so repetitive; nothing so determined. The proof of this is that it has vanished, replaced by a mechanical movement. Yet each fold, every braid, each folding over changes the starting set into a more complex set. The same square is preserved, and yet it's no longer the same square; it's easy to leave tracks on the space of the mixture reknotted in such a way. A strange onion where every layer comes from the mother mass and returns to it, a fetus that's elementary and folded over on itself. Let's follow the tracks that were left.

The baker, by kneading, ceaselessly redraws a new escutcheon; she makes successive escutcheons 'that cost her very little'.[18] Heraldry is useful to describe its divisions of the field and honourable ordinaries [*pièces honorables*]. Here is the baker's blazon, who in the morning kneads her quarters of nobility: bars, bends, saltires, fesses, pale and point, chevrons, chequy, lozengy, cottices, barrulets. The baker never stops; she doesn't choose one escutcheon, one pavilion or one flag; she passes through nearly all of them: the way one passes through language when one writes or talks; she imprints, she buries the great folded pavise in the dough. This can be said in topological language or in that of semaphore. But I'm speaking blazon or escutcheon, a much more ancient language, for it's a question of age. A new fold, an added folding over adds to age like a new quarter. The baker Penelope, up in the morning, ages with every fold; she weaves time, but in the other direction, as though the three sisters had come back up from the Underworld, the reverse of the instinct of death. The system ages without time escaping; it garners age; the young escutcheons are knotted, drowned, under the mature escutcheons; the baker moulds memory. Due to all the folds formed in the fetal state, what an incredible memory we are, what a stock of time to unfold; we are born old; we die infantile, with the exhaustion of our memory bank. Time no longer has a scythe; the Fate no longer has scissors. Analysis cuts; the baker folds. Time enters into the dough, a prisoner of its folds, a shadow of its foldings-over; it penetrates set theory, for the partitions cover each other; time can be marked in the layering of the dough;[19] estimate the immense time of our tissues; it can also be marked in the fragmentation of the escutcheons; it plunges into the mixture. The baker writes on, under the palimpsest of flour and water; she presses on the tablet; she imprints on the soft wax, matrix, imprint-recipient, the white womb of the virgin mother.

But no, the baker doesn't write; the fractal escutcheon isn't seen; the blazon remains white; the dough remains grey. The woman continues to fold, stretch, fold again, without anything ever being marked. Burying of the memory [*souvenir*] in the memory [*mémoire*], black box, silence. Let's now suppose that a fine-pointed stylus digs a point on this square, following it in its stretching, following it in its folding, following it thus ten times, twenty times, up to thirty stages of aging; it would write a bit of history, a monument or local remains of this always vanishing involution. We can try to read its path or the track it left. It is illegible. It's not a letter or a sentence; it's not a zigzag; it's not a book of magic spells kept in secrecy; it's not a trajectory; it's the flight of a fly or a crazy wasp. Each jump is clear and determined; the entire route seems random. The baker, in contrast to God, writes crooked in straight lines; she writes incomprehensible in luminous fragments. And that's why she doesn't write. And that's why we – simple blind men, simplistic or too short-sighted – haven't thought implication, the included, the fold; we have never known what a tissue was; we have never seen or heard women; we have never known what a mixture was, and we have never understood, or even thought, time. We have aligned it along analytical sequences. We have never looked at this path; we have never tried to read it.

Time is the writing of the baker or her absenting writing. Local time, from now to a moment ago or to a little before, is as clear, as determined, almost as necessitating as the folding over of the escutcheon, as the simple gesture of the baker. She holds it in her hand, like us.[20] It stretches, it folds, and I see where it goes and how it gets there. This can be conceived, deduced, calculated even. The fly goes from here to there, all of a sudden, by the whitest straight line, and this is how we act in space and time, and this is how we think in straight reason. Beyond this step, we are soon lost. The path from local time to global time, the path from the instant to time, the path from the present to history is not predictable; it is not integrable by reason, such as analysis has shaped it. It seems to go, crazily, just anywhere, drunk, and just anyhow. If the baker knew how to write, she would follow, lazily, the flight of the fly, the capricious folding of proteins, the shores of Brittany or Ushant, and the fluctuating edge of a mass of clouds. This writing is illegible. It's everywhere and yet no one looks at it, everywhere present and ignored.

A point in this dough is only a point. The point nearest the preceding one follows a path quite different from the first one, just as crazy, just as complicated, illegible. Time is not the path of a single point, but of at least several and at most all. A new inaccessible integration. All the paths soon cover all space; it becomes black with them; it becomes white with them; the dough remains grey; that's why the baker doesn't write. We have again found the tracks of the cattle.

She stretches the dough out and folds it over; she cuts it to fold it over as well. She is unaware of the Brownian trajectory of each of the points but nevertheless produces it as she folds the mixture. She is thus moulding the piece of wax of time, a tablet of unrepresentable history, a black jar filled to bursting with trajectories, a white jar in which they are erased. She folds and endlessly closes the black box, the black jar, the piece of virgin wax; she knots the malleable palimpsest; she presses, she imprints escutcheon upon escutcheon; yet nothing is imprinted on the grey dough, a white jar, a grey jar in the middle of the two jars; the essential thing here is indeed the circumvolution. If the trajectories, if the divisions, if the ages are erased in the common grey of the dough it's not intention, ruse or spitefulness; it's excess of complexity. Time is not a continuum, like this extendable dough; it is not discontinuous like layered puff pastry dough; it is one, it is the other, yes and no, white and black, shadow and light in a fine spectrum; it's a non-integrable graph that's crazily complex to the point of randomness, chance here being only the limit concept of the classical enterprises of reason, the concept that's discovered as soon as they are opened, since reason has simply, mechanically rejected it; it's a bee's flight, no, it's the thousand flights of a swarm of bees, no, it's the fuzzy set of Brownian flights, those of the little grains of the dough mixture. The baker involutes time – circumstances and fluctuations – in the circumvolutions of the piece of dough.

She stretches the dough out, and she folds it over, cutting it or not to fold it over, doesn't write. History writes on the tablet; the historian believes it to be virgin since he sees it as grey; he's unaware of the time of the dough and the fabulous books of magic spells that are prescribed in it. His track, for his part, a very simple one of little looped flights of human letters, lets the short laws and clear sequences be seen, analysis and synthesis. Yes, this can be said; others things can also be said, and still other things. Wide mesh nets also bring back fish. No writing will ever catch these present, patent and latent complections, black and white like the jars of Vesta.

You can always find a needle in a haystack, if you have the time of patience and a nostalgia for the lost needle. There's little chance on the contrary of finding a straw of hay in the hay of the stable. The hay is in disorder under the bellies of the cattle. Which straw do you want? Which straw do you know? They are indiscernible; they are undecidable, and how are you going to look for a straw in that uninteresting pile? Yet my hope lies in this straw, yes, in the run-of-the-mill chaos of the present; a fluctuation, tomorrow, has just engendered an infant who it is said will change the world. The other fluctuations or jolt-straws of hay have vanished, have remained straws of hay. I know of no other figure of hope than this straw that sparkles alone in the indifferent, the mixed, the ordinary, the disorderedness of the stable. Newton's hope shone like an apple in the middle of a common apple orchard; a single apple has just caught a ray of light; it shines with hope; it has understood the world. My hope lies in the unexpected; what can I expect from the dismal execution of laws? My hope is as rare as recognizing a straw in the haystack; my hope is this rare and common straw, as saturated with rarity as it is, in fact, ordinary and numerous, crammed to the gills with information; my hope is this genius idea drowned among the straw; it shines. My hope does not lie in that straight route, a monotonous and dismal method which newness has fled from the beginning; my hope is the interrupted path, broken, drawn at random at every halt, of the wasp, of the bee, of the fly in their flight. It's been thirty years and more that I've been watching flies, bees and wasps fly, against the teacher's orders, forty years of laziness in which I have seen hope fly. No, I'm not afraid of the wasp's chaotic and Brownian jumps. The teacher of the discourse on method would have been afraid. No, I can't find the straw in the haystack; no, I can't predict where the wasp will go; no, I can't understand the moted dust in the solar ray issuing from the crack in systems, but if I know, if I find, if I can one day predict, a tremendous fortune finally won at roulette, a major stroke of genius, a solar blast of intuition, what hope, no, my only hope. What hope do we have other than this circumstance? This latter cannot be thought except in and through adelos knowledge, a little black, not very evident, a bit confused and chaotic, black and white, in exquisite proximity to sleep, in exquisite, inchoative and happy proximity to wakefulness.[21] Why are you working? Hope shines, for these half-closed eyes, attentive and tired, in the twilights of the morning and evening, in the dance of the dust in the low-angled rays of light, in the wasp's zigzag flight, in the myriads of straw in disorder, *hope shines like a straw in the stable/what do you fear from the drunken wasp in its crazed flight/see, the sun is still moted in some hole/why didn't you fall asleep with your elbow on the table?*[22]

Who will describe the continuous spectrum, black and white, or grey of dawn, between Verlaine's poem and the theorem?

PART TWO

EMPIRE AND SUFFRAGE: DEATH

3 EMPIRE: THE FRAGMENTED MULTIPLICITY

Livy 1.16; Plutarch, 'Romulus' 27–29

Man is a wolf to man, violence. Man is a god to man, sacred. How can the change between the state posed by Hobbes and the one said by Spinoza be described? The history of Rome and the foundation of Rome answer the question. They anticipate the two principles. Romulus is wolf and god.

Romulus was holding a muster in the swamp of Capra when all of a sudden – thunder, lighting bolts – a violent thunderstorm burst. Prodigious disturbances, it is said; a black night descended in the middle of the day, furrowed with lightning and raging winds. The king disappeared from view, under a thick cloud. When the light returned, tranquil and serene, the throne was empty; Romulus was no longer there. Mute stupefaction from all. Cries then rose up from the mouths of a few; finally all were competing to acclaim the king become a god, son of a god and father of Rome. This is an apotheosis narrative. The apotheosis here is the passage from violence – thunderstorm – to the sacred: Romulus is a god. Yet Romulus was a wolf, the son of a she-wolf; he was violent, the son of a violation.

Listening, it sounded like this: the noise named *fragor* in Latin, a thundering fracas first; then silence; lastly a universal prayer of peace.

It was also said very quietly, and as though a great mystery, that the twin had been torn to pieces by the Fathers with their own hands. Each one of them, it was added, took a part of him in the folds of his robe and carried it away. Division of power, division of the corpse. The man became a god by being torn apart by wolves. The man is a god to men, that is, to wolves. He is a wolf-god among wolves; he suckled the milk of the she-wolf. He had killed his twin.

At the moment of the thunderstorm and beneath its clamours, the crowd flees; it disperses, but the Fathers, on the contrary, come nearer to one another, forming a tight group. No doubt tight around the king.

At the central point of the throne, at the instant of the circumstance, the wolf-god-man is said to be absent, present, invisible, visible, whole, divided into parts, hidden, exalted. The change happens at the middle point of this configuration, through these operations.

The event, subsequently, gave rise to a rite. The commemorative festival was called *Poplifugia*, that is, the people's flight. The storm bursts; the thunder roars; the lightning hits with a fracas; the corpse leaves in fragments; the crowd runs off in every direction. Nature bursts; the organism is undone into scattered limbs, and the collective scatters.

Distributed pieces of every type in the swamp of Capra, or, it has also been said, in the temple of Vulcan, he who beats the iron in the fire. It's the festivity of multiplicities. The pure multiple roams space; noise – force, energy, elements, bursts – fluctuates in the volume of the cloud and of the swamp.

No, this isn't dispersion in its pure state of noise, of fury, of fragmentation. In the volume thus considered, a figure, fuzzy, is drawn. It is centred. The throne is in the middle. The king's body is there, whole and visible, then in parts, hidden.

The storm bursts. No doubt it bursts in a point of departure. That it departs in fragments from here or there means that a same operation takes place in a definite point of space and time, I mean, the breaking into pieces. Our language is quite precise on this point: before the departure, there aren't any parts; the departure is, literally, the bursting or the dispersion of the parts. The flight of the parts is a clock, a time-counter. Our old age comes from having left several limbs in the four corners of the continents since the storm's departure. Consequently, it's understood that the origin point is empty, like the throne or site of the bursting. It is quite simply called the point of departure. The same figure, a bit fuzzy, is renewed in the sky or on the earth. The empty point from which a supernova bursts is easily reconstituted. Might the storm over the swamp of Capra be Rome's big bang? Its foundation, I don't know, but perhaps the point of departure from which the time of history can be counted.

The throne, in the middle, is empty, and the king is absent. Near this point a dense circle or a compact ring is formed. It will be said that these are the Fathers; it will be said it's a question of the Senate. As one moves away from the empty centre across the dense ring, said compactness weakens and distribution, dispersion, flight increase. In these zones, the crowd flees. Around the point of absence, a ring of system; around the dense torus, a distribution cloud. We have already encountered this form, at the beginning of the world.

This form has no concept yet; it has no definition. It lacks one because it has fuzzy edges; it is a fuzzy subset. In the periphery, the crowd flees; it departs to count time, and this form is a clock as well. It is not merely a form in space and time; it is a process of transformation. In the middle point, depending on the date, the body is absent or present, visible or invisible, whole or in parts; the local ring can be more or less compact or wide; and the fleeing distribution disperses or calls out to one another, as we are going to hear.

Noises, silence, calls, once again.

This slightly unformed form moves; it beats, it lives, it evolves and trans-forms. We have seen a wolf here transform into a god and vile murderers into senators of an empire. It is like a social transformer. And it beats its own time through density, through scattering.

Since the departure point can be empty – what is a point except this very emptiness? – sometimes, often, no one any longer knows why such a rite takes place. The origin, it is said, gets lost. During the archaic festivals of *Poplifugia*, the Romans go out to sacrifice in the swamp of Capra. Outside, they set about crying out the country's proper names: Hey, Marcus! Marcus! Hey, Lucius! Gaius … Here I am, Paul, Jacques, Jean, François, Michel, André, Pascal! The Romans shout out, call out to one another.

Much later, it was never known how the plebs set about seceding on the Sacred Mount. As usual, the historians quarrel. One says: this happened on the initiative of a single person whose name here matters little. But the other wrote: each hailed the other; they all called out to one another. Hey, Jacques, Jean, François, hey, Pascal! How can a collective be constituted? Cry out the names audible here. They form a chain, chains of calls. At random and in order. Whoever hears it, at random, sets about crying out names, too.

The women, the servant women, during this occasion, give each other blows and throw stones at one another. The stones separate them, and the names assemble them. Let's look at the moving schema again. The multitude flees. The more it flees, the more stones, it can be said, fly between each of them, or thunderclaps, or bursts of lightning. The crowd seems as if it were lapidated; its members scatter. But this movement, complex and noisy, produces chances for encounter. The elements, disordered, crash into one another. Encounters are produced when one calls out; names fly between the voices, known proper names, names from the country itself. Dispersion produces concourses; flight produces encounters. Stones separate; proper names assemble. Separation in every direction produces sets. As though the stones became signals, became calls, became proper names. Hey, Petrus! I'm calling you, Petrus; on you, around you, I will found the group. Peter's rock is Stephen's rock.[1] The rocks of the Roman servant women are the ones under which Tarpeia lies. And they are suddenly names. Hey, Tarpeia! Tarpeia, that is to say, the transformer, the tropeic. Attention: the people's flight, producing shocks, encounters, can be the origin of the people. Strictly speaking: the departure of the people. This logic of transformation, evident, cannot be understood, cannot be perceived, unless one considers the multiple as such. The process only takes place in the noisy, chaotic, fleeing movement of the multitude. I believe that here we are touching on an elementary form of the collective, on the simple, profound dynamic of its formation. It flees and encounters.

Music. The fleeing crowd makes noise, *fragor*. It flees in scattered fragments. These fractured pieces, these stones, make noise, let out calls, *fragor*, make acclamations. We aren't there yet. But we have to get accustomed to listening as well. The mob rushes; it noises. It assembles, it acclaims.

I have given the name joker, or white domino, to a kind of neutral or rather multivalent element, undetermined of itself, and which could take on this value, identity or determination or that one, depending on the system of proximities it is inserted into. I can say of the joker that it is a king, that it is a jack, that it is a queen or any other figure. The very first of the Italian algebraists had called this the *cosa*, the thing; and we have in turn called it the unknown = x. Neither the joker nor the thing are unknown; they are merely undetermined. As is said of the chameleon, they are determined by the environment. Or by a decision external to them. Or by the set in which they are put into play.

This joker can be found everywhere, from mathematics to the social sciences, from the theory of money as a general equivalent to every simple or complicated practice of deciphering.

Thus there are white elements.

Without them, we couldn't think the multiple, nor could we construct models. That's because incompatibilities increase very quickly with the terms put into play, their number and their combination. Noise, friction, interceptions, blockages invade the set, whether it be the pure multiple, chaos, or a well-formed system, ready to function. To eliminate the difficulty, Leibniz rigorously eliminated relations as well; the monads, without holes or doors, are blind, mute and deaf, except to God, the supreme exchanger and only centre. Reinject relations into the multiple, and noise, sound irrepressibly return: parasitic interference.[2] Leibniz's is the only solution to this problem that has been found, except for the lie told everywhere that a new proposed solution would be completely different. It's always the centre that propagates this lie and that makes enough noise to monopolize noise and impose silence on noise, that behaves enough like a parasite to cause the deaths of the little parasites, that won't tolerate relations between elements except for the very ones imposed by it. What is quite modestly called the monopoly of legitimate violence. I only know one solution that's completely different from that one: injecting these jokers, these white elements into the multiple, set or system. Locally they are repressors of incompatibility; they take incompatibility into themselves as their own determination; they therefore bring it to zero. The undetermined play the role of lubricant. The friction rolls over the white elements. As a result, they give the multiple a fuzzy appearance. Fluid. This solution is new, no lie.

Either a God exists in the middle, or archangels move, white, in the cloud. A thousand practical and concrete applications for this image of angels pass through my mind.

At the festival where the people flee, someone cries out: Hey, Marcus! Gaius! … No doubt several men with this name, with these names will begin to cry out two or three other first names, as though to no one in particular, and then several men with these names will … the chain is established; the network, regular, sustained, yet aleatory, expands and condenses. A certain collective appears. No, it reappears, for it must indeed have already been there for Gaius, Marcus to be right here as several persons.

It doesn't matter. Some person therefore leaves home and cries out a fairly common name. He is the transmitter of his voice, and he doesn't know its receptors. He knows them; he doesn't know them. He knows them, no doubt; he is Roman, he is Latin; he knows quite well who bears Roman names. The relation is a bit well-determined; assuredly, it excludes foreigners – Hernici or Etruscans, Greeks or Sicels. But it is undetermined in that the transmitter doesn't know who hears him and how many with this name hear him. The relationship is not yet white; nevertheless, it is, a little. We can imagine how to whiten it. He leaves, he cries out: Hey! Ho! Even if he cries out in one language – Here I am! Help! Au secours! – someone in some other language will hear him. And will help him or won't help him.

I call this link a white arm. A free arm. It has an origin; it has an undetermined end. It is a transmitter; it has undetermined receptors. Few sets are viable without white elements; few networks are reliable without white arms.

I believe that the theory of white arms was invented the day of the Pentecost. Here is a transmitter and fifty listeners, and each of them in his name, and each of them in his language. We must conceive a multivalent link. I'm not aware of any reliable network that is without one.

We don't think the multiple as such very much. The philosophical tradition gives it to us only to immediately take it back; it is destined to be subsumed. Hardly does it appear than it is captured by the concept, than it is, like Protagoras, driven underground, like a violated vestal, buried alive. The multiple is on the side of the unthought empirical; the unformed matter of form, it never receives its letters of nobility for entering the formal world. Everything happens as though philosophy remained fixed in the royal era of the concept or idea. Archaic enough not to be able to think a set and the abstract together.

The situation is even worse if the set has fuzzy edges, and if it's in full labour. The crowd here disperses and flees; just where, no one knows; for how long, no one has said; in what proportions, we don't know. And if the observer is in the crowd itself, he knows even less. The senators, in the circumstance and in a given place of this fluctuating set, draw closer to each other into a tight group. In this spot of the narrative, Plutarch uses an interesting verb, from which we could draw a word to say this thing. Plato himself uses this word on the page of the *Statesman* in which it's a question of turning the tow around the spindle and forming a solid strand from fluffy and soft-twisted threads. Through a turning and whirling motion, something is assembled, condensed, tightened. This slightly disordered, yet nonetheless torsional motion forms a thick set surrounded by a kind of cloud. One can waver between using this word, *systrophe*, and taking up the usual word, circumstance, to which in addition this new sense, a bit uncommon, would be given. *Systrophe* is under the sign of Tarpeia, the tropeic vestal. A ring of soldiers tightens around the vestal.

Systrophe is first of all an aggregate in Leibniz's sense, a conglomeration, a slightly compact mass, a swarm of bees, a flock of birds, a troop of soldiers. But *systrophe* is more than the aggregate, more than some subset. It manifests a work, a spending of energy, and the result of that action. The bees fly, and they surround the queen; the migrators are in a kind of rolling order; they float like a banner in the wind. This set is in order but in an order fluctuating through a work and a disposition of number and situation. *Systrophe* is a sedition, for example, a crowd in rebellion, a group in revolution. It is also a hurricane, a downpour and a waterspout. Here we are. What happens in the swamp of Capra, a hurricane, a flight or a sedition, the deposit, toward the middle of the vortex, of a knot or a density, what happens there is indeed the work of the multiple as such, when it remains in the state of the multiple. What happens is a circumstance, the slightly rounded movement of the Fathers around the throne, the contingency of fleeing movements all around, instability but relative stability of the whole.

This moving set deserves an old word, for it can be seen and located everywhere, in the natural and the human worlds; it deserves a new word however, for I don't know if it has ever been taken as an object or a phenomenon.

Let's re-examine this form and this motion. They have a pseudo-centre, empty or full, a dense zone that forms and comes undone, a cloud of flight and lastly of encounter. Each place is an exchanger, a converter, like a transformer. Someone is seated on the throne, there is no longer anyone there; he is whole, he is in tiny pieces; he is king, he is god; he is absent, he changes. It's dark, it's night, the light is there, tranquil and serene. Storm, beautiful weather. How to foresee the lightning strike? The ring, dense, advances: the Fathers, all bent over in mêlée, carve Romulus up into pieces; you might think they were forming the tortoise, back to back, together, every head in the black well, over the ignoble thing that soon will have no name in any language; the ring comes undone; each one of them conceals and carries off, in the black of the sinus, a terrifying piece of the king; the ring reforms; a few people let out a cry, a prayer, after the white silence of mute dejection. Oh, Romulus! Soon, everyone will follow suit, *fragor*, acclamation. The crowd flees around, encounters each other, crashes into each other, leaves in fear and returns in rapture. The crowd is fuzzy; it is a mob [*tourbe*]; it is turbulent; it goes and comes, disorder and order.

I believe this form, this circumstance, to be rare and stable at the same time. I believe this work is always recurring. The crowd is not the Brownian multiplicity of atoms in chaos, cloudy distribution as such. What I am calling circumstance – motion, work, drawing, result, exchanges and transformations – adopts this formation around another circumstance or when it arises.

We can see repetitions, copies of it everywhere, even on Sunday in churches or stadiums.

No one has ever seen pure royalty anywhere, a set united around a singleton. No one has observed pure aristocracy, nor an empire for all, ideal democracy. I'm writing nothing but banalities.

The form of *systrophe* or circumstance is stable; it is the basic social and political field, traversed with diverse movements, with complex work and noisy with transformations. It is always more or less centred, an empty middle or absent place, a full presence and whole throne; it is more or less equipped with a denser zone in which the parts of power are present and hidden, a thin or wide ring in which acclamations are unanimous, in which the links are powerful; it is always trimmed with a chaotic cloud of encounters and flights, in which stones and voices are exchanged without stop, in which relations float. A thousand names are given to the centre, whether vacant or occupied; as many names are given to the more or less thick torus, and just as many to the noisy periphery, but they are all compresent in space and time. The barons are always there, whatever freedom may be, whatever constraint may be; the centralism is always there, whatever the discourse may be, whatever the representation may be. What varies is the lighting. What varies, precisely, is the discourse. Or the variety of lie. What varies in fact is the complexity, the distribution, the displacements within this fuzzy and moving form. Energies are exchanged, parts, fragments, stones, calls, in this borderless force field; sometimes condensations are produced there. This form is the political or social geometral, and the geometral is now moving.

Let's try to understand stones and parts, and the zones of density.

The storm bursts; nature, in the middle of the fracas, departs in fragments; night falls. Romulus' body bursts; the Fathers dismember royalty; they hide the members in the black of the folds of their togas. The world and the king break; this action and this work remain hidden. The people burst; the crowd flees; to justify the rite, Plutarch recounts a story about a signal half hidden in the night sent out to Rome by a slave, Philotis, who had handed her body and those of her companions over to the enemy. I mean that in every case the passage to the multiple is a black operation. It's one of those works that are carried out by putting one's hands into the black box. Night, dark cloud, fold of a toga, torch.

The collective is a black box. But, if I dare say so, the blackest in the black box is the set of passages from the multiple to the one and from the one to the multiple.

The story tells us one thing in three things, one person in three people, or one in-stance in three in-stances. It is a natural story, a business of bodies, a movement of the crowd. Thus something that participates in nature and belongs to the living, and that is distributed like a collective in space, something for which these three realities are only images, comes to be divided, without anyone knowing clearly what this thing is or how it is divided. Without anyone knowing who could know such a thing either.

This knowledge belongs to occultations and flashes like the servant Philotis' torch behind the fig tree, calling Rome from the enemy camp. Black jar, white jar. Storm, and the return of the light, tranquil and serene. Are the Fathers going to open the folds of their togas to explain what they have done? This knowledge is white, evident; it hands itself over in simple little tales; it is black and concealed; it is kept in secret for the learned. The more you think here, the less you know. I mean: the less you think in the habitual way.

I am trying to name at least the thing to be divided, what the night was falling on when it was divided up, that before which the crowd fled when it burst, what the Fathers hid due to having cut it up.

It suffices not to be afraid. The Romans were afraid of the thunderstorm. The Fathers were afraid of both the king and the cut-up pieces they were transporting, ashamed. Caught with their hands in the fold, each of them risked quartering, in their turn. Or the ax. It suffices not to be afraid to speak clearly. Yet we are never afraid of what we have never desired. Of what we haven't done. Of what we have never prepared. Of what we have never obeyed. Of what we have never believed to be rare. Nor of what we have never taken or divided up. Thus the political philosopher must at least have no fear of storms, crowds or murders.

Or of empires. The thing that's abstract enough to be projected onto three in-stances is nothing other than the *imperium*, the empire. That is how it is named. The origin of the term *imperium* is still being quarrelled over. The classical roots – to prepare, to obey – are of a remarkable weakness: that which is acquired or that which is yielded to. The conjecture that it comes from *impair* [odd] is the difficult, interesting and combative reading. The origin of the empire is, to my mind, the very death of the king Romulus. I tentatively risk the hypothesis. The entire narrative lets it be seen and leads there. Empire is the part; the *imperium* is the *pars*, yes, the tearing into pieces, fearsome and hidden. The part, the operation of bursting, of cutting up into scattered fragments, and its impossibility, its interdiction, its being kept in secret, its unthinkable at the same time as impracticable nature. The empire denies being in pieces, or it covers its pieces over. The empire has burst; it has not burst. Empire says in a single word the entire apotheosis of the dismembered king in the black night of the storm, the entire flight of the crowd and its call back. Empire says, in theory, through its parts and through their negation, that the addition of the parts, their presence or compresence is not enough to make an empire. The empire thus cannot be divided and, if it is divided up, no one knows any longer where or what its parts are. Empire says in a word the unintegrable multiple. Romulus is not remade from his scattered limbs.

The empire, whole in the body of the king, the empire is undone through lynched Romulus. Each takes a part of the king. To do what?

This part of power is hidden. Power, empire, is always a part denied, like a cursed part. Ask him if he has it, and he will reply, covered in shame, in sweat, with fear, that he doesn't have it. He hides it in its breast, terrified of what he has done, terrified that someone might know he did it. It is known; it isn't known.

Who then killed Romulus? Someone or other? No. The Fathers killed him, no one in particular, everyone in collective. Who killed the king? The zone, the dense ring? Who holds power? The barons. No one in particular and everyone in collective.

What then is the 'we'? Who is this we, this set? No one in particular and everyone in collective. But what is this we?

It is known, it isn't known. No one in particular, nowhere, *imperium*. Yes, the empire is nowhere. And it denies locality: thus it rises to the universal.

This part of the we, do I have it, do I not have it?

All the Fathers, together, carved the king up into pieces.

Each one grabs a member and hides it in his bosom. The one who conceals it is thus marked; he is marked with the king's seal; he holds the scepter. Look at him, he is discovered now; he was hiding the king's cut-off hand, an end of a stiff finger, in his hand. So he is recognized. He is recognized as king; he is recognized as guilty. All the Fathers together are marked with the seal. Marked, they are all condemnable; all risk therefore being treated in turn as they treated Romulus. And as they will treat Caesar, the man, precisely, that is torn to pieces, Caesar in *diasparagmos*.[3] EMPEROR CAESAR, these two words form a nice black box in the now clear sense of an undivided division, a denied scattering, or the hidden *diasparagmos*. He who, among the Fathers, is caught carrying that denied part, that empire, he who is convicted of doing so, is in Romulus' state. A wolf from having killed, a king from carrying the part, a god from being put to death in his turn. They are, together, these hidden parts of Romulus. Each carries the impartitive empire; they are all this empire. Caesar, the son of the Caesar who was torn to pieces, the son of a torn women, of an eviscerated mother. Each for his part is this impartitive Romulus, the murderer of Remus, the wolf twin of the wolf son of a she-wolf, the king of Rome, the god carved up for the apotheosis, the son of Mars, god of violence, and of the violated vestal. Each here is a wolf, the twin of the wolf fathers in the city's Senate, carved up into some number of elders and conscripts.

Each one, each Caesar, hides his part of the empire; each denies being in possession of it. But everybody suspects everybody and keeps a watch on the fold of the other's robe. The black of his soul, as they say, or his unconscious. I know what the black fold of your unconscious contains. They hate each other for having torn up the seamless tunic. Each one hates the robe of the other and the fold of cloth, black. The ring formed by the Fathers, the zone around the throne, becomes tighter from this hatred, and loosens as well from this surveillance. They exchange names; they exchange stones; they all resemble one other without unanimity. The war of all against all is perhaps going to take place, and it assembles them. Nothing makes things stick together better than the glue of resentment. Hatred separates them; it reunites them. War moves them apart, and it brings them back together. All the evil in the world, it is said, is born from suspicion: the war here is born from the suspicion of empire, however this is nothing but an open secret. But what a contract, already, their war, their hatred and their suspicion are; what a pact their squabble is; what a glue their colloquy and their resentment.[4]

Each one knows, by himself, what all the others are hiding. Each one knows, thanks to the others, what he is hiding from himself.

Each one has stolen his part and conceals it; he is thus marked. Not all of them will be discovered at once. There they are, seeking out like dogs. They sniff like wolves.

Everyone suspects everyone. Who is going to discover who, now? And everything begins again. Everyone, again, discovers one of them and recognizes him. They recognize him as guilty: Romulus killed Remus, and this new one killed Romulus ... They recognize him as carrying the empire. His part hidden in the fold of his robe was impartitive; that which was to be demonstrated.

Power cannot be divided, and, when it is divided up, it is hidden.

The important thing is to open the black box of the toga. What is really there in the fold? That very thing enveloped there and which has no name in any language is repugnant enough that the fold has remained closed. Let's not be afraid; let's open the box. What's in the box? A quasi-object.

I am never alone in relation to an object. My attention, my perception are plunged in a social and cultural set. A theory of knowledge in which the subject, a monad, relates to an object, passive or active, is an empty utopia. The object is constituted in and through the relations of the group. A stake, for the combat of competition, a fetish, for vainglory and prosternation, merchandise, for commercial exchange, it is an object, more rarely. The subject of the object is always multiple.

Conversely, the collective never manages to form without that element I've called quasi-object circulating in it, the ball in the team, the peace pipe among the enemies finally reaching an agreement, the common glass at the feast where there is drinking, at the unanimous last supper, the small change at the market. This circulation is necessary for the distributed multiple to become a collective. It's not constituted by a contract – we don't know where it's written. It's not any will – we never find its subject. It is a token running from body to body, quite simply.

There is no object without a collective; there is no human collective without an object. Rome constructs the object.

The relations within the group constitute their object; the object running in a multiplicity constructs the relations and constitutes the group. These two complementary activities are contemporary. At the same time, the quasi-object transforms into an object, and the scattered multiple becomes a group. The quasi-object, still undetermined, is a joker.

These two works found the theory of knowledge and sociology. The progressive construction of the object, through a variable index, accounts for the birth of knowledge and that of the collective, accounts for their related evolution. The object, the luminous tracer of the relations established in the black box of the collective, fixes them, makes them stable, as unstable and fluctuating as they were; it dates, by its avatars, the state of knowledge. And the age of the group, the age of its works.

Perhaps it is enough to observe this object.

Perhaps history is its time.

I would never have undertaken writing this book without the intuition that inaugurates and envelops it. Athens and Jerusalem, bathed in the illumination of geometry and time, are both on the side of the subject, of the subject of knowledge. They allow us to understand, in equilibrium or in movement; they are white; they are from elsewhere; they aren't on the Acropolis or at the foot of the Wailing Wall. Rome neither explains nor sheds light; no light comes from its stone. It is black; it is on the side of the object. It is an object. It is here, on the shore of the Tiber, buried entirely in Rome, beneath the walls of its foundations. It constructs the object without shedding light on it or making it understood. That's why it passes for having no mind. The city, for it, is a thing, the *res publica*, the public thing. It founds, stubborn, deaf, mute, blind.

It is not enough to understand; it is not enough to be together in time; there must, in addition, be an object for these two operations to be practised.

The entire Mediterranean, at once, is necessary in order for us to be. The sign and the stone are necessary for us. And that shameful object in the black fold of the togas. That crazy object, that crazy man's object.

Something, it doesn't matter what, begins to circulate in the multiple; here already is the object. Quasi-object or pre-object. Romulus' death lets us see it. The Fathers hide a piece of royal flesh in the black fold of their clothing. Here the king is buried; here a piece of the king is enveloped, hidden. The Fathers invented at this time, inaugurated at the origin, this shameful quasi-object, scarcely exchangeable. Each of them have their part, and all of them have him in his entirety. Subsequently, in the rite, at the festival repeating that day, the servant women throw stones at each other, and each person calls the other by their name over and over again. The flesh, a fragment of the body, the stone, a fragment of the world, and the name, a fragment of language, fly from the ones to the others. The stones are visible, and the names are audible, but the flesh is hidden, buried in the fold. Plutarch: 'it is also said that Alcmene's body vanished, as they were carrying her to the grave, and that nothing but a stone was found on her bier.' The stones are the bones of my mother the earth. The flesh hardly circulates among the Fathers; the stones fly among the servant women; the names pass in the people fleeing in disorder. The states of the object – living flesh, inert stone, sign – let something like a transubstantiation be seen.

Yes, the foundation isn't far. In philosophy, some fathers have taught me that the foundation is in the subject, in the transcendental subject. And the sons of these fathers have replaced it with language. The foundation has receded into language.

Livy lets it be understood for example, in the chanson de geste of Coriolanus, that those who take cities are not necessarily those who take their name. He who takes the city doesn't found the city, even less so he who takes its name. And he who founds the city and gives it his name steals this foundation from the population. He is then cut up into pieces by his peers, and this abominable division and this black exchange and this concealment finally found the group.

The subject, on its own, isn't at the foundation of knowledge, and the transcendental is not in the subject. Knowledge is nothing without a collective that founds it. The collective is nothing without the circulation of the quasi-object. This circulation is concealed; the quasi-object itself is hidden. Knowledge is founded in collective practices that the collective is ignorant of. This black and white set of ignorance and knowledge can perhaps be called religion. The vestals buried an open white jar next to a closed black jar. The people were fleeing on that day too, that day of wrath.

There once was a fuzzy subset, the sanctuary woods; in its favourable shadow, violence calls a truce; wolves and she-wolves are found there. Bandits and whores, that's all our fathers and mothers were. It's not very important that the thing took place at some time, really. It's not a matter of writing history in the usual sense. It's a matter of seeing a set form. It must have formed one day, long ago, in the past, but it is forming again before our very eyes today; whether then or now, it's a matter of observing how it happens. Violence calls a truce in the shadow of the woods, in the shadow of knowledge; this is an image of ignorance; this is a black box. Images of violence always accompany the dark enclosure. It was night, and it was during a storm, and the thick cloud covered over the event. The same mystery in the sanctuary woods, black.

When the light returns, a transformation has taken place. Romulus is no longer there; the wolf has become a god, apotheosis. The Fathers have hidden a piece of the king in their robe. What is that object?

No human collective can exist without an object. There is no object without a collective; there is no collective without an object. The political animal is a fiction. The group floats crazily; it only becomes fixed for a time by means of an object. This proposition is no doubt generalizable: the more animals live in collectivity, the more they are forced to construct things outside their bodies, outside their group. These aren't the goals of their collective; they are its conditions.

The object was truly Rome's genius. Corneille constructs that object from a decapitated body in *The Death of Pompey*. Livy and Plutarch construct it slowly, without seeing it, as Rome is being founded.

The women and the people, on that day of commemoration, threw voices, names and stones at each other's heads. Might the stones be the bones or pieces of their unburied father?

I have called what circulates in a group and constitutes it through its circulation a quasi-object. It is sometimes hidden; this is the case with the slipper in 'hunt-the-slipper'. It passes. This is the case with the parts of the royal body, of the *imperium*, or of the empire. No one knows who is in possession of it, for he hides it; yet everyone is suspected of being in possession of it. It is this passage and this suspicion that constitutes the we, and not the addition of the Fathers, of the players who are present, their set as such. The quasi-object, this part, is the being of their relation. When it is discovered, its possessor becomes a singularity of the set. He is only one part of it, and he possesses the essence of social relations; he is only one part of it, and he possesses the whole. He holds in hand, in the exact sense, the empire. The quasi-object resolves the problem of the totality without addition: no, it's not their sum that produces the Senate or the set of the Fathers. It's the trace of blood on the insides of their togas. The king's body passes, part after part, passes from black fold to black fold; it traces routes in the black box. It is a tracing element; it reveals the network of unobservable relations in the box. Yet, the one who is discovered sees or can see all the quasi-twins swoop down on him to accuse and lynch him; he will therefore be thrown under them, subject, Caesar, Caesar at the Senate, under the conspirator Fathers. The quasi-object, a totalizing part, or tracing element, is an integrator. It can vary in form, nature or circulation, so the group varies with its variation. But in any case, it is the primary condition that allows an elementary form of society to be born.

This condition is not to be sought in a contract that precedes history. It is not in an abstract concept nor it is in a general will about which no one has ever known whose will it was. It is not in an idea or in a person, in a being or in a subject, in a preliminary writing or state. It is in an object. Neither the cloud nor the thunder has its law in the head or heart of a subject Jupiter, be he transcendent God or metaphysical Nature. Their law is in the relations of a charge. Things are no different here, except that neither the same laws nor the same objects are at issue. This quasi-object is a marker of relations; without it the relations would vanish and disappear. They float in the immediate. The quasi-object stabilizes time. While it is passing, the network is fairly stable. It is the first object of history.

It is the condition, the foundation of the group. As though the depositing of its first time.

It is the condition, the foundation of Rome. As though the impartitive part of the empire. It is a scattered member of Romulus' body. Analysis and synthesis, dispersion and centralization. The object here crystallizes an energy, sums up a dynamic, the one that disperses the parts and assembles them, the same one that made the people flee and that, through this flight, constructed the encounters, storm and fracas, return to the tranquil and serene light, stones and voices.

The Fathers, in their robes, conceal a part of the body torn to shreds. Who chose the best part, who chose the worst? This question has no meaning.

Each part, repugnant, is crude, is unformed; each part is unburied: *pars incondita*. Each part is hidden: *abscondita*, in the cloak's fold.

Since we are relating the foundation of Rome, *ab urbe condita*, we must begin again.

Nothing much has changed since the death of Romulus. Historians or interpreters, myself no doubt a distant and unworthy conscript, are around the text, Livy's or Plutarch's, around what remains of it or the last fragments, around the ancient or recent *corpus*. Different fathers for a different body. The one that goes from Mommsen to Corneille, from Shakespeare to Dionysius, and from annalistic to *fasti*. The immense software body of the city. Analysis rages; criticism and hypercriticism, dispute occupy the terrain; it's the new war of all against all. Everyone takes his part of it and considers the part of the others to be unfounded, crude and unformed. History has taken the place of empire. We have changed all that, and we have passed from hardware to software. We no longer take cities; we no longer take anything but names. But the murderous rule has nonetheless been maintained. The goal is to mark one's name and erase the others. Customs have passed from murder by sword to murder by language. The passage from the thing to the sign doesn't fundamentally change anything. We are all Coriolanus: taking the city by taking its name. And we don't hear the lamentations of the women. The historians become agitated, during the storm, around the Roman *corpus*.

Lamentation. Why must we still tear bodies to pieces? Why must we tear the corpus apart? Why must we always destroy the objects of knowledge?

Answer: in order to found. Silvia must be buried, Remus lynched, Romulus torn to pieces, to found the city. This is how it was founded. This is how. This is how knowledge is founded. This is how the institutions of knowledge are founded. The accord of the scholarly collective is isomorphic to the analysis into fragments of the corpus. Each scholar had a piece of the known in his robe, his discipline. He rules in his empire department. He rules in his reason. This is how Rome was founded. So be it. This is how the institution of knowledge is founded. So be it. This is how the collective is founded, and whichever it may be, urban, academic, etc. This is the true conflict of the faculties.

Lamentation: what good is it to seek to know this? Why open the black box? Why unfold the hem of the toga?

Answer: in order to found. We now know how to found. We can found a new city, a new knowledge, a new history. Do we want to? Do we want to cut up, analyse, tear apart the king's body again?

What do we want to found, what city do we want to found? That's the only question. What good is all of philosophy and all of history, what good are lives of work at the break of dawn without an answer to this question?

The answer is clear and simple. We no longer tolerate the thanatocracy or its acts, its discourses or the culture it brings about. The hatreds it spreads, the disputes, polemics, divisions, powers, resemble each other. The culture founded on death only returns to death, repetitively. The knowledge founded on murder returns to murder multiplied by knowledge. This multiplication was strong enough recently to absorb all that exists. Today we are at the point of no return. We have returned to the time of foundation, crushed by the thanatocracies of irrationality and rationality. We want to avoid a new repetition of the identical ancestral gesture. A city, science or knowledge that would no longer be founded, like ours, on death and destruction remains to be founded.

We no longer have anything but this work, apart from the dismal repetitions of history.

Romulus disappears, amid the storm, in the middle of the fleeing crowd; Romulus was analysed by the Fathers. He had killed, it is said, his twin. Did he really commit this murder?

It was the day of the inauguration. Remus, on the Aventine, was the first to receive six vultures as an augury. Romulus on the Palatine immediately observed twelve, double. And they were both first, one in time, the other by number. Each of them was therefore proclaimed king by his pressure group. Thus dispute, quarrel, exasperated anger, it ended in a murderous fight. There, in the crowd, Remus fell dead under the blows. *Ibi in turba ictus Remus cecidit.* In the middle of the crowd, in the middle of the mob, in the vortex of noise and quarrel.[5] In the slightly denser ring around which the crowd was fleeing. However the more common tradition has him murdered by his twin after he had jumped over the new walls of Rome with a leap. The two stories are contradictory because they say that two different things happened to the same people, at the same time, in the same respect. The two stories, it has been well observed, are two twins that kill each other. Either murder between twins took place, or lynching by the crowd; there is no third way. It suffices to think this simultaneity. It suffices to think it as an additional element of twinship. It suffices to displace it a little. The hatred between brothers goes to point of murder. This hatred between twins grows like ivy in the group; it goes toward extinction, and there is no foundation unless, stopping the reciprocal throat-slitting, the crowd turns against one among them. René Girard's lesson, the schema he has proposed makes these two contradictory stories compatible; it even makes them complementary. The fight between twins is an operator; the death in the middle of the mob is a point of articulation. The former is the motor force of a time, and the latter is the end of one time and the beginning of another. Hence the reference point for the foundation.

How was Rome founded by the founding family? Romulus disappears in the middle of the Fathers; Remus falls under blows in the middle of the mob. The twins are killed with a twin death. A double tradition is there so as to hide this. The one jumped over the wall, and the other disappeared from the throne during the storm.

How was Rome founded by the founding family? Rhea Silvia, a vestal, a mother, was put in chains for having been violated; she was thrown in prison. What chains, what prison? Violated vestals are buried alive at the Colline Gate. All the people stand up in silence and surround the action in the middle of a horrible sadness. On this gloomy day, the veiled vestal, held down with straps, hidden in the litter, blind and deaf, goes down into her little subterranean room where milk, a little water in a vase and some oil are waiting for her. Everyone is silent; no one can see; she neither hears nor sees. It is closed with earth. The black earth, a black box, is now blind and deaf to every pain. What prison? The tomb itself. What chains? All those that can hide what has just been done. Without Plutarch, without this description of the rites he said were imposed by Numa, we would never have known Rhea Silvia's fate. The history modestly says chains and prison. And is then silent. Silent about the ritual lynching. Silent about the possible parallel with the death of Tarpeia. Rhea Silvia disappears from history and the text; her disappearance disappears. I have read scholarly books about Tarpeia that explain everything about her except her stoning and her disappearance under the shields: they made her disappearance disappear.

How was Rome founded by the founding family? The mother having disappeared, Romulus having been carved into pieces, Remus having fallen beneath the blows of the crowd, the entire family is lynched. The criminal mother, a violated vestal, the brother who is a criminal for having killed his brother, the twin who is a criminal for having overstepped borders.

How was Rome founded by its founding family? Before Remus falls, before the twins and their group fight, Livy's narrative uses the verb *to found* three times and in different varieties of the future tense. The foundation is imminent. With Remus dead, the verb returns, in the past tense this time, and the city is founded. Between the two, the text recounts the inauguration, the two flights of eighteen vultures seen from the Aventine and the Palatine, the fight and the murder in the two twin traditions, one of which, more commonly believed, won out over the other; it had to be so. The hardware elimination of the bodies is answered by the software expulsion of the text. The foundation is death itself after the fight to the death. So Rome was named after the name of the founder. Which one? Rome's name comes from Remus, or from Romulus, indifferently; everything begins again, the fight to the death in the sign, and nothing is resolved. Was the founder the murderer? Was the founder the murdered? The answer to this question can be elegant; it says the lethal relation of the murderer and the murdered.

Become king, Romulus joins forces with Titus Tatius, king of the Sabines, and eliminates him. Rome never ceases being founded. Tullus, conqueror of Alba, joins forces with the dictator of Alba, Mettius, and he eliminates him. How were these twins eliminated?

So the king Titus Tatius was sharing the empire (we finally know that this proposition is as difficult to say as the thing is to do) with Romulus, king of Rome, the way the Sabine women were sharing the beds of the Roman men, when he has a dispute with the Laurentines. A fairly difficult affair in which the Laurentine legates were mistreated by his own relatives. The former protested by virtue of the law of nations; Titius played deaf and only heard the voice of blood; he only listened to his kin. Two groups are opposed again. The schema, mercilessly, begins again. So one day, Tatius went to the city of Lavinium, the capital of Laurentine, to celebrate a solemn sacrifice. A concourse formed, *concursu facto*, like an assembly, an uprising, and he fell dead. Assassinated. A concourse is the racing course of a mass toward a point. Here toward the place Tatius was. He didn't know that what was awaiting him, solemnly, in the city of Lavinium on this festival day was his own sacrifice.

The king of Alba is tied in the middle of the horses; worried, he is stretched out between eight horses; the king of Rome orders them to be whipped. The animals pull, walk, run; the king of Alba is dragged by the two times four horses; his flesh is torn apart by the horses. The king of Rome has distracted the limbs of the Alban dictator.

One doesn't share the empire with Tullus.

No one can be the guest of Hostilius.

The senators are around the king Romulus. The Laurentines around the sacrificer. The horses around the dictator of Alba. The horse-senators. It will be said: the equestrian order.

The three Curiatii are around the young Horatius: that he die! Always the same circumstance. Star, ring, the schema is always maintained.

The foundation of Rome, punctual, local, is this fight of twins finished off by a murder. Rome's name even lets us see that knowing who the murderer was and who the victim was is indifferent. It's almost never interesting to know such things, the things everyone seeks out so much that all the interest in the world seems to take refuge in this mystery. Romus kills Remulus. Why not? Either this murder takes place with equal culpability, or a lynching takes place. The entire founding family passes here and goes through this.[6]

Once the foundation of Rome is defined, we must define the path along which, precisely, it never ceases to take place. This path defines a time, the primary time of history: the constitution of a collective, of its elementary form, constitution and disaggregation. Remus, perhaps, or Rhea Silvia begins; Romulus begins again, and Titus Tatius, and the quartered one, but also Tarpeia, but the young Horatius as well (whose avoided lynching and whose reversed sacrifice mark the passage to the judicial state, founding the institution of tribunals), and this doesn't stop all the way up to Julius, Julius in his toga in the middle of the senators, Caesar first of the Caesars, and this doesn't stop all the way up to this very day. The assassination of the first king of Rome in the middle of the popular concourse, amid voices and prayers, in a dense ring of guardians, dates from yesterday morning.

This path is that of *fundamental history*, of history defined by the series of foundations. The crowd forms in a ring; the crowd breaks up; the people flee; the crowd forms again. The multiple lets its fundamental beating be seen. The deep pulsing in the heart of its black box, of the city and of the people of Rome, the accords and disaccords of the Romans, their greatness and their decline as has been said. Not the struggle of the orders described by history at another level, but the multiplicity's secret beating. This beating is cadenced with founding murders, by eponyms of assassins, of victims. There is, in the beginnings, something like an accumulation point; or rather the dense site where the murders multiply is the departure itself, the foundation, the beginning. Subsequently, they space out; they happen less frequently, or rather this spacing out is the sequence itself, that is to say, fundamental history or time. The collective is more solid; it is surer of itself; the institutions endure; objects have taken over. Crisis is the moment when a multiplicity no longer has confidence in its objects. It changes, it is going to change quasi-objects, the objects that create its social relations. The crisis is one of objective transubstantiation. This is fundamental time; it runs from founding murder to founding murder.

Each founding murder imposes a discontinuity, a break. Conversely, the break is barbarous, and every theory that lets it be seen is a theory of the sacred. Not of science, but of the sacred.

These breaks are all the same, of a bleak repetitiveness. Being killed, killing, carving up, stoning. It is understood that the death instinct is iteration, and conversely. The fundamental time of history is marked by death. It appears to be discontinuous, but it is merely the time of the Eternal Return. It comes back either over itself or over the same form of origin at close intervals, as though panicked, or at wide and patient ones. You might say that the motionless motor of time is hidden there.

The reason why we see this clearly: we have come back to it. The thanatocracy is set up in proximity to the return to the foundation. We have found it again. Here we are. The multiplicity that trembles, broken up, to be created, is now the global collective – universal – the possible victim of the new lethal quasi-object, the bomb. He was holding a muster in the middle of the plain when suddenly a thunderstorm accompanied by violent thunderclaps burst. A thick cloud enveloped us ...

On empire, once again, and see how, from the beginning, it forms regionally. Tarquinius arrives, Superbus, at the assembly of the principal Latins with a long day's delay.[7] Impatient, the petty kings complain bitterly; they blow up at him. Turnus of Aricia is at the head of the anger; he inveighs against Superbus, the ferocious, the arrogant. The king of Rome, having arrived, is at the centre; he is a scapegoat. Look at this empty place, empty due to delay, due to the king's absence. Tarquinius arrives; Turnus leaves the assembly. Now look at the substitution. Tarquinius takes the place of Turnus; Turnus takes the place of Tarquinius, the first in the assembly, the second as the absent object of hate. Given some plot fomented just right, a mass of weapons deposited secretly at night in the residence of the prince of Aricia, and the collective ire abruptly changes head, leader, subject. The operation is so clear and simple that it almost becomes abstract. Tullus, in danger, in the middle of the crowd, makes Horatius fight and remains king. The victim is a substitute: Tarquinius or Turnus and vice versa. Turnus is a vice-Tarquinius, or he is his vicar. All these words are equivalent: they are substitutable; the truth remaining intact.

The vicar undergoes a terrible punishment affirmed by the historian to be without precedent or of a new kind. He had already said the same thing about the quartering of the Alban dictator. Proof that he doesn't see the long dismal series for which these murders are merely the repetitive links. Turnus is thrown into the Ferentina spring; everybody throws a hurdle loaded with stones over him. If this is not the beginning, it's assuredly the schema of the empire. Tarpeia's body is beneath the shields covered with precious stones. Turnus' body is beneath the wicker hurdle whose interlacing is hidden beneath the rocks scattered on it. Did each Latin prince carry his stone to the edifice? To the dismantled edifice, dismantled into fragments, under which a woven fabric holds fast, under which a corpse is hidden? The hurdle intermediate between the bodies and stones is a good image of the social bonds then woven. And the scattered stones say that the king of Aricia, beneath the acclamations, profited from the suffrages. A clear organization chart of the empire.

Ab urbe condita. *I admire Livy's title; I wish to leave it untranslated. What is said here is the foundation of the city and designates the book that follows the foundation. Yet the city is never completely founded; the thing is never assured. It's the same for us, I mean for knowledge. Everything said here is said at a distance from the founded city; everything only has existence through this distance, through the length of this separation. The essential thing is the ab, or the from, which are, in fact, a starting from. A reference point, a point of departure, a bursting place. The explosion into parts at the swamp of Capra indicates a departure in every direction. A new geometral of possible directions.*

With the distance measured along one bearing, along one direction, the city seems to disappear, as though its foundation were becoming too distant. So it returns. Relate a series of events, follow slowly its consecution, see how, departing from the foundation, it moves away from it, and how, all of a sudden, it brings you back there in an instant. I don't know how things really are with history, real or recounted, but I do know, but I do see that it has a fixed point and that it moves away from it so as to return to it. No, there isn't one foundation of the city, one real, ritual, historical act, one myth or one representation, one dream, one imagination; there wasn't this unique and definitive thing starting from which a history, a time of great length, unwinds its course, as though there were a source and a flow, as though a mark existed and, starting from its unicity, a computus. No, I see an equilibrium, a stable state; this invariance is the foundation. The city-state is there in its stable seat. That said or that posited as thesis, time, history and circumstances diverge in distance around this position. Livy measures the distance to the foundation: however far we seem to be from it, history, recounted or real, doesn't lose sight of it. Distance from the in-stance to the circumstance.

With his title, Livy invites us to measure the distance or interval and to assess a slow moving away. Along this path, then, an abrupt fall stops it and throws everything toward the state of equilibrium; everything returns, one might say naturally, from the environments of said circumstance to the in-stances of the foundation, from the distance taken to that zero state where distance is nil. Rome never ceases being founded; its history or its time is simply what happens between two occurrences of the founding gesture. Here it is freeing itself from it, climbing, rising in relation to its stable seat, sometimes for a long time, then it falls there; it falls back there. Rome begins. Even when it becomes the city of Augustus, it is still a city of auguries; Rome is the city of beginnings. The beginning that we know is simply the time in which many beginnings accumulate.

I see a thousand festoons around this position, a thousand capricious distancings around the thesis, or rather and precisely starting from the thesis – festoons, distancings that are irregular, quite short, medium, lightning fast in brevity, or not particularly long, sometimes interminable, a twinkling star with rays that are dead as soon as they appear, with shimmering light all the way to a time of adolescence, piercing immense distances as well, endowed with a powerfully attractive black centre in which the beginning is involuted and endlessly restarts, endowed with a deep pole, that of foundation. Rome begins again and is founded; at its beginning it was founded often. Hardly visible little distancings, weak rays, narrow festoons. Its proper time is this false rhythm, in which the brief borders the long, in which the immense is next to the aborted. This time is close enough to that of life, near that of genesis; it's astonishing that it has long been confused with eternity.

Rome rarely leaves the time of beginning; it endures by returning there.

The redundancy sown on the multiple is the return to the foundations.

I see here for the first time and clear as day the primary link between the eternal return's time and the unicursal, monodromic, irreversible, linear, ordinary time of history.

Rome enters into history, at least we think so. I mean: if we are in history, and we do think so, Rome must be as well, for we entered it thanks to it as well in those days. Yet Rome is mired in the sacred. Its feet are tied up in the snares of the sacred. Blind, its attempts to free itself are visible; it is inexorably brought back. Drugged, intoxicated with violence, it can't escape the sacred. The eternal return is exactly the return of the sacred, the return of the forgotten, of the buried, the return to the light of the head with the intact face at the top of Capitoline Hill. Who could have buried who, dead or alive, on this mound, in this hill? The return of the founded, the lightning-fast return to the abominable gesture of foundation. The sacred comes out of the black box, and it calls back, while Rome, like Hercules, has its back turned. They flee, trembling, this not very certain place, and the cattle's mad baritone calls them back. The city then returns, blind, crazy, to the cave, to the cavern, or to Numa's grotto. It falls into the foundation trench; Rome always has one foot in this grave, and it falls back in. Return. It leaves it due to the abundant and perennial spring. This: the false rhythm of its time, the irregularity of the luminous arms around the star come from the compromise of the irreversible

time of the water-pourer – spring, Tiber, Albula, the time-counter without
return – with the monotonous, repetitive, legal time of the sacred. Should the
linear carry it along, the festoon will be long; should the return impose itself
in its turn, the ray will become short. The time of invention comes to terms
with the time of repetition. The time of newnesses comes to terms with the
returns of sacred redundancy. No, the negative doesn't produce any work, any
movement; on the contrary, it annuls all movement by the return to zero, by
the eternal return to the act of founding. Killing is nothing but monotonous,
and this law produces nothing. The work of the negative is a null work; it
nullifies itself at the point of return, at the sacred place of foundation. Real
work only comes from diverging from this position, only comes from distance
from this return, distance from the fragile disequilibriums around the thesis,
only comes from separation in relation to the foundation, in relation to
the inexorable invariance of the sacred, with zero information. Livy holds
together, in the palm of his hand and from the origin, the question of the
foundation, that of the negative, that of the return, that of the sacred. One
little word resolves them: Ab. There is history only in tearing away from there.
Rome can do so, Rome can't do so. Hence the ruleless beating around the
thesis. Ab urbe condita. *An impaled insect struggles madly around a thorn.*
Culture is, quite simply, the distance from this foundation, barbarous.

Are we so sure of being so far from this centre, well, or black hole that we
are never caught in it? We are, quite to the contrary, assured of the contrary.
Atrocious returning ghosts sometimes called reason or the work of history,
the foundation and its barbarous gestures never cease to repeat themselves,
sacred.[8] Can we imagine a distancing that would be definitive and without
return? Can we conceive that culture begins? It has perhaps begun without
our knowing. We have heard an explosion into parts, universal, and all our
work is to avoid its return …

4 SUFFRAGE: THE ASSEMBLED MULTIPLICITY

Transubstantiation. Romulus, the king of Rome, and Mettius, the dictator of Alba, are torn to pieces, by quartering or another method. Tarpeia and Turnus are visibly stoned. Rhea Silvia no doubt is buried alive.

These murders first of all form a series; the founding family begins; it gives a global image of it: the mother is buried; one twin is lynched; the other is carved up. This series never stops, all the way to Julius Caesar, all the way to the foundation of Christianity and after. It is the current foundation, recurring throughout time; it could be used to delimit eras or periods. It is rarely made visible. The arrogance of our culture suffers from its barbarous foundation.

This series, impressive in its returns whatever the degree of culture might be, is endowed with a simple reason. This reason is a law; this law has meaning. The king, the dictator are divided into parts. They are unities; they are cut up into parts. The stones on the hurdle at the Ferentina spring, the precious bracelets on the left wrists of the Sabine soldiers, even their shields, are fragments, parts, splinters that a multiplicity throws into a place and toward a point: the parts return together, convene, converge toward unity. The law is quite simple; it follows a star schema: the one becomes multiplicity; the multiple becomes unity. We have to think together lynching and stoning, a mob pouncing together upon a body and execution by quartering. We could even name this law: the law of empire.

This law has meaning. I have described, as you will recall, the dynamics of the flight during the storm in the swamp of Capra. The people disperse, and it's in scattering that people encounter each other. They move away and scatter through thrown rocks; they assemble through voices. I'm saying that the stones become voices; I'm saying that the precious stones become names, pretransubstantiation. This is no mystery; on the contrary, it's easy to understand. Beat the cream, and it will set. The distribution ends in gathering. What I have called *systrophe* above is this exchanger, this dynamic converter of the multiple into the one and the one into the multiple, this crucible in which energies spread, expand, that is to say, move and condense anew.

Two things are to be distinguished a bit: the group as such and the quasi-objects that circulate in it. The group explodes and reforms under the action of these forces, diastole and systole, atomization and moving closer again, and the quasi-objects vary: stones and voices. The stones separate. Stoning: they converge. They are suddenly like the parts of the royal body returned to their place. They will tear another body to pieces as well. The quasi-object, at first an unformed part hidden in the fold of the toga, the quasi-object becomes objectivized, if I dare say so. I am a part of my group; I carry in my breast a part of the king's body. Sociobiology tells of our barbary. The organic model of the group is perhaps originary; it's originary enough to make you vomit in disgust. I am part of the Leviathan or the large animal; I am as Agrippa Menenius said one of its members; the Fathers around the king have just carried out the fable of the stomach. Blood circulates; they are covered with it; each one of them is or has a member. There is no human collective without an object. Here is the first object. Each of them thus participates in the same body. This object becomes transubstantiated; this means that the relation of the group becomes transformed. This object becomes stone; it becomes bracelet; it becomes shield; it is always related to the object it comes from. It is always fragment; it always comes from unity so as to return to it. It is the tracer, the tracing element, which reveals, in the black box, how the energies that make it a converter move and condense. It is fragment, and it is sign, a hardware fragment and a software sign. It is a fragmented piece: he who is under the pile of fragments has received the suffrages under the fracas of the acclamations. He is stoned in a hardware kind of way; he is elected in a software kind of way. The transubstantiation is there: the stone becomes bread, and the bread becomes body. No. The stone becomes body, and the body becomes sign. The transubstantiation never ceases. It precedes itself in the text in which it occurs: what if your brother asks you for bread and you give him a stone in its stead? This separates you from your brother. The stone becomes bread, or the bread becomes stone. In any case, they are signs. The discussion about the mystery is part of the mystery, that is to say, part of history. Yes, the quasi-object remains quite real; relation is a being among us, and without this being, there, there is no relation, that is to say, no group, but the being of this being evolves and fluctuates. It is flesh, it is stone, it is voice. It goes from real presence to symbolic presence, and that's another transubstantiation. From flesh to voice or from stone to noise. What must be understood here is a series as well, a series of transubstantiations, of which the one we have canonized is only one stage. Flesh, stone, bread, body, blood, voice, sign, and so on. And changing substance signifies changing being: the being of the relation, the being of a null being, the being of the collective.

Tarpeia. Tarpeia lies beneath the precious stones. She dies beneath her own price. Tarpeia lies underneath; she is motionless, underneath, stable, dead, stopped, for eternity. In the literal sense of the Latin language, she in the position of substance; she is substance; she is underneath. The Sabine soldiers buried her alive beneath their shields; they stoned her with their bracelets. How much is Tarpeia worth? How much is the capture of Rome worth? How much is the violation of its walls, of its gate worth? How much is Rome worth? How much is the city worth? How much is the body worth? Tarpeia is worth her weight in gold; she's worth her weight in gemstones. Or at least a weight sufficient to knock her over, to cover her over, to hold her below, lying.

The coloured stones shimmer on the surface. They are the price, the equivalent of the body; they are now its appearance. The fragmented, colourful, sparkling, noisy multiplicity covers over she whose site leads us to call substance. Phenomenal stone, accidental stones, circumstantial stones, awarded by the Sabines to Tarpeia. They are the appearance; they are the accident; they are the circumstances, held above and all around; they are the attributes of the thing underneath, that no longer has a name in any language. A multicoloured painting, blended, tiger-striped, striated, mixed, motley, traversed with sound, fury, a screen of substance.

How many Sabines are necessary to take the city? How many precious bracelets are necessary to pay the vestal? How many accidents, attributes, circumstances are necessary to exhaust, to name substance? How many suffrages are necessary for the contract to appear, for harmony to be heard, for the unanimous soul to make the social body? How much silver and gold is necessary to equal the total, reserve, stock or capital? How much time, how many words, sentences and books are necessary to finally say what I have wanted to say for so long? There must be a theory of infinite debt. Never will I write enough to discover the very source, ceaselessly covered over by what it produces; never will I give you what you have given me; never do I find what I'm looking for; the accidents, the attributes never reach the sum, nor do the parts of the bodies reach the body; nor do you, or me, or them reach the social body itself; nor do the Sabines reach the captured Rome that absorbs the Sabines; nor do the scattered jewels reach the priestess, nor does the phenomenal reach reality; multiplicity does not reach unity; it is most often unintegrable. It must be believed that if it were integrable, history would stop. History flows, and time flows across that divergence from integration. The staves of the barrel of the Danaids are disjointed; through this opening, I die and can't say everything; through this fissure, the eternal return doesn't go back over itself; through this irrational, newness occurs and perpetuates multiplicity. Why are we endlessly stoning?

Never does suffrage reach substance; suffrage always returns.

Who is underneath? Who is under the fragmented pile of stones of light? Rhea Silvia? Perhaps, but who else? Tarpeia? Perhaps, but who else? Turnus? Perhaps, but who else? Stephen? Perhaps, but who else? Galileo? Galileo condemned for the law of falling stones? Who is underneath? Even if the mass of stones were lifted, even if this tomb of stone were opened, even if the immense stone in front of the tomb were rolled away, even if the scattered ashes, the bone fragments of the one who was covered over were searched, substitution, again, would cause the end to flee. A goat in a bush, encountered by chance, always takes Isaac's place. Taking the place and ceding the place, again, cause time to run. The culprit is endlessly being found; he is endlessly being proclaimed innocent. Substance is another name for substitution. Substance stops; substitution flees.

No, Tarpeia is not a name. Tarpeia is the name of a law. Historically, the name of a Roman law that, around 450, permitted moving from cattle to money in the assessment of fines. The Tarpeian law transforms an ovine, a bovine, into pieces of *aes rude*. The assessment is a transubstantiation of the animal into the stone. I was going to say of the animal into the fragments that are thrown onto it, into suffrage. Or from reality to sign. Any of these will do. No, don't look any more to see whether the author, the eponym, a certain Spurius Tarpeius, consul, existed or not. That's because the death of Tarpeia, a vestal, is already a Tarpeian law. That's because the name Tarpeia is the law itself. The tropeic vestal is transformation; she is transubstantiation; she is the series of equivalences that endlessly attempt and miss the exact equalization. I even wonder whether she isn't the law of history, I mean the law of time.

Struck by the first stones, Tarpeia, the young vestal, collapses in the flowers. The Sabine soldiers still see her, long and beautiful, a bit battered. The rain of bracelets beats down on her, making her lose form little by little. She would soon be nothing but a pile of unformed pulp, if the precious stones didn't modestly cover her over. The Sabines see her, they no longer see her; they see her disfigured; they deform her, transform her; they drowned her. Around her, scattered stones, here and there, frame the painting on the grass of the mound, a cutting out of the repugnant scene, hatred of the given beauty.

The Sabines see the thing; the Sabines see the icon. Tarpeia is there, living; she is surrounded by her forms. The first stone breaks the first form; many bracelets deform her; more bracelets cover her over. The Sabines see the representation on the icon vanish under the volley of stones, after the burst body has been hidden. Precise, sovereign, bewitching, intimidating with beauty, now rendered fuzzy under the sparkling of the cut stones, a detail, soon to be carved up, ravaged, under the complete torture of the cutting;[1] an impressionism and later a pointillism, lastly a geometrism of little ruby or sard cubes set in the Sabines' bracelets, each jewel showing an infinitesimal window of flesh to the microscope, finally an abstract painting when what has no name in language or no longer exists except as analysed, destroyed, ground up, finds itself covered over by the iconoclasts.

To recognize the priestess, to decipher her name, lifting a few shields is not enough; the fracas of battle calling a truce is not enough; who is she who, opening the door, has allowed all this noise and this fury? There, beneath the dazzling mosaic, beneath the thick and chaotic material of the abstract masterpiece, she dies, the noisy beauty, perhaps letting her foot be seen, perhaps letting her foot stick out beyond the precious stones. There again is a geometral. Who is she, the unknown vestal?

Tarpeia, her name is Tarpeia. Is that a Latin, Etruscan or Greek name? In Greek, τροπαία designates she who makes turn. Who turns away ills, certainly, another name for the goat or the *pharmakos*. But above all she who transforms. She makes history, time, becoming turn; she changes; she converts; she converts the multiple into the one and the one into the multiple, *diasparagmos*, stoning; she converts a piece of information into value, a word into money, a stone into jewellery, a sign into another sign; she is a trope. Trope and transubstantiation.

The tropeic vestal exchanges empire and suffrage in her body.

Kings. The kingship of Rome is a banal, ordinary, legal kingship, one such as India had or other collectivities, a kingship like Alba's, savage. The savage kings of Alba seem to draw their name from localities, rivers or hills. These hills, on the contrary, these rivers are the kings' first tombs and are named from that. Kingship finds its foundation in the king's tomb. Kings everywhere, kings always, are the excluded, the expelled, are victims; to be king is to be put to death by the multitude, the kingship, the reign existing from deferring the day of drowning in the middle of the Albula, the day of wrath when the *diasparagmos* explodes, the day when the crowd pushes the king from the top of the execution rock, the day when divine wrath strikes the king down with lightning; the gods are on the earth that day. The king is nothing but the death of the king; he is the moment of his collective death; he is sacred due to his expulsion; he is sacred due to his lynching; kingship is nothing but the waiting time until this day.

All the power is in the hands of he who can, of he who is going to die at the hands of all. He polarizes the collective violence. He holds the potential monopoly or mono-pole of collective violence.[2] He holds the capacity, the power of the social accord.[3] He doesn't hold it in the order of the sign, in the order of the contract; he holds it in the real order of energy and force. The energy is directed toward the one, he who is capable of every energy, of the whole of force; he holds this knot, potentially. He waits for this capacity to pass into act. I'm taking the word *capable* in the geometric sense.[4]

The historian's interrogation of the merits and projects of Marcus Manlius Capitolinus, the judicial interrogation of his intentions fall under the forgetting of this banal law: Manlius was pushed from the Tarpeian Rock – this very thing made him king. Likewise, Caesar was lynched in the Senate – this very thing made him king. The suspicion of wanting to be king comes from this. To reign is to live the distance from the Capitol to the Tarpeian Rock, a short space, a brief, fairly long or very long time, an interminable reign. It's the distance from the possible to the real: from power to its being put into execution. Power – that's its name – is restrained potentiality, restrained until the passage into act, into the act presupposed by this capacity. The very expression 'exercising power' is fairly ambiguous, for one doesn't exercise a simple capacity; one only exercises executions. When Rome, at the end of its kingships, throws the kings out, it doesn't expel kingship; it defines it. The same ambiguity, the same impossibility to think: how to exclude exclusion? When Rome forbids ever saying this execrated title, it defines the sacred kingship. The two twin consuls, each year, quickly abandon their place and power before arriving at the due date for payment, I mean before being at the edge of the rock, before killing one another, before being killed by all, before acquitting the price of this power. The price of power is the act that power restrains. Kingship directly, carnally, savagely, takes on being put to death, which is like paying off the debt for power. The other exercises cheat, a salutary cheating that assures the passage from human sacrifice to the symbol or sign, from social energy to the contract, or from the thing itself to representation: any given form of power takes on the putting to death temporarily and passes it quickly on to some other just before having to pay its just price. Should this being relieved be lacking, the putting to death is there. Power is transmitted like a red hot coal, the red flower of the wolves in the depths of the jungle.

I'll return to the kings of Alba, to the time of Tullus' reign. The Alban army attacks; it arrives at the gates of Rome. The king of Alba, Cluilius, digs a trench around Rome and his own camp. Let's remember the trench dug by King Romulus at the time of Rome's foundation. Yes, the foundation begins again for a new city that's going to include the Albans. Remus, murdered for having leapt over the first trench, is perhaps buried inside, beneath the walls of the city that bears his name. The second ditch is named after the king of Alba, Cluilius. Here everything speeds up. First Cluilius dies. Livy says that the Cluilian trench was called such right up until time erased it. Lastly the Cluilian trench is the cloaca itself; it's the same word, it seems; it's the Cloaca Maxima or the great sewer.

As it is being dug, the king dies. He is expelled. Is Cluilius, like Remus, at the bottom of the furrow in the ground? The cloaca is a tomb. Conversely: is the trench in which the kings are lying an evacuation conduit? Is power only thought, only thinkable, in the beginning, as social refuse? And the expulsion trench is itself expelled; it is erased as a real presence; its name as symbol and sign has been forgotten.

The trench under the wall, foundation, the border trench or the boundary trench of the city, of the sacred enclosure, of space, definition, the trench of the religious, of logic, of origin and of power, is the maxima route of the cloaca, the great feeder, the sewer, the expulsion canal, the exclusion conduit.

It is low, underground. It follows the lowest low points; it recruits all of the possible. And that's why it has capacity, power. It is the tomb. It is exclusion. It is the place of the king.

Here we see the rigorous place of power defined by its nature as limit, by its minimum site, by its redoubled function of erasing and expelling.

In the depths of the den, a black box, the lion receives the blows from all the animals.

Theory of universal suffrage. I think that suffrage is universal. By this I mean that it is just as much royal as it is democratic. On the nether side of the *res publica*, which is unified in this way, suffrage is rooted in anthropological customs. It accounts for the birth, real or imaginary, of the hero. Perhaps it announces a logic of the concept. Perhaps it organizes the collective representations … Let's get to work.

Look at the word *suffrage* and read its root. The Latin *fragor* is our 'fracture' or our 'fractionation', from *frangere*, breaking, smashing, splitting up, putting into pieces. Under the fracas of the bursting storm, king Romulus is thus carved up, cut into pieces; the crowd breaks up in fleeing. Lucretius uses the word *fragor* for the fine fractionation of the atoms. The dictator of Alba, Mettius, is disarticulated by the horses. The world was quartered into simple atomic members. Someone or something lies under the fractures, suffers under the fragmentation, remains under the fractionations: I already hear the word 'suffrage'.[5] What snaps, what breaks produces noise, and *fragor* is again this fracas or this bursting. When the Alban houses, destroyed, collapse into powder, they let this cracking be heard. So 'suffrage': what lies under the fracas. Here is the thundering noise of the storm and the tumult of the crowd. Again Lucretius often lets the clamours of the world be heard. The set as a whole loses, gets lost in the disorder; it gets cut up into a set of elements, the elements return to the set through collisions and concentration; unities go to the multiple, and multiplicity returns to unity, a material, collective and conceptual pulsation. This doesn't happen without noise. The language says it, lets it be seen, and our old history recounts it. The passage to disorder and the return to order, the transformation, taken in general, occurs beneath the clamour, the rumbling, sometimes deafening. There's no apotheosis without a storm, no king or god without cheers, no thinking without hubbub; without chaos, without confusion, there's no world. But what makes noise is sometimes endowed with a meaning [*sens*], even if it's only the direction [*sens*] going from the multiple to the one, in the star. This *sens*, quite simply spatial, like that of the inclination, a rarity in the parallelism of the white falling, is perhaps the first meaning. So *fragor* is a message; it is a rumbling, a diffuse noise that first runs like a quasi-object; it quickly becomes acclamation. This is how it happens in the swamp of Capra; this is how it is heard. Suffrage is a putting to a voice vote, beneath the voices, a designation by ovation. Here we are, it's the vote. The king, the elected one, the hero, or that unity, covered for a moment beneath the multiple itself, lies beneath fragments: stones, money, votes, cries, election by acclamations.

He has been elected; he has benefited from our suffrages: things or signs.

Yes, suffrage is universal. Romulus is king, non-elected, a god beneath the fracas of the thunder, carved up into fragments by the enraged crowd, beneath the clamours: suffrage. Some candidate – white is the sum of colours, the synthesis or unity of their brilliant fragments – is elected beneath acclamations or votes: suffrage.[6] Royal or republican, designating the one, god, king, hero or unity in general; yes, history is slower, more repetitive than was thought. But let's leave politics where things are so simple – where the funerals of a few heroes are paid for by the people, at so much per head. The hero lies beneath the coins [*pièces*].

Suffrage is deeper, it is more subtle than substance itself. This latter lies beneath; it is what remains, what stays, durable and stable, across the multiplicity of the attributes or accidents; it is precisely an invariant across variations. Substance is static. Suffrage is the corresponding concept for what belongs to anthropology, the collective, or the social sciences. Is there a social invariant? Can social substance be thought? Evidently not. No one has ever found or seen there that which doesn't vary. No one has ever conceived any invariant there. But if substance can't be thought, suffrage can be conceived. It can be conceived universally.

Suffrage is not stable, it is not a thing, it is not an idea; it's an action, a transformation, it's a work, a functioning. It goes toward unity; it doesn't remain there. It requires fragments; it returns to fragments. So these latter come to unity, to the unity said to be underneath, said, acclaimed, represented, conceived to be underneath; whether the unity be god, victim, king, hero, tribune or even idea, the fragments cover it over, but they don't remain there; they don't reconstitute it, whole; they remain fragments when they find it and cover it over. Suffrage is universal. We must try to understand it in relation to substance; we must give it just as much importance. Substance is a concept. A concept subsumes the multiple under unity. The concept is royal, divine, heroic, that is to say victimary. For each of your concepts, tell the murderer who founds it. Substance is either the first or the last unity, hidden beneath, permanent across the diversity of attributes or accidents. Substance is royal, divine, heroic, that is to say, sacrificial. The hero, the king, the god, the victim, the substance, the concept, these are unities founded beneath the volley of stones, the rumbling of the crowd and the peal of thunder, these are unities of representation, the multiple by the one and the one by the multiple. Archaic and savage philosophy. Suffrage is not a concept; suffrage is not substance; it never ceases to vibrate from the unity to the multiplicities or conversely. It shows or it is the functioning of transformation. Contrary to substance, it gives the multiple a chance; it gives it its free rein; it gives time a chance and produces its flowing.

Substance, most often, is outside time. Time is in its attributes or its accidents. Suffrage is an arhythmic pulsing from the one toward the multiple and from the multiple to the one: the relation of the vestal to the fragments of the Sabine stones, or of the price of the betrayal to the precious bracelets, or of the violation of the Roman enclosure to the covering over by the shields or to the burying alive under that hill, a relation of a sum to small change, of scattered members to the whole body that was torn to pieces, a relation of a social body – present, absent, represented, imaginary, and yet real – to those we call its members. Our group is at our suffrages; our group is our suffrage. It is hopelessly divided up; it tends toward unity; it attains it, it withdraws, it is multiple. Suffrage is this beating. This beating is the motor of time. Time descends the decomposition; the course of time flows toward dissolution; time falls into fragments and dust; time climbs toward unity; it shoots out toward the cohesive and the organic; it gushes out toward harmony. Our history's time descends from the social body toward us; it goes from the scattered members of our collective to its unanimous body. To its present, absent, represented, divine, imaginary, dispersed body: Romulus. Suffrage is this beating that ceaselessly starts up again, always disappointed and always full of hope. Suffrage is the motor of time. Inflation toward the multiple, rare deflation toward the one. Inflation is only one figure of that law.

Thus history is made at our suffrage; thus its time is at the suffrage of certain of our actions and certain of our signs. The world is at the suffrage of the atoms, the group at the suffrage of the men, all thought in the process of forming at the suffrage of the multiplicities.

Substance is metaphysical. It is said in a domain so named for being situated beyond physics and the knowledge of physics. Substance is said in a language seeking stability; it is said in its metalanguage. Suffrage is voluble, unanimous and noisy; it beats from the concept to the multiple as such. I would like to say it, to pronounce it somewhere else than in its elected domain, politics; I would like to generalize it, universalize it. Can a space be conceived that would be to the social sciences what metaphysics was to physics?

This space no doubt exists. It can even be said that nothing existed before it. The history of religion says the social sciences in their nascent state, in their inchoative and archaic state, in their fundamental state. It's in a conflictual and founding relationship with the whole of the social sciences the way metaphysics was with physics. Physics, sometimes, physics, nonetheless, returns to founding questions; it returns to philosophy, via the demands of crisis, moments of invention, of renewal. The social sciences, established against the religions and in foundational conflict with them, from Richard Simon to Renan, from philosophy to political theory, sometimes return, nonetheless, to founding questions opened in and by the history of religion. Hence I read the book of Rome's foundation the way others open Genesis, the Prophets or the corpus of Greek myths, to ponder the foundation of our social sciences. But the conflict of physics and metaphysics was only a conflict inside knowledge and the scholarly corps. The debate over substance didn't spread beyond certain walls. And yet it was necessary to put substance to death in order to found science again, to remain at the appearances and describe their relations. That was a foundation in the sense of this book. The debate of the social and human sciences against religion was, on the contrary, open and historical. It isn't completely finished. It perhaps began with the Presocratics; it endures up to our time. It is much less clear and defined than the first debate. The symmetry of the questions ends, but it instructs us. When I try to think suffrage, when I seek a parallel with the notion of substance, I let the ancient founding relation be seen, still present here and now, the relation of our practice and our positive knowledge to the most ancient practices and knowledge of our history. The great scene of suffrage by things, signs and sounds, by the world, the body and acclamation, is the death of the king Romulus; the great scene of suffrage is the stoning of the vestal Tarpeia; the great scene of suffrage is the synthesis of the two scenes. A tragic beating, in a fundamental time, in which pieces depart from a body and return there, transubstantiated into stones before being being transubstantiated into signs, in the middle of the clamours and voices. Suffrage traverses the history of religion, the slow and heavy thickness of our myths; it comes to our social sciences. It is there in our rites and practices; it is our relation to the body of the collective, through voice. The conflictual relationship between the two domains, between the priests who are priests and say so and the scholars who are also priests but don't want anyone to say so, this conflictual relationship has a common consequence. Everything happens as though the conflict was hiding the relationship, as though the conflict was only there to hide the true relationship. The conflict is only an appearance. I am returning, by the path followed by suffrage, to the foundations. Suffrage leads me to fundamental anthropology, here told by the history of religion.

So I stand by what I wrote, even if the symmetry I'm depicting here is neither complete nor precise. This symmetry is suggestive, like an intuition. Physics would be to metaphysics what our social sciences would be to the history of religion. Suffrage traces a transversal path from one domain to the other, as substance did in times past between its two closely connected domains. So I now see where the symmetries are lacking, where the theory of knowledge intervenes. The hope for unity has never stopped on the one side. The social sciences irreducibly have multiplicities as their object. They are not sciences in the sense of the hard sciences; they don't have objects in this same sense. Like religions in times past, they proliferate, become fragmented, and the fractal landscape in the Northwest Passage is that of suffrage. From one sea to the other, we never stop advancing toward the multiple, time and history. This makes a philosophy of multiplicity necessary. I'm making one.

Subject, substance, suffrage. Substance is said to be metaphysical, beyond the physics which deals with the things of the world. It is stable beneath the variable and shimmering distribution of the inert. The subject likewise lies beneath the crowd that tramples it. It lies beneath the squalls of flying thoughts, of deceptive veils, of partial messages. It is thrown underneath like substance; it is not said that it is invariant in this site, as substance is. Suffrage is a double-napped star; it is the action of the multiple when it infinitely goes toward unity; it is the action of unity tearing itself apart toward the multiple. Thus suffrage is unstable; it vibrates and goes. The subject lies beneath the suffrages sometimes. Substance and the subject are metaphysical; suffrage and the subject are metapolitical; I've come to detest such grand words. The subject lies beneath the scattered fragments, stones that were flesh or members, thrown by a scattered crowd, beneath the fearsome fracas of noise and scattered clamourings, calls and voices that were stones. We have no word corresponding to suffrage to say, in its site, this change, this beating that never stops and is called transubstantiation. The fragments are transformed. If the substance is made of stone, the subject beneath suffrage is king; if the substance is call or voice, the subject beneath suffrage, temporary and substitutable, is whatever you like: consul, tribune, elected in any case. The king is on the side of real presence; the elected, by transubstantiation, is on the side of the sign. What changes is the quasi-object.

Noise. The rumbling always bathes the multiple; it surrounds it; it circumscribes it like a circumstanced aura; it bathes and penetrates it. The collective is immersed in noise; noise is its milieu.

The swarm vibrates with bees and buzzing. The latter announces it and follows it. The herd of bulls shakes the entire land with its stampede. The echo of the dull trampling of legions has been in my ears ever since childhood. The crowd in the stadium thunders its ecstasy and despair in the city. Atoms vibrate in the black box, white noise. The background noise of the world is inextinguishable, like the panting of the sea and the wailing and bitter murmur of my burning coenesthesia. The multiple isn't mute. Only the solitary are silent; only the isolated observe silence; only the forsaken glide through the bushes without a whisper. Don't send spies or emissaries in groups, and observe all alone. Work alone. Above all don't gather together in the hubbub. Yes, if the monads are what they are, unique islands, then no one hears them, then nothing is transmitted by them;

they can't listen to or talk to each other; Leibniz is right, metaphysically, and I find substance again. And if he is right, as though reciprocally, the multiple is saturated with doors and windows; everything enters it, everything leaves it; it is perforated, fragmented, fractal, full of fracas, sound and fury, a transmitter, a receiver, bathed with noise and messages. Substance is silent, suffrage is thundering. How could Leibniz make a system of harmony integrating monads that are deaf and mute at the same time? The harmony seems to me to be a zero sum whereas suffrage is not integrable.

The group is never heard being quiet except to hand down its noise to an orchestral or choral subset. This latter becomes the set for a moment by proxy. Music, theatre, spectacle are transfers of the tumult. The entire group quickly seizes its rumbling again, it rapturously plunges into the background noise again with its applause. Musical harmony is a metaphor for social peace, quite simply in the physical sense: the transport of noise into harmony, the transport of the collective into its little model; these two transports are parallel, transports of multiplicity into unity.[7] The collective doesn't stay in this disequilibrium for long; in return for transfer, the harmony suddenly fragments into the bursts of clapping hands; they crush up the unity, break the music; the collective plunges with sheer delight into its noise again. The musicians have our suffrages twice, through silence and through this sea noise. We break the unity like the senators during the storm.

The multiple is the seat of movements that do not stop, that vary like squalls; one might say it's a hot network of communications – ordered, disordered – whose heat also varies. All this language would be by images, if the noise heard was not alone in informing us about the state of the multiple, was not alone in alerting us of either its disunion or its unanimity. The unitary ovation and the return to scattered conversations are recognized without further information. The multiple makes noise – forest, sea, atoms, universe – the social multiple makes noise as well, and we only have this global information about it. This noise and this suffrage form direct and global information on its current global state. The harmony lost in little pieces in search of a body is audible. The variable murmuring of this finite and fuzzy space fascinates me.

I hear this clamour, even if I'm immersed in the group, drowned in its fury and its movements. Noise has no need for any point to be perceived, the way sight enjoys points of view or can vanish without them. There is no punctual listening centre for this noise; listening centres only exist for messages. Sight can be blinded; hearing is irrepressible; it's an open organ. Sight can be oblique; the rumbling is like the air, a milieu of the multiple without hiatus; it crosses waters; it goes through walls; it gently, delicately, shakes cuirasses. If Cain had only had to escape from the eye, he would have succeeded in the end, but it was the call, the tumult of God that he had to avoid; there is no place to flee from the breath. It's necessary to go farther from the collective than one might believe to finally rest beyond the reach of its clamours, its requests. They go beyond its fuzzy borders; they fluctuate and form its second boundaries. Boundaries lost today beneath the diluvian growth of the noise. The global information it gives us seems to signify that nothing more than a global fracas will be heard, another name for universal suffrage. The swamp of Capra, the first name of the tragic scene (τράγος [tragos] is the male of the goat itself), extends to the world map.

Of the collective, we only know this suffrage. Of its scattering and its unanimity, we only know the modalities of its clamours, of its acclamations. Suffrage comes out of the black box; it gives information to the scrutineers about what happens inside. Of the black box, we perhaps only know this chaotic and sometimes meaningful coming out.

I listen: storm, bursts, noise of thunder, thundering fracas. Silence. A clamour rises, prays. Hesitant, solitary, uneasy, in suspense. Two, three, twenty clamours succeed it, a little recruitment. I don't know if they are going to quiet down. Perhaps. Is it a return to silence, or to the scattered squalls of the sonorous fluctuation? No, no. A hundred, a thousand cheers burst out together around the name of Romulus, a god, a god, son of a god, apotheosis. The background noise broken up by silences and by rare, high, medium, sharp points, giant spiked peaks, abruptly becomes a unanimous litany. It's always the same contingent chain. The litany is rare, the way kings are; the clamours never cease; the intermittent rain of suffrages never ceases. They are the multiplicity of voices.

Death penalty. The death penalty is only necessary against royal power. The death penalty is necessary against the sovereign. The sovereign, beneath the suffrages, is lynched. The suffrages are stones, are money, are signs. They are transubstantiated. The sovereign is king, beneath the stones; a candidate, he buys the voice votes; he is elected, beneath the acclamations.

The death penalty is a memory, a trace taking long to be erased of old histories of kings. The death penalty is a leftover from the time when the spectacle wasn't a substitution, but a reality. The body of the man condemned to death is the king's second body, his real body of flesh, his real presence. A sovereign that suspends his pardon above it has the first body, a software body or sign body.

History, at least the history of power, has patiently changed flesh into stone, gold, silver or bronze, and value into signs, writings or voices. But things remain longer than they matter; they remain interminably after their meaning or their function or their utility has disappeared. Power has two bodies, the real presence and the sign. So the elected sovereign possesses the pardon, the performative word, the one that even makes life and death; the condemned has nothing more than reality. Power, in all, is the relation of the sovereign, deferring pardon, to the one who's going to be executed. Power, as we know, resides in this suspension, in this postponed time, the wait for the execution. This is the king's double body. The sovereign always has two bodies, but the second one is in the dungeon. All universal suffrage is suspended from this relation.

If the death is real the group lives under a kingship. Royal history is marked with corpses. Let's pass on to the sign, no more kings. If the sovereign refuses the pardon, he must not stop refusing it, for deprived of the real body, deprived of this second body waiting for death, he is immediately and because of this in danger of death. The frequency of political assassinations is nothing but this anthropological constant. Certain people never stop looking for kings.

If progress in history exists, and we are old and wise enough to doubt this a little and to note, when it does happen, its rare occurrence, it's this passage from the real body to the symbol. That is to say, from the king to the temporarily elected. That is to say, from the death penalty to every software penalty.

Don't touch subjects; don't touch substances; mobilize suffrages.

The abolition of the death penalty is the moment when a country truly frees itself from its kings. What had been said on this subject in the history books or picture books was nothing but a lie. The king's double body was always there.

I prefer to be governed by a sign. Elected in the middle of the suffrages, in the last of its meanings, that is to say, amid the acclamations.

Treasure. The quasi-object, by its movement, marks the relations, floating, in a group. An abject piece of the royal body, a bracelet set with jewels, a voice that hails a name, the quasi-object is transformed. Fascinated by her, I return to Tarpeia, the triste tropeic. She lies beneath her price, beneath the equivalent of her sale. She opened the gate of the city or the gate of time that sleeps between her legs, the chaste vestal; the nymph Danaë opens her capital, her coffer, to the golden rain. The Sabines cover her with jewels. Are money and value the divisible equivalents of bodies in the same way as stones? Is this an origin of payment? When we pay, do we stone?

The people divided up the costs of the funeral, at a sixth of an *as* per head for example, at the death of some hero, Camillus or Agrippa, dying in poverty despite his grandeur. The costs are fragments, are another name for suffrages. The Romans cover the heroic corpse with coins [*pièces*]. Camillus or Tarpeia, substances or subjects, lie beneath other suffrages than stones or voices. Here lies their value.[8] Here lies their collective evaluation, the small change, finely divided and scattered, of their bodies. Are one hundred maravedis equivalent to one piaster? How many lice are necessary to eat a lion?

In other words, money would be the transition between thing and sign, between stone and voice, a third suffrage. Kill the king or buy the candidate or acclaim the elected one. Money is the sign-thing, sometimes close to the thing, still a stone but precious, sometimes near the sign, the broken symbol. The sign-thing takes on its price in the vicinity of the corpse. Death would be the reference, hidden, of value; of the value of the stone and of the signification of the sign. Damage would be the reference for the gift. The body would be the first value or the well of value. The tropeic vestal gave her body. No one ever has anything but his body to give.

She was corrupted – that's an admission by language. Corrupted, that is to say, ruptured or broken. To corrupt with money is to break with it. The fragments return, the costs and the suffrages, again: pieces of a body that are powerless to reunite, a mosaic without possible mixture, small change from the transcendental treasure, scattered cheers in search of meaning – god! son of god! – a collective working at its sum. Integration: the body, the treasure, god, meaning, collective unity. All this is unintegrable.

Money is a quasi-object, seized or stopped, in the course of said transubstantiation. The quasi-object runs in multiplicities without integration; it runs after their unity. Money doesn't circulate for exchange at first, but to mark out or to fix relations. Before exchange, this mobile and fixed marking out is necessary. Before variation, before fragmentation, a tropeic power is necessary. Here it is: Tarpeia. The transcendental treasure and motor for transformation, the tropism of signs.

PART THREE

THE EXCLUDED
MIDDLE OR THIRD

5 AENEAS, SABINES, TARQUINS, CORIOLANUS: THE COMPOSITE MULTIPLICITY

Livy 1.1.1

By means of a horse introduced, a foreign body, into the city walls, the Greek soldiers have just occupied Troy. Burn, pillage, rape, sack, kill. Flames take over space; bodies are strewn across the ground. Only two men are spared the massacre, Aeneas, the head of the Roman line, and Antenor, his antonym. How and why did they escape unharmed?

The Greeks subject the Trojans to the law of war, *ius belli*. We know how things are: destruction. An exception is made for the two heroes, counselors of peace over the course of the war, because they never stopped wanting, during the whole affair, to give Helen back. They are an exception thanks to the law of ancient hospitality, *vetusti iure hospitii*. The destruction of the city and the death of the people belong to war; Aeneas' safekeeping and flight have another reason. Helen was a guest; a guest must be free, free to go home.[1] Aeneas found himself free to leave and flee.

Well before the beginning of Rome, at the red twilight of Troy's rule, from the first lines of Livy's narrative, the opposition of two laws appears: the law of war, of hostilities, and the law, said to be ancient, of hospitality. No, it's hospitality itself that's ancient. If I understand correctly Rome owes it to hospitality for having come to see the light of day.

It is not uninteresting to see Aeneas' antonym disappear from the origin. Antenor gets lost in the forgetting of a second Troy, on the Adriatic shore of the Veneti, dead as soon as it was born in the narrative. A bifurcation, two branches: the one colossal, the most colossal in all of history, the Roman Empire, and the other one immediately aborted. It's the chain of genesis: how many Antenors are erased when there is only one sole Aeneas? How many little balls of clay and one enormous termite hill?

Or, by intuition or dream, another idea: the historian beginning to write was born in Padua, near the Veneti. Did he have the acute and secret arrogance of giving himself an ancestor? The bifurcation changes then: on the one side, the colossal history of Rome gets lost in wealth and luxury before collapsing amid the ruins; on the other, the thousand time more colossal history of historians piles up in books. This will kill that; the book will kill the edifice; written history kills lived history; the historian writes death as well as life; Antenor is stronger than Aeneas; the latter takes the risk of building the fact; the other writes without risk the book. When destruction is interrupting the life of the city, nothing prevents the book of destruction from being written; it's a fair bit easier. The empire of signs is more terrible than the empire of Rome. It invented immortality. Rome is no more, or almost; Livy is still here.

Of the two pseudo-twins of the origin, we don't really know who truly wins out over the other. We don't know; we know. What we end up knowing is unexpected. That the little energies are greater than the great energies, and often more malicious.

Troy was captured and destroyed for having introduced a horse into its walls, for having given hospitality to a large foreign horse. Astonishment: it was filled to the eyes with enemies. A brutal resumption of hostilities, the death of the old capital. At war for having introduced a stranger, Helen; in ruins for having introduced the enemy.

Two violations of the law of ancient hospitality, from which the hostilities ensued: the abduction of Helen on the one side, the bait of the large horse on the other. The law of peace collapses into the law of war.

But hospitality, conversely, can sometimes ensue from hostilities. Troy sees two heroes who each land in a place called Troy. Troy near the Veneti, Troy on the shore of the Laurentum. Aeneas, upon arrival, makes war on the king Latinus. But the lines of the two armies, ready to come to blows, stop; the leaders leave the ranks and parley. A spectacle. The very first spectacle of this kind known in these pages of history. Latinus holds out his hand to Aeneas; he invites him; he gives him his daughter. Aeneas founds Lavinium from the name of Lavinia, his wife. General hospitality.

Which immediately collapses into hostility. Turnus, the king of the Rutulians, engaged to Lavinia, can't endure having a foreigner preferred over him. So he enters into war.

This never ceases. Rome doesn't make war as one believes.

The uncertainty principle – which causes the law of hospitality to turn into war or which causes, by a sudden miracle, a spectacle between two hostile armies, an implacable enemy to become the husband of the opposing king – the principle of hostility-hospitality, the double law, is at work from the origin, from the beginning, from the collapse of Troy.

From the beginning, the law of hospitality is already old. Hospitality often, almost always, is said to be ancient. You who enter, you are the bearer of the tessera, the symbol that shows that one of my old forebears was in times past received in the home of one of your ancestors. And when he entered that home, perhaps he was already holding in this hand a symbol of the same type. Hospitality always refers back to the one who's called the third man, to a previously contracted obligation. You who enter with your hand empty, be welcome as well; I know that the transfer of the symbol was long, so long that one day by accident it must have slipped from someone's hand. I would be afraid to break a legal chain that only lost the sign of its law, but that maintains its law all the same. You who enter in poverty, welcome; I would be afraid, by closing the door, of not giving the gods my due. The previous obligation is so long that it can do without any trace, so long that at the limits it is absolute. Nothing is so old, so archaic. Every question that refers back to the third man argument can be rooted in a tradition.

The law of war is current, brutal; it takes effect at the point of a sword over the overturned enemy; the law of war is said in and applies to the present: it is the present itself. Alas. The declaration of the laws of hospitality is the discourse from before; it lingers in the traditions: it is the entire tradition, when there is one.

The twins, nourished by the she-wolf's milk, found Rome via the crime we know; amid an enterprise, peaceful at first, the ancestral evil intervenes: the desire to be king. As though there was an evil running in the family, something like a royal illness, something like a hereditary disease, a first sin of ruling.[2] A little after Troy fell, amid the ravages and crimes of the captured city, an exception intervenes, the law of ancient hospitality. As though a welcome existed running through our memories, a hospitable gentleness, a residual and rare peace, a lifting of assuaging. What is most ancient in the ancient origins of the city, *avitum malum*, the ancestral evil, what is most ancient at the end of the ancient city, *vetusti hospitii*, the archaic hospitality, what is oldest is said, there, right from the newness of the origin. The ancestral evil puts kings to death, makes kings. The ancestral evil makes people kill to rule. The ancestral evil is the desire to rule, the appetite for power; it's the old machine for manufacturing kings, murder; the ancestral evil is the desire for power and domination, violence and glory, the current disease of history, and making our history, from generation to generation, producing, as it is said, our history, an ancestral evil or hereditary disease or original sin – why hide its other pure and simple name? – yes, the original sin of history is written there by Livy: one king kills another and thereby becomes king. The original sin is quite simply the equation of power and murder. This ancestral evil has come all the way down to us. Facing this simple and ignoble motor is that thing that's as simple and as ancient and as originary: welcome.

The law of war and the law of hospitality, contemporaries of the capture of Troy, already refer us back to dealings from before the war; and these laws are there, both of them, at Aeneas' departure; they are there, still, on the shore of Laurentum, at the first spectacle, in the front of the troops, when the enemy gives his hand, opens his door, offers his daughter, when the first guest becomes the enemy.

If a certain designated evil is said to be ancestral, if welcome is said to be ancient, this instructs us about the primitive, about what our ancestors thought of the ancestral, about what the tradition reports about the tradition. This primitive recorded by them is war; this primitive reported by one of the oldest texts of our tradition and which tells its most archaic legend, this primitive is the return of violence and glory, its repeated equilibrium. Its morbid equilibrium sometimes lifted by gentle hospitality. The primitive is this uncertainty. Everyone is always and everywhere subjected to the law of war, barring exceptions. Barring the exception of the safe and sound Antenor, in company with Aeneas. Barring the exception of the Roman Empire. Rome was born from this exception, from this exception to the concept; Rome was born from this rarity, from this deviation from the equilibrium of war. The primitive, transhistorical, from before, from immensely before, from legendarily before, is this uncertainty in which Aeneas finds himself during the sack of Troy. Law of hostility, he dies – no Rome; law of hospitality, he flees – Rome is born. It will remember this. This uncertainty endures; it is the primitive, but it's always there. Constant. The hard equilibrated certainty of murder, perforated, lacunarily, by rare liftings of welcome. The history that is beginning is going to unfold the uniform massif of these hard certainties. A few liftings, uncertain, sometimes traverse it, which are the birth of everything. The law is one of death; the concept is death; life is the exception.

A different horse marks the origins of the city. Rome, around the sanctuary woods, is now nothing but a pack of whitened scoundrels. It is deprived of time; it has no women; Rome is going to die from lack of love. It lacks love; this is the ordinary state; this is the lasting stability of death.

Rome is looking for women; it cries out its lack of women everywhere; this is what ordinary language says; this is what carefully chosen language always sings about; everyone keeps them away from their women; open a sanctuary woods for women, they are told. Whores and bandits, the sterility might perhaps not have stopped.

So the king of the scoundrels organizes the Games, in honour, it is said, of Neptunus Equester. Here is the horse already.

And here are the women. It is again or in the first place the festival of omnitude. Whoever you may be, enter and be blessed. So the Sabines enter, equipped with their Sabine women, daughters, sisters and concubines; the festivities begin. The city offers the Sabines hospitality in private homes. Neptunus Equester was not yet, in those very ancient times, lying on his ceremonial bed, feasting. The spectacle begins, and the Sabine men are watching with all eyes. So the Romans, spreading out in the streets, seize the Sabine women. They have suddenly violated the laws of hospitality. The *hôte* has turned enemy. The inviting *hôte* is the enemy; the received *hôte* is the enemy. War is declared by the Sabines. A state of war, a collapse of hospitality into hostility.

The law of uncertainty, expressed thus by the Latin language with simplicity, always shows its effectiveness. Rome is indebted to it for its vital time; Rome will have children. Rome will have a history. Will it have love?

War breaks out, and the Sabines, passing over the body of the stoned vestal Tarpeia, take the citadel. The Romans are in the plain. The two armies, the next day, are face to face, high and low. Engagement. On the Sabine side, Mettius Curtius attacks a routed Roman army across the entire space of the forum. The two heroes are face to face, not the two kings, but the two heroes. Facing Curtius, who has the advantage, Hostius Hostilius falls. He falls, and his army flees. So Romulus prays to Jupiter Stator. During this time Curtius cries out: we have beaten these treacherous guests, these cowardly enemies. A bad translation. I'll start over: we have beaten these deceptive hospitallers, hostile and yet poor belligerents. *Perfidos hospites imbelles hostes*. The principle said here is dense with meaning: Romans without faith in hospitality; Romans without pugnacity in hostility. If you choose the law of war, make war; if you decide for the law of hospitality, then keep the faith. There is good faith in welcome, as there is courage in belligerence. Never has the principle of the double law, called for right from the origin, been better recalled: the principle of the law and its two distortions. For the Sabine hero, the Romans, beaten after having abducted the Sabine women, violated both laws in turn: that of hospitality, by the theft of the women, that of war, by their cowardice. Facing Curtius is a hero named *Hostius Hostilius*. He falls. He falls, and his army flees in disarray. I don't know whether this hero ever existed; I don't know whether this is history or myth; all I see is a fine conceptual symmetry between the name and the cry, between the two heroes face to face. Hostius is the name of the host; Hostilius that of the enemy. Two assonant and related names upon the same head, two breaths for the same mouth or two men in one. From one word: Rome's strategy. From one cry, its unveiling: no faith nor courage. Facing Hostius, *hospites perfidos* is said and facing Hostilius, *imbelles hostes*. It is understood that the hero falls. An extraordinary twin combat between the one advertising or announcing the originary double law and the one accusing him of the double sin, a surprising battle in which it is nonetheless the Sabines, by means of the Sabine women, who have entered the Roman home, a floating fight of two principles themselves floating, heroes floating around Jupiter Stator, the unshakable fixed point. Symmetry, again: the combat is uncertain; it stumbles and shakes around the site promised to the unshakable god. Hostius, the Roman, fell first, but after his cry of triumph, Curtius, the Sabine, was shaken in turn. Romulus attacks and the Sabines are routed. They will soon return. In the valley between two hills, in equilibrium, the combat resumes, to the Romans' advantage however, disequilibrium. The symmetry or twinship floats around Stator; it isn't straight. Two generations will yet be necessary to become devoted to a twin war. Hostilius' grandson, the Roman king Tullus, will have erased the mark of Hostius in his name, and only enemy will be read. Against Alba things will be clearer and more twin. For the moment, the relatives, no, the battling in-laws waver around Stator. The Sabines scatter; Mettius Curtius is driven back into a swamp by his frightened horse. Here is the horse already.

And here are the women. In the middle of the uncertain combat between in-law families and in the name of fuzzy principles, the women, bareheaded, semi-naked, throw themselves between the lines. Spectacle. The hostesses stop the hostilities. They were the object of the violation of hospitality; they were the cause of the war. They are Helen of Troy translated into multiplicity. They are double as well, sisters or daughters of one side, mothers or wives of the other. They are introduced into the war system; they make it rock, bifurcate. Emotion wins out; silence falls, calm spreads; a treaty is concluded. The Sabines are invited to join with the Romans; the two states will be made one, governed by two kings. Yes: hospitality at first turned into hostility; by the same operator, hostility turns into hospitality.

But for this an element must be found that can take on many values: the Sabine women. Abducted, they are at the first crossroads; come back, they are at the second crossroads. They make history bifurcate twice. The two heroes, like the battle, float around the two points of decision, where the women are.

How the war against Alba started is rarely said. Who was first to enter the lands of the other, who was first to pillage its goods, God knows. The grounds or causes of war are the same on every side: each side accuses the other of having started it; it is therefore justified to have armed recourse. This shared belief, this symmetrical illusion, is better said by myth than in history; it is said by the twins, Curiatius and Horatius, twins of Rome or of Alba, and twins among themselves. We have given much time to observing that opposing powers, on the eve of war, look so alike you can't tell them apart. They both say that the other started it, the enemy is completely in the wrong, we're waging a holy war for justice and good laws. Wars, whether external, civil, familial or hereditary, war, quarrel, battle, divorces, polemics, dialectics, apologetics, clashings of arguments and swords, vociferations, always oppose Horatius and Curiatius; thesis and antithesis are scarcely discernible, never surpassed, except by a new combat between two other twins, the monotonous nightmare of history.

Alba and Rome start together; the war started before, long before, transhistorically before the belligerents accused each other of having started it. War is anterior to the search for causes; war has always anticipated its grounds. The warrior only searches for the grounds or cause after the decision to come to blows. War is the cause of its causes. It is the first positive feedback. A thousand philosophies are reducible to this feedback. While war lasts, it fans the flames of its causes, makes them weightier or reinforces them, causes them to be reborn when they wear out, revives them when they become erased, makes sure other causes will take over for them or, as is said, surpass them; it feeds them in return. War is not only the fathering of all things; it is a successor that feeds its predecessors. These logics, without seeing it or saying so, have quite simply laid their hands on the common and barbarous example of the alimentation of predecessors by successors along some given chain. The effect feeds its cause again. War makes its grounds be born, is the cause of its causes, surpasses them if need be. Having laid their hands on this simple image, these philosophies profit from it; they invade, in this way and in their own field, space and time, as though inevitably. Nothing can escape them. They are the continuation of war by other means, the consequence of barbarism in and through culture. Horatius and Curiatius, twins the way thesis and antithesis are twins, nourish in return the fury of the old Horatius, who wants them to surpass each other.

How the war against Alba started is rarely said. This latter sends its delegates to Rome; Rome sends its representatives as well. These latter promptly return, mission accomplished and with war declared to take effect in one month. Receiving gentle and kindly hospitality from king Tullus, the Alban delegates do long justice to the royal table; they linger. Everything is the same in the affair; every cause is twin as well as every action; all the champions are twins and all the wrongs too, except for this dissymmetry of time, this gap at the long feast. Thus Hannibal, is it said, lingered in the delights of Capua after Cannae; thus I no longer know which captain lost I no longer know which battle for having tasted I don't know what fruit for too long. Tullus' table was delicious; here is the law of ancient hospitality, facing the law of war. Before being hostile, Hostilius was hospitable; he signs there, with his name, his first kingly act: he has just been named. Perhaps he is hospitable the better to become hostile? No matter. The Alban war that's sown with symmetries everywhere is ruptured here; the ambassadors are being entertained at table. Tullus Hostilius will only invite them to speak their request later when he hears the report from his own delegates. Alba, as usual, hesitates, loses time; Rome gains time; at issue is a gap in time. Alba will be taken; it is already taken by surprise. But the time is that of a feast. Rome violates, again, the laws of hospitality. It announced a hospitable king; it no longer has anything but a warrior king. Conversely, and in passing, an old legend will teach us that it takes a hard and rare conversion to transform a soldier, a hunter, a ferocious killer of animals into a hospitaller saint.[3]

The war against Alba starts with an invitation, with a royal feast, with a convivial celebration. Rome takes the hospitable advantage; Tullus Hostilius, quickly informed by the return of his people, sends the Alban delegates back, making the responsibility for the hostilities fall squarely on their shoulders. Rome declared war first while making it seem that Alba had started it. This double shifting is obtained by the table and the princely board.

Alba attacks, invades the zone of the city. And digs a trench all around named Cluilius, from the name of its king. The future cloaca, it is said. Cluilius dies. No one knows why the king of Alba died. I imagine that this death bears some relation to the trench; I have spoken about this. Did the king cross over it, leap over it?

When someone defines a space with precision, he traces out its edges. Here is the cordon drawn by Alba Longa, and Rome is circumscribed. Those inside are friends; whoever is outside is enemy. Such is the law of war, distinct, precise, well-defined. The first person who, having enclosed a piece of land, took it into his head to say, 'this is mine', killed the first person who crossed that enclosure. Killed the first person who pulled up the posts and filled in the trench. Whence crimes, wars, murders, miseries and horrors. If you are outside and you penetrate inside, you are a dead man. If you are inside, if you go out, you are dead. Thus Remus, the brother, and thus Cluilius, the relative, were subject to that precision, to that decision.

But here is it again: the uncertainty principle *hostes hospites,* or better, *hospites imbelles hostes,* causes the wall to be porous, blurs the boundaries, causes the definition to be fuzzy. It opens doors in the threshold's trap: whoever you may be, enemy, friend, enter or leave and be blessed. At your risk and mine. At the risk of returning to the precise, exact definition, to the cut divide. At the risk of the Sabine women, at the risk of Tarpeia beneath the Sabines' stones, at the risk of the Albans. In the vicinity of the trench, along its route to the left and the right, a narrow or wide band, wide perhaps to the point of covering all of Rome, to the right, and soon the universe, to the left, *urbi et orbi,* a kind of grey zone leaves the name of he who stays and lives there fuzzy, Alban, Roman, ally, enemy; it's the zone of the *hôte* where fuzzy subsets are invented. It's the law of ancient hospitality, which Rome always leaves next to the law of war. Roman multiplicity is fuzzy, and its walls are porous; the city is a sanctuary woods, always: who, soon, won't have right of citizenship here? This is the true secret of the empire.

Let's ponder the exemplary episode of the three hundred and six champions named Fabius. Here is the ancient city-state's ideal, the aristocratic idea, the Greek ideal: this is mathematical ideality, a perfect set, precisely defined, well counted, in which the generic element is perfectly marked out. This ideal is dead in Rome. Inside this army, everybody is related, friends, and gives his life to everyone; outside, without shaky lines, the enemy is put to death. This army can only die in its entirety, too perfect.

Rome has no unity; perhaps it has never existed unitarily.

Rome is a pack. It's nothing but a pack of repentant thieves in the sanctuary woods or, along the shores of the Tiber, of she-wolves in brothels. Rome is not only a mixing of whores and former murderers, it's also and above all a mixture of people come from outside.

The ancient city-state, surrounded by walls, is closed to foreigners; it religiously expels whoever is not of the good blood, of the good law, whoever bears impurity. The law of the excluded middle or third draws the city on the terrain; it is its logical definition, and it presides at its rites.[4] Every third comer must be excluded. Nothing is more ancient than class, than family, than order, than hierarchy and classification. Nothing is more ancient than the excluded middle or third, to be understood at once in every sense, drawing, discourse and religion. The excluded middle or third is the scapegoat: the scapegoat is at the foundation of anthropology, the excluded middle at the foundation of our logic. They bear the same name.

Rome doesn't know the excluded middle or third; it wanted to exclude it.

Rome is Greek; it bears a Greek name, perhaps; it is Hellenic through Evander, a refugee from the Peloponnesus and son of Hermes, through the cult of Hercules and perhaps through Carmenta. But it is also anti-Greek, I mean Trojan since it was founded by Aeneas. Rome is Alban, it comes from Alba Longa; it is anti-Alban since it destroyed that city and quartered its king. It plunged its sword into its mother's womb. Rome is Sabine, governed by Titus Tatius; it abducted the Sabine women from the enemy. Rome is Latin; it ravages Latium. And Rome was Etruscan, governed by Etruscan kings, beautified by Etruscan art, educated by haruspices, and it was anti-Etruscan; it only saw itself free after having driven out the kings. Rome is everything all at once; it introduces contradiction. Not perhaps all the way to the Semites, by whom Aeneas was loved, in Carthage, whose mark and countermark it bears at the same time. If Rome is asked what Rome is, it itself does not know. It answers according to who is asking. It doesn't have that unity one notices in the rigour of the excluded middle. Rome has never existed except as multiplicity. It needed to be founded ceaselessly.

Facing the Greeks, Rome can say it's Greek, can say that it says that language; facing the Sabines, Rome says that it's the daughter of the Sabine women; facing the Latins, Rome speaks Latin; facing the Etruscans, Rome lets its auspices and monuments be seen; hostile to Carthage, Rome remembers Aeneas' love. Rome is not a fixed subject; it is not a defined subject; it is deprived of any well-formed definition; Rome is a mixture: tiger-striped, streaked, many-coloured, motley, blended, constellated. Rome is a multiplicity. It resembles those paintings that, seen from here, present themselves as a seascape, seen from there, reveal a naked woman, seen from elsewhere, represent another scene. Seen from here, I mean Greece, Rome is Greek; seen from Etruria, it is Etruscan; seen from Alba, it is Alban; seen from a dozen Mediterranean cities, it is Trojan, and so on. So Rome doesn't have the ordinary unity that the excluded middle would ensure; it doesn't have that logical unity allowing the usual representation; it doesn't have perfect bounds; it welcomes other gods and non-native religions. Rome is a tissue of others; Rome does not strictly exist as a subject; Rome is an ichnography. Divide it up, and it is still Rome; a mixture can be divided up without ceasing to be a mixture; it can grow for the same reason.

I seriously believe that its history, its growth and power came from this inexistence. Everything squeezed like sardines in the stiffness of the excluded middle, every city surrounded by walls, every existent put in a closed system can only play stability, can only play by leaving time. It has been very profoundly said that India had abandoned history; this is due to the caste system, a fine lamination of the principle of the excluded middle. These beings play perfection; they play being; they play fixity; they play eternity. Rome was historical; it invented time, not as a concept but in the moving reality of the mixture. The difference between a mixture and a system is the difference between Rome and India.

Time doesn't know the excluded middle; Rome didn't know it. The Spartan aristocrats lived from the excluded middle, and it's in this way that Sparta left history. The ancient city in general dies from this exclusion. The cities subjugated by Rome, by the sword and fire of Rome, the ancient cities that were destroyed or vanished, were all getting ready, more or less, to leave historical time for this simple reason. Or they returned into the time of history by regaining mixture and inclusion inside Rome.

Livy 2.48–50

I don't know if Rome knew it; Rome in any case recounts it. I know, I can say it in abstract terms; it does so in narrative. Rome is a non-standardized multiplicity; a well-standardized multiplicity only promises to disappear; the excluded middle makes it leave time. Here is the corresponding narrative: it is a crucial experiment, a reductio ad absurdum and a reasoning to the limits at the same time.

Faced with the Veiian banditry, the Fabii, then at the height of their glory through military exploits and public good deeds, decided, through the mouth of one of their own, a consul, to form an army composed of their family and it alone. Starting the next day, the entire *gens Fabia* in arms, inspected by the consul in campaign clothes, parades through the city with its leader at the centre, passing before the Capitol and praying, and leaving by the Porta Carmentalis, followed by a mob of kinsmen and friends, followed by the blissful public.

Here is the cloned multiplicity. Three hundred and six aristocrats; these are the best; each being able to aspire to preside over the Senate.

This troop is exceptional; this story is unique in Rome: this army would have been ordinary in Sparta or elsewhere; its story would merge with the history of these city-states. The multiplicity here is well-standardized: all of them have the same name; all are of the same blood; they are all bearing the same weapons; the one at the centre, the consul, is entirely replaceable by any of them. The army is only made up of generals, of lieutenants rather, and it is the best. Not only is the set standard, but it is also optimized. The Romans understand the experiment: if Rome had three families of the same stamp, it would subjugate the Aequi and the Volsci at the same time as the Veientes, the people remaining tranquil and peaceful, they say.

The experiment begins, and it succeeds. The *gens Fabia*, near the Cremera, comports itself valiantly. It wins, it vanquishes, and it grows confident. The experiment is succeeding, but it does not last. A few Etruscans draw the warriors into a trap: a wide and distant plain in which scattered livestock are dispersed. The perfect order collapses before disorder; it is neither flexible nor adaptable. Standard multiplicity is stiff, doesn't know how to evolve, repeating its conduct when that conduct brought it to victory, without concern for floating circumstances. Here is the *gens Fabia* scattered like a procession of calves in the meadow. The Etruscans then leave their ambush positions. Battle. The family is seized in a circle; it gets free; it takes refuge on the heights; surrounded again, it is exterminated. Only one remains. A strange detail: three hundred and six die out of three hundred and six; only one survives, of a very young age, to start a line. The Remainder.

This story is not a history; it is an exemplary narrative, a legend. It says how to read the history of Rome. A crucial experiment: standard multiplicity can't withstand time. Only mixture withstands time since mixture is time. It is a reductio ad absurdum and a reasoning to the limits. Nothing is better than the name Fabius, than Fabius blood, than Fabius counsel, than the religion, the experience, the sense of duty, of war, of state, of strategy in the Fabii. And yet if each of them follows this model and only this model, all of them die.

Consequently, the best multiplicity is non-standard. And Rome was made in this way. That which was to be demonstrated.

The Roman plebs facing the patrician order is a pure multiplicity. The nobles form a class. They have been perfectly organized and for a very long time: attached to agricultural property, domestic altars, the tombs of ancestors, familial hierarchy, cadet branches, clients, servants and slaves. This is an order. The plebs has no social order, no agrarian land boundaries, no religion, no law, no magistrates. It is not a people; it is not a body; it is not a group; it is not a true collectivity. It is pure multitude. Crowd, aggregate, population, cloud, confusion, a herd of animals.

No, Rome did not know class struggle. Class struggle assumes two classes, two composite, organized, ordered, disciplined armies. Just as the war of all against all is not a war, so class struggle, or the *certamen ordinum*, the confrontation of the orders, is either an optimistic or a false way of speaking. It hides history.

A class and a non-class are face to face. A nucleus of order is surrounded by disorder. And this is the real problem or question. The history of the Roman plebs is the set of fluctuations that disorder experiences while it is becoming ordered. The patrician order, classical, resists, comes undone, is remade, falls toward disorder. Plebeian disorder fluctuates, becomes organized, ordered, comes undone, is remade, goes toward order, falls back into disorder.

Pure multitude is the subject or the object of history; order and the relations of order, even if combatant, are only the objects of stability. Thus the three hundred and six dying men named Fabius leave Rome surrounded by the mob, the throng of the public. This circumstance, this cloud floating around a standard set is a good concept. Order leaves Rome, and the mob stays there to continue time.

Understand now why the ancient city-state is dead, and from what. It died from its ideal, from its strict reason; it died from pure blood and pure reason, from its definition; I was going to say that it died from its pure mathematicity. The three hundred and six champions are good Spartans, excellent Greek aristocrats; I was going to say good mathematicians. As such, hopelessly condemned. You understand now why the Greek city-state could invent abstract mathematical purity and why the Roman city could never attain it. The city-state was pure, the city was impure. The former is defined and the other fuzzy. Rome is always a sanctuary woods, that is to say, a fuzzy set. Who is truly Roman here, since the entry of the Sabines, the Albans, the Latins, and the Etruscan kings? Rome lives in mixture; it lives, floating, varying on who is Roman. The ancient city-state, pure, died from desire for eternity; the City was eternal from never having desired such a thing. Rome has no strict border, no defined edge, no precise limit; it only has undecided proximities; it is fuzzy. Therefore it has no ideas in the ordinary sense; it has as few concepts as it has mathematics. But this kind of grey zone, which is not merely abstract, which can be mapped by populations, migrations or the evolution of the right to citizenship, this zone is the life of the city, and it is its history. It is still there, floating, among us, ghostly and mobile, but surprisingly present and living. It is the secret of the empire.

At the outset, I said that Rome was an object. No doubt. Rome is not a subject in any case. Who am I? Roman, Celtic, Iberian, Latin, what have you? No one has posed the problem of the subject here. Undulating, fuzzy and diverse, mixed. Borderless, undefined. Who is Sextus Tarquinius? Roman, Gabian, Collatian?

I'm going to return a little to war and the link of fighting to its causes. War is the cause of its causes; its current excesses ceaselessly incite its motives; its true dynamic is a positive feedback; the mêlée of Horatius with the Curiatii feeds Horatius' old father's fury, who incites him to die, who cries out for superslaughter. War is a very good perpetual motion, and most often history is right to see it as what maintains its time. I am saying: war or its avatars, economy, the sacred, even culture. Jupiter is an avatar of Mars; Quirinus is another. In brief, more than just maintaining itself, war maintains and feeds in return the reasons that drive it. This is hostility's law of expansion. Hostility feeds its old father.

The law of hospitality is different, which however is also a feedback. It is a negative feedback. The guest kills the host differently than the soldier kills the soldier. The host feeds the guest and not conversely; the arrow is simple; it is not double; the one gives, the other receives, without reciprocity. The one who is fed is fed all the way until the host's resources are exhausted. The beneficiary lives on the death of the giver; he devours him. In other words, the successor continues along the chain on condition of causing the disappearance of the predecessor; the downstream exists through the destruction or erasure of the upstream; the parasite feeds on its conditions up until their disappearance. The guest is the cause of the disappearance of its causes. Hospitality maintains itself from the erasure of the causes that drive it. This is hospitality's law of expansion. It kills its old mother. We are going to hear the cries of Coriolanus' mother; they echo the appeal of Corneille's Sabine: you are plunging your sword into your mother's womb.

Hostility feeds its father, and hospitality kills its mother.

The expulsion of the Etruscan kings causes the primitive history to bifurcate abruptly; it's the new foundation of the city. We don't know – will we ever? – under what exact circumstances the Tarquins – were they really called Tarquins? – seized the kingship. We do know they were foreigners. Lucumo came from Etruria, it is said, with his wife and all his belongings on a wagon. Very rich, he came from Tarquinii, bought a house, changed his name. Lucius Tarquinius is the name of a city, like the name Coriolanus.

He came from Tarquinii where he was already considered a foreigner. Twice a foreigner: in his adopted city, in the city of his birth; he was born of a father expelled from Corinth. Already. Demaratus of Corinth had been driven away by a revolution. Already. The Tarquins are foreigners, sons of foreigners to the places they left; foreign sons of foreigners, expelled sons of the expelled, immigrant sons of immigrants.

As far as I know, Romulus was Alban; Tatius was Sabine; Numa was not Roman; they went and sought him out in Cures. Aren't kings native-born? Is the exception the rule or law? Ancus is a descendant of Numa; Servius Tullius is of dubious birth: either son of a slave or son of a foreign woman, come, chased out of Corniculum. Tullus Hostilius remains. All of them are foreigners; all of them are guests, except Hostilius. This latter is only marked by the law in his name. Rome will only expel, will only exclude exceptions. What I wanted to demonstrate.

It isn't certain that we have to see here a retrograde movement of the true: as though it were easier to drive out a foreigner. It's not only for the Republic and for so-called liberty that the kings aren't native-born. It's their definition and the secret of their function. They are never from the city; one among them could say that he is not from this world. The king rules by being excluded, by suspending his expulsion. Being struck with exile is conversely the chance of being king one day. The concept of king is this very exception; it is the concept of its own exception. The master of the place is not from this place; he forms a hole in space like Romulus' absent body after the storm in the middle of the ring of Fathers and the fleeing people. Kingship could be drawn as a spatial variety equipped with a well, or a stercoraceous door or a trench or a sewer, *cloaca maxima*. Concept and exception together describe the same situation as the double word *hôte* or as hostility, apposition to hospitality. The apotheosis of the kings is only a theoxeny. Hence I recount the entire history of the Tarquins in two words only: a guest [*hôte*] come from Etruria, a rich host [*hôte*] inviting the notables, he had a welcoming table, a guest invited by the king and become the tutor for the princes, the parasite's masterstroke, a guest finally king, detested enemy guests, hostile to everyone, enemies expelled. History in two words, pure and simple logic. This is nothing but a canonical history of the king. So Rome enters into history with liberty when the principle of the excluded middle or third no longer takes place. The king is the excluded third.

The adventure and misadventure of the Etruscan kings: a former guest, the law of ancient hospitality, a guest become *superbus*, that is to say, insolent, arrogant, an enemy to drive away; the final misadventure is told starting from the misadventure of Sextus Tarquinius, the youngest of Suberbus' three sons. This sixth-generation adventure is still the same. If Tarquinius is named Tarquinius because of Tarquinii, if Demaratus of Corinth is so named from the city he was expelled from, if Coriolanus takes the name of Corioli for having captured the city, I mean its houses and walls, Sextus should be named Gabii. Sextus Tarquinius is the guest of the Gabii the way his father is a guest in Rome. Superbus, the father, lays siege to Gabii; the assault fails; he is indeed the enemy. So the son, feigning to be angry with his father, therefore becoming the enemy of the enemy, flees to Gabii and takes refuge there. And holds forth against Superbus: his cruelty, he says, is practised on foreigners.

What must we understand by this? Who, here or there, is the foreigner? If Tarquinius has indeed remained slightly Etruscan, perhaps he is cruel toward the Romans themselves, who he treats like slaves, like construction workers. Where is Sextus a foreigner? Is he Etruscan in Rome and Roman in Gabii and Gabian again in Rome? A logic with many values can indeed be seen here. Since the Gabini can't see anything there, Sextus is admitted to political debate; he speaks with the notables; he poses as an expert in military matters. Certainly. He knows well the strengths of the opposing parties, having fought with each side. Sextus is third everywhere.

I have always observed that the very people who intend to kill their father end up, in getting older, by killing the adversaries of their father. It's the most common way of becoming a father. This is how the good sons ensure the expansion and preservation of their family. The sons of the family revolt, apparently to kill the father, but in reality so that the father might also have a share in the revolution. This is how the great families progress, to the right through the father, to the left through the son. The little guys of the little families sometimes encounter the little guys of the great families, either on the right through power or on the left through opposition, but they only encounter them as their leaders; they will never be anything but their retinue. Sextus has power in Rome through his father as prince; he has taken the counterpower in Gabii, where he has the counternotables killed. Don't believe, if you are a little guy, that you will ever be the leader of the little guys. The position of leader of the little guys has long been held by the little guys of the great. The father of the masters is the master of the masters; the son of the masters is the master of the slaves. Don't trust the dialectic, if you are little. The two-value dialectic, crude and rough, is nothing but the logic of the masters. It has shown this well ever since it was invented. If you are humble, guard yourself, left and right, against every possible dialectic. It doesn't work for you; it's neither said nor made for you. It's the logic of immobility. Of stability, of repetition in the appearance of movement. It's the logic of empire. It is stupid. If you are little, be intelligent.

The misadventure of the Etruscan kings, repeated in Sextus' adventure in Gabii, who does nearly the same thing in that city that the Tarquins do in Rome, the two adventures finishing similarly, the misadventure of the kings is now going to be explained by a specifically Roman misadventure on the part of Sextus Tarquinius. And again the same structure appears. A grand narrative, for the history of Rome; a reduced model in Gabii, a little local narrative of the rape of Lucretia in Collatia; whatever the scale, it's the same narrative law.

Everything begins with a feast, continues by feasts, develops during a feast, is resolved after a feast; it's a parasite story. Beneath the walls of a hard siege, that of the city of Ardea, the young captain princes, idle, are killing time at table. That evening, the meal was held at Sextus Tarquinius' tent. After drinking, the men boast of their wives as is common with the mediocre and the foolish. Another must indeed desire to be assured in one's own desire, floating. Each of the braggarts has the most beautiful and the most well-behaved wife. 'To our horses,' they cry, 'let's go see. Let's go surprise our wives to decide which is the most well-behaved.' The wives were all, like the men, sitting in front of lavish feasts. Foolish men and foolish women, banquets or feasts, soldiers and whores, the score is even; it's the norm. The exception is Lucretia, the winner, Lucretia the wife of Tarquinius Collatinus, son of Egeria the poor, Lucretia surprised seated amid her maidservants, working hard on the wool very late into the night, Lucretia, the image of a vestal. Collatinus, the imbecilic winner of this imbecilic competition, invites the morons to a third feast, during which Sextus Tarquinius desires Lucretius. Ranking has never existed except to order desires. The most moronic only desire the most beautiful; the stupidest have never read anything but the most read author, have never voted for anyone but the winner.

The fourth feast, Sextus Tarquinius returns to Collatia, unbeknownst to her husband. Lucretia receives him, a good hostess, makes him dinner, leads him to the guest chamber, *hospitale cubiculum*. Here we are. Lucretia remains a hostess, invariant in her role, straight. The state of war, beneath Ardea, persists, the state of plague is instaurated. War, it is said, rots. What plays out on Lucretia's bed where Sextus appears, armed, in the middle of the night, when everything is sleeping, what plays out at the point of a sword is a rape, the rape of the quasi-vestal by a little quasi-Mars, an aborted repetition of the death of the founding Rhea Silvia, but without any generation of kings; the kings will be driven out tomorrow; what plays out is a substitution, is a mistaking. Black box of the night. Rhea Vestal believed that it was Mars, or so she wanted to make us believe. Alcmene believed that Amphitryon was returning from war; no, it was Jupiter; she will give birth to twins, one of which will be a god, Hercules, and will in these sites precede the twins, one of which will be king. Lucretia believed that it was a question of a guest; no, it was an enemy. It was perhaps Quirinus. It was an enemy; she says so. The culprit is Sextus Tarquinius, the guest acting with hostility; *hostis pro hospite*, she cries out before dying. What is played out on Lucretia's bed, where Sextus threatened to put a naked slave with his throat cut so as to make others believe it was an ignoble adultery, what is played out is substitution; the same substitution that the same Sextus Tarquinius had played elsewhere, in another enemy and hospitable city, Gabii. What is played out is the fuzzy.

Everything is always, everything is everywhere the same thing, give or take a degree of size or perfection. The kings are foreigners; Rome is their host; now they are enemies. The Tarquins are Etruscan; the city invites them in; now they are expelled. Sextus, a little Tarquin, is a guest in Collatia; Lucretia receives him; he abuses her, *hostis pro hospite*; he violated the law of hospitality. So it's the same on all sides. Here is Sextus in Gabii: an enemy, introduced, a guest, a quasi-king, delivering the city over to Rome, lastly expelled, killed, an enemy again.

Superbus couldn't manage to complete the siege of Gabii. The state of war drags on; as in Ardea, it rots, and the state of plague returns. Failure in the assault, failure beneath the walls. The king pretends to withdraw; he devotes himself to his construction works; he consecrates his time to the foundations of the temple. We don't leave the narratives of foundation. So Sextus plays his role, the one that can no longer be called anything but Rome's role par excellence, I mean the logic or strategy of the joker, or of the hole in compact space, or of the fuzziness of the set. It's not merely a double play, but a play with numerous values. Sextus has a value for Rome; he has a value for Gabii, but he also has a value for Lucretia. For capturing cities, Gabii or Ardea, for taking women: the Sabine women, Tarpeia and the walls and the gates. He can be introduced into any system. He is not the two-value indecision of the undecidable double game; he is the many-valued white game, infinitely-valued, if you like. This is perhaps not Rome's game; it would rather be Alba's game. Rome inherited this white from Alba. Sextus, the sixth, is a white element. He can be introduced into Gabii as into Lucretia's bed, as into her house; he can be introduced into a system; he makes its evolution bifurcate; he is an operator of change.

Only the white domino, the joker, the token with several values can take on any number, any code, any figure, any appearance or any other. Sextus is Roman in Rome, even a prince, and Gabian in Gabii, admitted to the political debates, Collatian in Collatia, invited to a meal by Lucretia. When Tarquinius Superbus takes the path of exile, Sextus takes the path of Gabii again, which was like his kingdom, *tamquam suum regnum*. He returns there, despite his high treason. Livy has just said the word 'kingdom.' So Sextus, hated, is murdered. That which is to be demonstrated.

Rome is the city of the object; Rome doesn't pose the question of the subject.

Who is now, well after the rape or abduction or the maternity, any given Sabine woman abducted long ago? Has she remained a daughter or sister of the Sabines? Has she become a Roman wife or mother? She is at the bifurcation point, the crossroad knot, where the system changes in time. Who is Corneille's Sabine, Roman or Alban? What is the womb's identity? What is the virgin's or mother's white identity? An itself undetermined womb that determines who is who, in which everybody's identity is determined. Who is Alba the White, who is Rome, daughter of Alba? This Roman woman, here, now, is Sabine or Alban; she comes from Corioli or Collatia, and we are lost.

Who is Sextus Tarquinius, a foreigner descending from a foreigner in Rome, a Roman, from Tarquinii, an Etruscan, from Corinth, a foreigner in Gabii, a foreigner in Collatia in Lucretia's bed, a foreigner beneath the walls of Ardea, a prince, notable, refugee, spy, senator, captain, victor, victim, vile rapist, driven out, dying murdered? Ceaselessly a guest and a parasite. Excluded, expelled: king. King, that is to say, in the end put to death. He takes on every value; he bears the entire ichnography of values. We return to the old myth of Hercules, even before the foundation. Sextus – many-coloured, mixed, shifting and diverse, a phase transition between two states – can make the system bifurcate into a thousand, into every conceivable, possible direction.

Before the foundation, the Herculean legend describes a mixed state, a mixed system in false equilibrium; it depicts an ichnography; yes, it says possible worlds; it draws possible narratives, and the written narrative is one scenography of it; this world where Rome, this city, is founded, in this way and by such-and-such, is one determination of it. Sextus Tarquinius is undetermined like Hercules; he is dedifferentiated. Certain Roman heroes, it is said, are strongly dedifferentiated. Before the advent of the Republic, the adventure of Sextus Tarquinius describes the same mixed state, another mixed system in false equilibrium; it also draws an ichnography. Sextus, in equilibrium, could have ended up king of Rome or giving Rome to Gabii as well as Gabii to Rome; Coriolanus, in the same circumstances, will be well on the verge of giving Rome to the Volsci; Sextus could have decided on a Lucretia who was a bit Sabine; he could have abducted her; we see all the bifurcations surrounding him like a star. I see Sextus Tarquinius as Harlequin, the joker daubed with a thousand colours; the future will be blue, red, pink, very black; the future will be green.

We don't necessarily pass from the myth to history. Who can judge or decide such a question when the referent has melted into time? But assuredly history, real or recounted, never ceases passing from the possible to the real. This birth never stops. It takes place today as before Rome's foundation, as during the time when the Republic was being formed.

In the beginning, on the morning of the foundation, here are two twins, the battle, the murder; here are two parallel narratives, two groups, two hills, two flights of vultures.

In the beginning therefore is violence; only one god exists, the god Mars of combat; everything comes from him, resides in him, passes through him; this book, like Livy's, shows it.

In the beginning, at the foundation, is the bifurcation of the twins. Remus perched on the Aventine, Romulus at the Palatine, watching out for the auguries, birds. This is not the beginning; the paths already diverge. Let's slowly return from the bifurcation to the point where the roads part, to the formation point where two figures are superposed, to the point where the two twins are one single and same person, the King. The beginning lies there.

Let's reason about this point, according to this identity point. In the beginning, at the foundation, one twin kills his twin. Romulus remains king from having killed his brother; he remains king up until his own *diasparagmos* beneath the storm, beneath the mêlée of the senators. Therefore the twins are twins from having been killed, from having been driven out, excluded, erased, both of them. We have to begin again, continually return to the point of departure, to the point where 'Remus is Romulus' can be said without contradiction. Thus when we go back up along the two generating lines of a cone to its point, to its summit, when we reach the point, exactly the point, it's possible to say that said point is an intersection circle of the nappe of the cone, that it is a limit circle. Here, the point is a circle; here the circle is a point; here, at the limit, the principle of the excluded middle suspends its legislation. Starting from this point, the generating lines, the paths bifurcate; starting from this point, difference appears: a point is a point, a circle is a circle; no one will ever be able to say any more that a circle is a point. But at this point-summit, the point is a circle. This point is also a non-point; it is a limit point. Likewise, Remus is on the Aventine, Romulus at the Palatine; they conquered their identities. From the beginning of the bifurcation on, identity requires the excluded middle. And Romulus is king from having excluded Remus. The principle of identity demands the principle of the excluded middle or third. Yet at the point of departure itself, it doesn't require it. The twins merge. They haven't merged through a third; they are one and as though melted together.[5] So we must take up history again; we must return to the instauration, to the centre of the cross where the paths converge.

Romulus remains king up until his death; this is a redundancy. Romulus remains king for the time that suspends his *diasparagmos*, his erasure: when the tranquil and serene light returned after the storm, the king was no longer there. The throne is empty after the storm. He was there, he is no longer there. This is not the reason for the cessation of kingship; this is the reason for kingship. It is sufficient to understand Remus at the very point where he is Romulus, at the point of departure, where and when the twins are merged. Remus was king from having been killed. Yes, Remus remains king for an instant, the time that suspends his erasure, the instant, brief as a lightning flash, when he tumbles into the trench. When he falls into the tomb. When he collapses into the expulsion sewer. We are at the foundation. The first king of Rome, at this point, is Remus, killed amid the mob, the way his twin will be carved to pieces in the senators' fury. Remus is the first king of Rome, that is to say, the first one expelled – Tarquinius was the last – his reign will last an instant. In the beginning is this point, this limit place where everything is shaken up, this hyper-dense point or black hole where the two crowds, the vulture flights, the twins sons of a she-wolf, the death given, the death received, are all involuted together. This point is the duration of an instant; it's the duration of Remus' reign. In the beginning is this point, this instant. The king Remus lightning flash.

To understand this dense place, we must understand how to suspend the principle of the excluded middle. By returning back over it to the limit of the bifurcating roads. Conversely, starting from it, in the direction of evolution, the resemblance of the lineages becomes clear. They come out of a source where there's no excluded middle or third. They still bear its mark. Hence the twins, for a short while, in the vicinity of the source.

Romulus is not king from having killed Remus; Remus was perhaps killed by the crowd. Remus is king from having been killed, by Romulus or by the mob. And Romulus, the second by the name, is king from suspending a bit longer the instant when he too will be erased. Remus, the first by the name, is king as much as Romulus and identically to Romulus, for the same reason, by the same principle, during the same time, I mean a duration of the same nature, even though not of the same measure. The two twins are king, likewise, from having been killed, driven out, expelled; they remained king while the expulsion was suspended, a brief duration for the one, a lightning fast instant of sacrificial lynching, a long duration for the second, thirty-seven years, the thirty-seven years of waiting for the lightning bolt that fell vertically from the storm in the swamp of Capra. The thirty-two years of waiting for the day when Tullus Hostilius was struck by a thunderbolt. Struck by this Jupiter Elicius about whom Plutarch tells us, in a terrifying text, that he demanded the heads of men. In brief, the long years of waiting for the expulsion of the Tarquins are the definition of the royal history of Rome. The king is dead; long live the king; and what if it was the same king?

Sextus Tarquinius, a prince of the blood, nearly king in Gabii, son of the king in Rome, Sextus Tarquinius, quasi-king, soon to be king – in which of the two twin cities? – Sextus Tarquinius, sacrificed, excluded from Rome, killed in Gabii, Sextus Tarquinius is the last of the kings of Rome, as Remus was the first. Driven out, assassinated, each of them reigns for the time of exclusion or of being put to death, the time of letting the law of the king be seen. Remus rules over the first point of space and at the first instant of time; Sextus is at the apex of the pyramid of the possible. He announces the series of kings without reign, from Manlius Capitolinus to Julius Caesar. Those who only ruled the instant of the execution like those who ruled waiting for it lie at the foundation.

At the foundation point or origin point, time is involuted; time doesn't know the excluded middle or third. The middle or third is involuted in the same dense point.

Sextus Tarquinius is at the apex of the pyramid, the tomb of kings, at the singular place where its edges flow together, where the principle of the excluded middle suspends its legislation. A singleton bearing the total and minimal evil, he climbs toward the singularity of space. That is where the throne of power is; that is where the sacrificial altar is. That is where the end, the apex of Leibniz's *Theodicy* is. That is where the Capitol is, that is where the Tarpeian rock is, absolute power and the thunderbolt that falls. Here again are the true twins. The summit of the figure is abstract or geometrical; the Romans knew this place in the concrete, this point where Manlius Capitolinus hesitates: triumph, erasure, crowning, execution, the point where the principle of the excluded middle suspends its legislation. A point hardly visible under the Republic, the Republic being precisely the time when this point is hardly visible, when the point of kingship seems to be erased, when the space of kingship is reduced to this point, when this foundation point is almost hidden, when the point without the excluded middle seems lost. This point or pole, exactly halfway between the Capitol and the Rock, this pole where the Capitol is the Rock itself, is the site where the monopoly or mono-pole of violence is understood, the monopoly in one hand, on one head, of violence to be legitimated, insofar as the hand wields it and the head receives it. In this mono-pole, the violence done and the violence undergone are the same violence, the principle of the excluded middle suspending its legislation. Violence only becomes legitimate under this punctual contract: the mono-pole accepts what it gives, and receives what it hurls; it is threatened by what it threatens; it is threatened punctually and at once by everything it distributively threatens space with. All the lines departing the point toward all of space converge toward this point; it is an intersection. This monopoly or mono-pole is swollen under the kings and of long duration, and visibly exercised; it is brought back to this punctual and almost invisible site under the Republic, where the people who occupy it substitute one for the other, quickly, before the thunderbolt falls on them. It always falls if they stay there too long. So the mono-pole is visible. Always follow the path of said thunderbolt.

Power [*pouvoir*], the mono-pole of violence, integrates active or passive violence into its singularity, whether visible or hidden. Power is the welcome to the same place of the thunderbolt that leaves and of the thunderbolt that comes. It is called power [*puissance*]; and, of course, it manipulates the departing lightning. But it is above all the capacity to receive the lightning as well as to handle it. It is this potentiality; it is this potential. It is this possibility in which the excluded middle is lifted. It is the excluded middle or third itself. A hole that receives lightning and hurls it.

Sextus Tarquinius, at the apex of the tall figure, is right to turn around, imploring, toward the Capitol, the moment when he sees himself, at least in image, pushed from the Rock; others, on the contrary, long to descend when they climb. At the pole where Sextus Tarquinius stands, the two possibles, twins, stand together and are born from the same animal. It's the pole of power; the double-faced mono-pole of violence.

The king is the excluded third; he is the spatial singularity, apex, trench; power is the excluded third.

All the violence of Rome and all that of the Gabini pile on his head. Rome will be free of kings. It expels the Tarquins.

The philosopher's figure and the historian's narrative together say the same legend. Rome, long ago, was founded on murder; it was born from this evil. Rome has never had anything but one god and one father: Mars. Royal Rome is founded on death; republican Rome is founded on exclusion. The Gabini, more archaic, more deeply thrust into the mythic age, are still in the age of anthropology; Gabii lags behind Rome: it kills Sextus, and Rome expels him. Rome excludes him without killing him. Banishment here is a measurable advance over human sacrifice. The city excludes the Tarquins without ritual murder. Royal Rome is founded on this rite; the Rome of the Republic at least for the moment does without corpses. The operation is the same, without the repugnant referent. Is history born when Rome delivers itself from anthropological horrors? Perhaps. Has it then begun today? It is taking so long to disengage from them that philosophy perhaps is only this slow, patient waiting.

Sextus Tarquinius is sacrificed in Gabii; his corpse is at the summit of the pyramid. He is expelled from the City; the apex is the site of his exclusion. Of his presence and his exclusion. This site is the site of foundation. In this knot is the closure. Here is the condition of the new liberty, says the historical narrative. Here is the sacrificial mechanism of the social pact, the anthropologist would say. Here is the requisite for the constitution of the world, the philosopher said.

Several foundations are accumulated one above the other at the same point.

For the world to be created, for it to be the best possible, a minimal grain of evil is necessary – the sacrifice of the singleton Sextus. Violence is done to him. This is the philosopher's lesson.

He is from Gabii in Rome, he stems from Tarquinii; but he is from Rome in Gabii, distantly stemming from Corinth, a foreigner; he is third everywhere; he is third in Lucretia's bed. He is the third of Tarquinius Collatinus. Either Lucretia dies or Sextus. Either Sextus dies or Rome is enslaved. He is the third, he is excluded.

For the world to be created, violence has to be done to Sextus. And Sextus is the third. And Sextus is excluded.

There exists something rather than nothing. The reason for the coming into existence of these things is the death or the exclusion of this Sextus. Of this third.

The principle of sufficient reason merges into the problem of evil. Reason is related to evil. They are both related to the excluded third.

It was the foundation of the world; it was reason; it's now the foundation of Rome. This is the historian's lesson.

The history of the city begins, or begins again. The Tarquins are expelled, this family of foreigners. To exclude kings, to drive out Sextus Tarquinius is to bring about liberty: the easiest reading. The most difficult reading: it's to make history possible. To expel kings is to close myth, to be done with legend, to stop the era of anthropology, to erase the space of sacrifice, to bring space back to a quasi-invisible point, to put an end to the book of foundation. History begins from forgetting kings, that is to say, foundations. From covering tombs over with earth, as at the mound by the Colline Gate, when a living vestal was left to suffocate in the dark. With the foundations covered over, it's possible to pass from legend to history, from myth to narrative, from the possible to the real.

To pass from the possible to the real and from myth to history, Sextus must be excluded.

Theology: creation of the world. Ontology: principle of reason. Mythology: the kings of Rome. Or anthropology: Sextus sacrificed in order for the collective to form.

In order for the collective to form, for the city of Rome to enter into history, in order for the world to be world and for it to be the best, in order for the things as such to attain existence, for all this, violence is necessary, this evil is necessary: that Sextus be excluded.

Who is this third, excluded?

What is this logic? What is this logic whose genealogy we have just traced? This logic, this principle, this pure form of the excluded middle is not so pure or so formal. This principle, in the principle, beyond ontology, beyond classical theology, goes back to mythology, to the anthropology of sacrifice.

In order for me to be able to speak, in order for me to be able to think, in order for me to be able to write, the middle or third has to be excluded. Otherwise I wander, unstable, I say just anything and no one understands me; never do I conclude. Never do I close my reasoning, or my text, or my language. Sextus is at the point of the pyramid of worlds, or of the hopper of the possible, the condition, the foundation of things, of groups, of time; he is also at the summit of languages. In order for us to understand one another, an excluded middle or third is required. For the principle and in the flesh. As though there was a flesh of languages, a conditional flesh, the founder of their flight. Sextus lies, sacrificed, at the foundation of logic, too, of logos and communication. His corpse lies at the sharp point of language and its rigour. I understand why the Tower of Babel remains without a top; it is good that it remains so. If the Tower of Babel were completed, it would be closed, in the unity of languages, in the unicity or accord of the logos, over the corpse of a Sextus, over the exclusion of a third again. No one is killed, no one excluded on top of the highest of the terraces in ruin, vertiginously overhanging the mixture of thoughts, the mêlée of languages, opening as many third ways as you please; the Tower has remained open; society, as they say, is; invention and freedom are open. Excluded Sextus, on the contrary, closes the naval figure of the singular point, of the summit. He is the flesh ancestor of the logical principle of the same name as him.

The book of foundations is a book of history, perhaps; who knows? It is a book of myths, legends for anthropologists. It is a book of philosophy from which figures for the creation of the world are drawn. Surprise! It's a book of logic, from which the oldest of the genealogies of the principle of the excluded middle is drawn.

Friend or foe? Choose. Be with us, otherwise you are against us. The injunction of this choice is a threat. Be Horatius or be Curiatius, from Rome or from Alba. Terror doesn't come from combat, but from the terrifying obligation to take part in it. I am a survivor, profoundly wounded, of such terrors. I am a survivor of the physical terror during wartime, when no one escapes the choice. I am a survivor, even more wounded, of the terror of warlike police detective philosophers who track you down everywhere to subject you to this choice. Against or for? There are few free spaces: whatever the discipline, groups and ideas exclude some third way. The master subjects you to a terror, his terror, but the terror grows to the heavens if he subjects you to his battle: you are under the terror of a terrified tyrant.[6] Your money or your life, the middle is excluded.

'I am free' always means: I can finally not fight. Not fighting is the first of freedom's demands; the first of its requests. The deepest servitude is the slavery of battles. The slave drools before the pantomime; the battle enters into his body. Polemic is the most atrocious of necessities; hell is the dialectic, which is the necessity of death, of destruction. Life flees the battleground; freedom follows it, perhaps preceding it.

No one fights for freedom. He servilely obeys the passion for combat. When one fights for freedom, necessity quickly returns, worse. Slavery has not stopped.

The terror comes from the excluded middle; you don't have the choice; there is no third way. For or against, your money or your life, no or yes. The great times of terror are the times of the excluded middle. Classical logic occupies the place; it divides it up militarily. That which is rigorous in discourse or useful in working with things can be deadly in human relations. For example, being forced into having no other solution than the one being imposed. The third way would be freedom. So the majority, recruited by terror, start to fight for their existence, as they say, dressed in armour borrowed from the theatre. Including science's armour. For science too has served and serves as terror. If you aren't for science, are you against it? Even the worst stupidity is engendered by the terror of the excluded middle.

I have never fought. The first condition for thinking remains the freedom of thought. There is no freedom in battle, which closes third ways, the inventive ways. I want to stay free, an educated third.

As soon as a third is excluded, the group is formed; thus the Book of Kings opens with Remus, thus it closes in that way with Sextus Tarquinius. Sextus who is excluded because third, a foreigner in every place, a third in Lucretia's bed. The group is formed, founded, is demarcated; it draws its limits; it recognizes the opposing groups; foreign wars begin. Alba, Veii, and others were formed on neighbouring sites, in successive times, in the same respect. The third is expelled into a vague land – one unrecognized, not marked out, undefined – through the sewer, through the trench, through the cloaca; he passes through the stercoraceous door. Sextus is expelled from Rome, killed in Gabii, guilty in Collatia; Sextus has no place. He is king, quasi-king, a joker that can have the value of king.

What then does the exclusion of kings signify, if the kings are kings precisely through being excluded?

One doesn't get rid of them so easily. Whether there are kings or not, there are always some. There is no third way.

This seems to me to be new, that the two ways work or go in the same direction. A rectifier is hidden there.

There are two sexes, there are only two; I'm not qualified to talk about these things, not having studied the deep sciences; I nevertheless think that there are only two sexes: mothers and the rest.

The parasitical relation is a simple arrow, an irreversible flow, without return. The parasite takes and doesn't give back, receives everything and gives nothing. A semiconductor. The parasite's discourse is held to make people believe that he gives back; he never gives anything back except in discourse. Hence the fact that all discourse is most often parasitical: it is demonstrated in it that words are worth just as much as the things taken; when arrogance comes, when all the places are taken, the things themselves are expelled. Second generation: it remains to be a parasite to the parasites. And so on. Nothing more than this noise is heard any more.

The discourse held by the *hôte* is rarely heard. By *hôte*, for once I mean: he who gives and does not receive. We don't notice that within the symmetrical situation of the word, a minor divergence is produced, scarcely perceptible. If *hôte* has the two meanings of host and guest, *hôtesse*, in the feminine, does not. A hostess is not a woman who is received; she must always be the woman who does the receiving. We also don't notice this other symmetrical situation for the verb 'to receive'. If I receive a gift, a letter, gold, I'm obviously not giving. If a hostess receives someone in her home, she is giving. What is called the active or the passive sense, different words that explain nothing. A hostess thus receives: this sentence has an assignable and single meaning; but if the *hôte* receives, we are lost, hesitant, at a crossroads of possible meanings. The hostess's discourse is rarely heard.

Don Juan takes; he doesn't give; he speaks interminably. If he were making love, he wouldn't speak so tirelessly no doubt. He who doesn't make love is forced into theory. Into a theory as long as a thousand and one chaste nights. He talks, abstractly. If I had the time – let's run a short life's race – I would like to write the life and adventures of Don Pedro, he who gives without ever taking: he is almost mute. Mute as a stone. He doesn't receive, he isn't received. Never invited. At the first formal invitation uttered by the one who doesn't give, you might well think that he, although a stone, will find his tongue again. But, come to think of it, he isn't a man. The hostess, insofar as she is a hostess, receives: she gives and doesn't take. Is it possible for me to call her Doña Petra? But this situation, which has no name, is realized in life by the mother. She is a woman, she is a hostess, for the body's lodging.

During the years of *The Parasite*, I missed the mother's rare discourse. I didn't know how to do it. And yet there are only two simple arrows: taking without ever giving back and giving without receiving, the parasitical arrow and the hostess arrow. Two arrows, two sexes: mothers and the rest. *Genesis* and agenesis.

I missed Alcmene's discourse, who receives, at night and the dawn, the god and the king, who contains in her womb the hero and the man. Alcmene's lodging is capable of Jupiter and Amphitryon, of Hercules and his false twin, a very ordinary person. A fabulous capacity, which goes from the earth to the heavens. When you miss a thing, you recognize it when it appears. Here it is. Listen to the discourse of the mother of the parasite Coriolanus: the discourse of the good hostess.

Who are you? What is your name? This is the question of the host, the Volscian Aufidius. Coriolanus has just entered his home, where the feast smells good from wine, but he doesn't look like a dinner guest; his head is wrapped in a hood; he's dressed in rags, exiled. What is your name? Marcius, Roman, or Coriolanus, Volscian? From Corioli, which Marcius took as a Roman soldier and which he is going to retake from the Romans soon as a Volscian general. Who are you? What is your real name? How can Coriolanus know? A soldier, a hero, a scornful patrician hating the plebs, seeking perhaps to starve them, a candidate to the consulate, condemned, exiled, an enemy of his country, a hero before Corioli, a traitor before Corioli again, an enemy of the Volsci, a guest of these latter, a general of the enemy, giving Rome victories, holding the conquered Rome under his foot. Who are you, Marcius Coriolanus? Who am I? At Aufidius' house, Coriolanus replays Sextus Tarquinius' strategy at Gabii. In reverse, perhaps. In reverse, are we sure? The host in the middle of the feast recognizes his worst enemy who has become his guest; he suddenly recognizes a friend who shares his hatred of Rome. Does he really recognize him?

The scene written by Shakespeare is not in Livy, even if it is in Plutarch. But Livy wrote a similar scene. We return to those grand games, to those games of instauration, during which in the morning a slave was seen being whipped with his head in a neck yoke; we return to the fundamental games; we return to the bifurcation. Even before the games' opening, the Volsci came there in droves. They receive hospitality in private homes. Yet the same Aufidius, Tullius in Livy, the first by far of the Volsci, is going to tell the consuls, who are going to tell the Senate, that his fellow citizens, presently guests of Rome, risk sowing disorder there, are even preparing to do so. So the guests, reputed from then on to be enemies, are expelled from the games. They leave the city in a pitiful file; Tullius waits for them near the Ferentina spring. He intensifies their already full anger; he impels them to war; he cries 'down with the enemy!'

The lesson is the same everywhere. Inclusion: Marcius enters into Corioli during a sortie by the Volsci; he enters Volsci territory while he is its sworn enemy; the Volsci are the guests of Rome for the games … Exclusion: Coriolanus departs for exile, the Volsci are expelled from the games. Hospitality includes the enemy, hostility excludes the guest. Tullius or Aufidius is justified in saying: who are you, and what is your name? And everyone is deceived. The guest deceives everyone, everyone is deceived by the guest. He himself perhaps deceives himself.

Only the hostess isn't deceived. Gaius Marcius Coriolanus is known for loving his mother. All his exploits are for her; he scorns recompense and only endures his mother's congratulations. Coriolanus has no father. He becomes a war hero in order to be great in his mother's eyes. Coriolanus becomes great, very great. Exiled from his country, finding refuge with the enemy, an enemy of the plebs become an enemy of Rome, translating class struggle into foreign war, he wins, he wins just as much for the enemy as he won in the past armed for Rome. He takes one town, two, five, ten towns; he takes twenty cities on behalf of the Volsci; he camps five miles from Rome, at the edge of the Cluilian trench. This was inevitable, for it is his place. From which he ravages the surrounding area, sparing the lands of the nobles, further intensifying the struggle of the orders, already hot. Expelled by the battle between the pressure groups, Coriolanus returns to make it flame up even more than before. He waits.

He waits for the system divided against itself to fall on its own. Then, just as the Sabine women did long ago, the matrons exit the gates. Here are Volumnia, Veturia, Marcius' mother and the mother of his children. For once, the discourse of the hostess-mother is heard. The discourse of the one who gives and doesn't take is heard. Where am I, she says, where am I here and now? With my son, or with an enemy? Who are you? What is your name? If you win the battle, if you take and destroy Rome, I lose, for I am Roman; if you lose the fight and your life, I lose; I lose you, for I am your mother; in both cases I lose. The hostess always loses. The parasite always wins. The hostess gives without receiving; the other takes without ever giving back. The hostess can't be deceived while the parasite always deceives. Coriolanus recognizes that he is recognized. And he breaks camp.

The second expulsion from Rome. Coriolanus' second birth. The real one no doubt. The mother, having delivered, has just delivered Rome.

The mother has pinpointed the name and the thing, the place, the word and the being. But this is not enough. The mother always says the law. She said the thing itself: if I had never been a mother, Rome would be free. You die, and Rome is free, I lose in both cases; you live, and Rome is besieged, lost. She said the word of recognition; she now says the law of functioning: you ravage the land that gave birth to you, you destroy what fed you. She is certainly speaking of the Roman land; secretly she is speaking of herself. The land is this mother; the mother is this land. You are ravaging what fed you. Corneille's Sabine, another matron, says: you are plunging your sword into your mother's womb. Let's look at this law with a bit more attention.

Or rather these two laws.

Pleasure and pain, joy or distress, misfortunes, an opportune life – ordinary time divides the odds; no one knows any system for constant fortune. And yet, there are strategies for winning at every stroke. The parasite is fed and lodged whether the host is feeling well or ill; what does his ruin or prosperity matter to him? His position is the best; it appears to be beyond setbacks. The king speaks: if you are in danger, I am here to save you; if you are fortunate, look to my popularity; thank me in both cases. God rewards you, God punishes you; pray to God in misery, pray to God in the elation of happiness; God only hears your prayers, of thanks, of joy, of supplication. It seems to me that there are places in space that redress bad luck, where the same result occurs whatever the antecedents may have been. The parasite has a lively expression and a ruby mouth even if the hostess has a headache and needs to be bled. Theology and politics cause the negative and the positive, famine and abundance, slaughter and peace, horror and pleasure, to work in the same direction: a good dialectic suffices for this. What does recounting the history of tragedies or successes matter to the historian? Tragedy sells rather better. Scarcity and massacres ensure the front page of the gazettes and reviews. A record of equilibrium or a record of crisis is always only a record. Is it sufficient, in order to secure such a place where said rectifier functions in your favour, is it sufficient to transform the thing into a signal, the hardware into software? The word that says evil is no worse a word than the one that says luck; the word hot is no hotter than the word cold is cold. The word blue is not very blue. If you tell that somebody died in a fire, the text won't burn you, and you will fascinate populations. Somebody has nevertheless had the bad luck to die in a fire. Thus the best reason is not always held by the strongest, but by he who has found this place in space where the orders of things change. Where the things of the world give out signs. The winning strategy changes orders. It refuses the battle at the level where it rages; it changes levels. It passes to metalanguage. To the level of metalanguage, to the level upstream from the given level; the blows are rectified wherever they come from. The battle dead reinforce the interest of the story, appeal to the saviour of the country, cry out for vengeance or pardon to the tutelary gods, make deep the philosophy that speaks about them and that, through them, conquers all space.

If you don't have any talent, move on to criticism. If you don't have any critical talent, manufacture texts, take them simply as objects. If you don't know how to build anything, move on to commentary; destruction itself works in your favour and for your renown. If you can't invent truth, move quickly on to epistemology. If your philosophy isn't worth anything, move on to metalanguage, where you will be able to say what philosophy is worth. If you don't know how to do anything, do advertising. Change orders: the semiconductor works for you. The uncircumventable strategies pass through such cheatings. If you are worthless, make yourself king, make yourself god, speak in any case.

I want to say that the world of things, a host for mankind if there ever was one, gives everything to science and that science gives nothing back to it: science is right, always right, that's all. The peasant gives a landscape to his land and receives from it, in good years and bad, bread and a roof.[7] He doesn't always win, but the land doesn't always either, a game with divided odds, sometimes unequal, unpredictable. Science has discovered a system for always beating the world; the scientist is a peasant who no longer loses at the game of things. The peasant remains at the hardware or material level of the hardware game, sweat for rain, work for germination; the scientist changes orders; he transforms the world into information, high energies into little energies: scientific experiment is not work; work remains in the the order of things; experimentation is the place where the game changes orders; it moves to software. The peasant is of course a bad scientist; he remains in his software muteness, but it is never said how much the scientist is a bad peasant; he gives nothing to the world. The peasant gives a landscape to the land, Gascony, Umbria or the Loire valley; the world as such receives nothing from knowledge. Do you know a single place in the world unforgettably transfigured, beautified merely through science? And yet science's truth comes to it from things, the way bread comes from them for us, peasants.

There is indeed a parasite strategy for taking without giving anything back. He who invents it places himself upstream from he who remains subject to good luck and bad, but in between the upstream and the downstream there is a threshold, like a threshold of transformation, like a change of levels, or of orders of things. At each level, the game changes rules. He who always wins, he who is always right, the uncircumventable one, isn't playing the same game as he who loses and wins, depending. The game of truth entails risks; it's very important to be able to, to know how to make mistakes. It's by error, it's by failure that research is recognized; it's by error that fairness is recognized; it's by error that science is recognized; more and better, it's by error that humanity is recognized. It's by the constant and faultless truth that the devil is recognized, or the clever one or the imbecile. *Errare humanus est*, error is hominid. I demand the right to err; it's a human right. Change levels, and you obtain systems for winning at every stroke. Metalanguage, metaphysics.

Coriolanus: I don't know if he took the city, but I do know that he took its name. Hence the hostess's discourse, who gives without receiving, and who recognizes him: Coriolanus, tell us your name. It's by your name that we'll know why you win all the time.

Second law: you ravage what feeds you. I've already said it: hostility feeds its old father; hospitality kills its mother. Coriolanus, camped on the Cluilian trench, is going to destroy Rome, his female progenitor. Only his mother, ready to die, can still say so. This is how Rome acted against Alba in the past. This is how you will act in order to found. We are very familiar with processes that, via a reverse feedback, advancing along their own sequence, destroy their antecedents, covering them over, erasing them. We have already encountered them enough in the parasite world. We don't need to return to this.

We are evidently entering into new spaces. The lines vibrate, fuzzy; uncertainty about just who is hostile or hospitable transforms borders into margins; points, poles, mono-poles are limits and paradoxical; they stretch out or are holes; we are evidently entering into new logics. Perhaps we are slowly discovering, in the book of foundations, the fundament of our logics. Here the excluded middle suspends its legislation; it shows its foundation in what precedes our social sciences.

Let's consider these new spaces.

I will have to speak about the strange logic of sacks and the hard logic of boxes. A canvas sack folds easily into a canvas sack, and it can conversely contain it as well, whereas if a wooden crate contains a wooden crate, the latter cannot conversely contain the former. Thus there are conditions of inclusion dependent on the material of what is included and of what does the including, steel, wood, marble, fabric, jute, dependent above all on the space where this happens. This space is extensible or it is inextensible. Canvas is deformable enough at leisure; wood is little; marble is not. It seems to me that I see a kind of topology before logic, a space that's prerequisite for its operations. Depending on which space inclusion is immersed in, it changes laws. The space is deformable for example, or it is not. The usual logic assumes a space that is not deformable; it sides with the wooden crates, the steel tanks, the marble boxes. Yet the case where space is deformable cannot not be envisaged. Here is some fabric, some cloth, something pliable, something elastic; we have rather more of the malleable on hand than the hard, rather more of the flexible than the rigid, more leaves than ingots, more flesh than skeletons, more fluids than invincible rocks. I have a feeling that human experience or what are called the social sciences most often refer to the textile space of sacks, of variable invaginations, and that the sciences said to be hard quite simply refer to the space of hard boxes. Just as we have succeeded in conquering rigour in the non-metric, we will learn the reasonable in the non-rigorous, I mean the non-rigid. A logical future is promised to the malleable, to the extensible, to the textile and the fuzzy.

Jupiter induces us to think that religion and sovereignty envelop war and economy. Jupiter implicates Mars and Quirinus, and he explicates them.

Mars induces us to think that war envelops religion and economy. Mars implicates Jupiter and Quirinus, and he explicates them.

Quirinus induces us to think that economy – production, capital, exchanges, money – envelops war and religion. Quirinus implicates Mars and Jupiter, and he explicates them.

They are all three gods, on Jupiter's side; they are all three of the sacred, stemming from violence, and freezings of violence, on Mars' side; they are all three social classes, on Quirinus' side. They are all three from all three sides.

They are all three theoretical classes, classes of interpretation, authorities. We have seen theocracies, polemarchs, plutocrats, all sorts of regimes in which priests, armies, their generals, bankers or producers dominate. Ideocracies, theoretical regimes, the dominants of interpretation, linguistic, speculative or software power are spoken of less often. Who commands is a question, sometimes, often, a question of force. Who is right is another such question, sometimes the same one, a question of legitimacy. Who is right is the one who can silence the other. The priest explicates history; he was right. The military man explicates history as relations of force, and he is right. The economist explicates history, and he is right. Each of them implicates the two other explications in turn. The implication turns around and becomes reversed. They all wanted to be right; they desired to right history; they are right; they are all right.[8] They are all three right *modulo*, the logic of sacks.

They were, they are, they will be right, de facto, through force, when they seize sovereignty, when they occupy Jupiter's place and all of Quirinus' productive space through Mars' force. They have rights over history and are right in doing this, when they take it and produce it.

But they are, in addition, right de jure, if we suppose to be well described the extensible, deformable, elastic space in which explication, in which implication both turn around, reverse, and become reciprocal. I am barely beginning to understand the importance of this space. I believe that history develops in it. I believe that the time and direction or meaning of history are not thinkable without it.

The multitudes spread throughout this book – in the sanctuary woods, in the Roman forum, in the middle of camps, in fairground esplanades – fluctuate in such a space: sets with fuzzy edges, that expand or tighten.

These multitudes include, they are agglutinating. They are included; they almost disappear into another multiplicity that they contained. They are open. To be open is to be in such a space.

Should they exclude a third, they will close up. They will enter into a hard space, undeformable. Excluding is closing up. As soon as there is an excluded third, inclusion is not reciprocal. He who closes is either the excluded third or the third man standing at the gates and inventing another game than the one inside.

Likewise. Let there be an operation here in the process of being decided. Let there be a battle, a game, a work, a negotiation, in brief, some evolution going toward an outcome. This outcome is good or bad, unlucky or favourable, false or true, winning or losing, the bifurcation sometimes letting us see more than two ways. We never take into account the space in which this operation unfolds. Everything happens as though the space were transparent, as though it were everywhere homogeneous. Everything happens as though the space in which the evolution takes place were also the space of its proximities as well as of its distances, as though a universal space of immersion existed, in which we too would be immersed, here and now, as well as the operation that's said and done. In other words, as though everything is always and everywhere, from far or from near, concerned in this local work or this temporary evolution, and concerned directly in their laws and their outcome. Then and then only can we conceive that this operation, this game, this work are everywhere motors, that there even is a motor.

The universal space of communication is of an extreme rarity. In general, most spaces are not homogeneous; they are not everywhere the same. I'll explain.

Here is a game that unfolds and takes place in a stadium or a circus, for example a game on horses in honour of an equestrian god. Whether the greens or the blues win or lose the game doesn't matter to the Romans or the god: those who abduct the Sabine women behind the backs of the spectators win, not the game, which no longer takes place once outside the circus, but rather the Sabine women, a different stake. They win all the more when the game of the greens and blues is close, when the game involves risk, or is undecidable and long; the crowd is standing breathless, one of the players is perhaps going to expire on the duelling grounds. In the space of the stadium, a game takes place, on horse or otherwise, a race or battle, a win or loss, a spectacle, but in the space nearest the stadium gates a second game is also taking place which answers to different rules and is instaurated in order to win no matter what the outcome of the first one. The first game captures a space; it defines and closes it; it leaves free a second one in which an entirely different law appears. While the Sabine men are standing and gaping at thesis and antithesis making sound and fury, the Romans are taking their women. The battle of the two theses in the space of the circus, amid the dust raised by the horses, is separated by a trench or by a rectifier from the space where the Sabine women are stolen or violated. What I'm calling a rectifier is that semi-conduction operator that causes the blues to win when the blues win, but that also causes the blues to win when the greens win. Or rather what I'm calling a rectifier is that semi-conduction operator that causes the Romans to win whether the blues win or lose. The Romans have placed themselves outside the space of the stadium in which the blues and the greens are striving to the death. The space is not homogeneous; the law of the battle of the greens and blues, of the antithesis and the thesis, and its outcome don't directly affect the one standing at the stadium gates: he has invented a different game, a different space, in which he wins no matter the fate of the greens. Theorem: there is no work of the negative (the work of the negative is only local, in the space thus drawn or closed), there is only the work or the fascination of the representation, of the closure of one space and the invention of a second one. While the philosophers are fascinated by the spectacle of the dialectic unfolding in a single space, the work of history, behind their backs, is happening in a different space and according to different laws and with different outcomes.

We can speak differently and displace the representation. In the space of the thing and the dirt, he who works and gets his hands dirty loses or wins, and he risks his forfeit and his hands; he puts his flesh and his glory in a precarious position, but outside the space of the dirt and the forfeit and somewhere in a new space, another site exists separated from the precarious position by a rectifier, in which the games are engaged differently, in which the logic changes, in which the rules have no relation to the first rules of risk and in which a third man wins no matter what the outcome of the game engaged above, decisive on the duelling grounds. It is never, it is rarely that the winner wins; he only wins very locally or temporarily; the real winner is this third man located, attentive, in the second space, the inventor of the rectifier.

An example. Write a beautiful book, write an ugly book, a true or false, long or short book, which required a thousand dawns of attention and ardor, or thirty minutes of chattering – what does it matter to the person selling it, to the impotent critic who talks about it without having read it, since their game is one of money or hot air? The games are separated; the spaces are different; the book is transparent for one person, it's an object for another; it's an object for one, it's a means for another. What does the one who, covered in blood and deeply scarred, captured the city in the course of the assault and siege's game to the death matter to the historian? What does his name matter, if the one writing can change it, can cite it, can cross it out with a stroke of the pen? The battle of Corioli, taken by Marcius or by the consul, taken by Rome, retaken by the Volsci, the multiple battle of Coriolis in any case works for him: whether a real or a represented battle. And it's him, when all is said and done, that history trusts. He always wins. Someone takes the city, someone takes the name.

In the case of the games of Neptunus Equester, the ruse consisted in leaving the space of representation. While the Sabine men, with all their popping eyes, are watching the theatre, placing their bodies into the representation, the Romans, in real space, are really taking their real women. So real they will have children. In Coriolanus' case, the ruse is to invent a space of representation. While the soldier is risking his life on a ladder in false equilibrium at the top of the city wall, while the hero is entering the city during an enemy sortie, while he is exhausting himself in exploits, the one who is writing and dramatizing these exploits is taking the profits from them, all the more so since Coriolanus is dead.

The essential thing then is not to distinguish the real from the represented, myth from history or the concrete from the legendary, or to reduce the one to the other or the other to the one, easy exercises; the essential thing is to see these differentiated spaces form, the essential thing is to see that there isn't only one space that's either real or represented, again a very singular battle, but that there are numerous spaces, finely imbricated into each other, inextricably. This is difficult to think, now: the multiplicity of spaces.

The game is not one of winning or losing, of saying the true or the imaginary; the game is only dialectical, the game is only to be decided or not for those who think that there is only one space. The winners are rarely those who win; the strongest is not strongest for very long. The winner and the strongest are most often those who find a site outside the game where the work of the game and not its outcome is capturable, is conceivable, is rectified by them. No, the slave is not the slave of the master, nor does he ever become the master of the master; it was ages ago that this combat, if it ever took place, was cut out into its own space, as in its vignette, and then rectified in a hundred ways, in a thousand different spaces and in a thousand sites.[9] The slave remains a slave, for example, by being loyal or faithful to a god, or militant in a party or elite in a science, and he can become, Aesop or Epictetus, a professor of wisdom, respected by kings, a bishop or historian, a banker for nations or for ruling stock markets: ruses proliferate. Leaving the boundaries of the game, finding another game that collects the profits from the first one no matter the possible outcome is the good strategy. Changing spaces, changing combats, changing rules. And this begins again often.

The strongest gladiator ends up dying or at least growing older, and he quits the circus. The journalist is always there. What does it matter to the financier who sells the tickets at the window that inside the stadium the blues or the greens win? The more the game is in suspense, deadly, undecidable, the more the onlookers flock, the more the business figures climb. The open ticket window is a good rectifier: it transforms the game to the death into a game of money or a game of Sabine women.

What does it matter to the historian that Rome or Alba dies, that those who lie bleeding in the area of the Porta Capena are named Horatius or Curiatius, with even the tradition mixing them up? What does it matter? The fight is in suspense; it has held us breathless for centuries; Livy wins a beautiful text from it, Corneille a beautiful poem; this is not the same game.

What does the economic crisis and its effects or outcomes matter to the politician? If it grows worse to the point of poverty, call on me as saviour, he says; if its ravages stagger out a little, if a semblance of prosperity returns, like a kind of sunny spell, thank me, he concludes; and here he is elected beneath the cheers. He won in both cases. He's playing a different game in a completely different space. Politics rectifies, when it can, the economy or violence. Direct determination is lost.

The gladiator loses or wins, his hand, his skin, his life; the barge worker gambles his life in the middle of the waters, furious or tranquil, high or low, clear or loaded with what it carries along. What does it matter to the financier? What does it matter to the accounts? What does it matter to the economist? The figure will be put to the right or the left in the columns of the balance sheet; the economy is only a paper game that creates a nice effect of the real for intellectuals, for those who believe it to be as transparent as a divine language. And again, what does it matter to the politician where the figure is? He will only be a true statesman if he discovers another space in which to rectify the other results in favour of his new game. Rectifiers are scattered everywhere, invisible: they cause the passage from the game of life and death to a game of accounts or books, from a risk taken to tranquility of mind, from one representation to another one, and so on ad infinitum.

To believe and say, for example, that the economy determines or conditions the political game or the direction of history, to believe and say, for example, that a given combat brings about a global movement, history, through a chain of struggles is always to suppose that a single space is posed, is given, one common to two neighbouring or distant combats, to the economy game and the political game. This can of course happen, but happens if and only if the economy puts itself in power. If it imposes its space. Like just any pressure.

In general, the spaces I'm talking about are mixed, with contingent proximities. Many of them, I suppose, have still to be invented. It would be a great miracle if only a single space existed, common to every game, work and action; if this were so we would know universal laws, uniform chains of determinations that would run through places and times. If this existed, it would be known. There isn't a single space, but rather a landscape. A landscape is a mosaic of spaces and not a set of objects placed in a common space.

It is sometimes believed that these spaces are fitted into each other like Russian dolls, the winner always situating himself at the top level. This is one particular case of the single space envisioned already. It's the illusion of the *Leviathan*, the double opposing illusion that causes us to believe, on the one hand, that a living organism is built according to the organigram of power, according to the imaginary organigram of institutional or social power, and that causes us to believe, on the other hand, that a given collective, built from this organigram precisely is a semi-organic body. The construction is simple, and it uses a chain of rectifiers. The spaces hierarchically placed, level after level, are separated in such a way that at each level the game changes rules. Noise is rectified into information; change is rectified into equilibrium, etc. That the rules change at each level is a bit contradictory as a principle; for it presupposes an invariant rule, the one that piles the levels one on top of the other: this rule doesn't change. There is a game space, and this game is played in this space by changing the instructions.

I repeat: for a single space and a single game to take place, one space would have to have won out forever over the others in a time that precedes time. The universal space that contains the fitted together levels, in which this Jacob's ladder exists, takes shape and functions, the universal space that we've lost in the exact sciences for several decades, long after Newton had formed it in God's image, the universal space in which everything is played, is what is left of God for us in the social sciences, still in their childhood, or in the sciences of the living thing, adolescent. The parallel existence of a time, a single time, a universal time in which every living thing is immersed, in which all of evolution stretches out and ramifies, is also what is left of God in Darwin or the historians, when it's a question of history. The hierarchically constructed space of the levels and Darwinian time are the *sensorium Dei* of the life scientists; the space that's common to every law of determination starting from a first or final authority and the direction of history are the *sensorium Dei* of the properly human narratives. The most atheist among men thus use a theology. The single space is absolute, divine, universal, so is this single time.

A landscape in which different spaces mix must be imagined. All the rules change and all the games, from space to space. Of course, two neighbouring spaces, linked by what I've called a rectifier, are related to each other through this rectified game. But the transitivity is quickly lost. By the nth rectifier, the risk that was first taken has been lost forever. Better to conceive a kind of puzzle, better to see a land.

This – what I'm describing – is a mixture, that is to say, a space and a time. This – what I'm describing – is a space-time. It's one of the space-times of history.

Rather here is a map, a sort of world map. The lines drawing the different spaces, as on any map, are traces of nature or history and so fringed, entangled, inextricable. If the spaces or the levels were wisely, simply ordered, it would be easy to establish a site for laws to last, to be won, to be conceived. This is not so easy, as we know.

Sometimes the loser is the one whose body stiffens in the fascination with the representations, intoxicated with the imaginary; sometimes on the contrary he's the one who works getting his hands and body dirty in real risks. The winner is sometimes the one passing abruptly to the referent, to the thing itself; he is more often the one playing representations, playing the first naïve representation or the supposed final one, or whichever one is well-situated at the moment. The spaces on the map are different, and their difference goes semi-continuously from a quite real real that's generally indexed by the death of bodies – that's the criterion of the real – to the multiplicity of the fanned-out representations. This continuous spectrum is scattered across the map, like the thousand colours across a world atlas.

Don't look for what is myth and what is legend, what is history and what has happened; the thing isn't decided by yes or no; too many ways to play different games, too many rules intervene. At this very moment, the invention of new games is continuing on. The map is becoming complete, modelled, transformed, extended; it's one of the space-times of history.

I see how history progresses; it progresses the way a fly flies. It's true that a fly progresses, sometimes.

Having left, if you like, now, from here, from some space, whether real, represented or imaginary, history abruptly bifurcates under the attractive grip of a site that's become favourable or that rectifies with profit the contentious games of the first space; it halts for a long or short time, a flash, depending; it abruptly bifurcates under the attractive grip of a site that's suddenly become ...

Coriolanus progresses in time: he takes Corioli, perhaps he only takes its name, a warrior beneath its walls, a historian in the archives, in the annals – history, legend? No, apologue; here is the fable of the members and the stomach, so frequently repeated in Antiquity, a fable recited in the single-voiced spectacle given by Menenius – fable, spectacle? No, circus; here suddenly are the circus games and the game in the game, that slave who passes by in the morning being whipped and the dream of this game, and the interpretation in the dream of this double representation, a spectacle, an apparition, an epiphany of Jupiter in the dream itself; what level are we at in the *mise en abyme*? Can we distinguish between myth and history when a variety of legends abounds here – apologue, fable, spectacle, dream, theophany, interpretation? But Coriolanus continues, a candidate; he gives himself as spectacle; he refuses this representation; a given sword stroke kills or leaves a scar that allows the candidate to become consul; the Senate plays its part on the stage of the Curia in the middle of the enraged plebs, and Coriolanus is just about to be lynched; all the spectacles are born together; the dancer trembles like the whipped slave; the slave whipped in the centre of the circus and at the beginning of the spectacle is the first dancer; he is Coriolanus himself, Coriolanus half-lynched, Coriolanus the candidate who failed to make the consulate and who, thanks to this failure, reveals the real functioning of suffrage; it was almost a dancer who received the suffrage that day; it's always a dancer who receives it in this sense; so the almost lynched quasi-consul leaves the city the way the enemies left the city where they had been invited for the games; he pays a visit to his double, associates with him, his host, in order to become hostile to Rome; he takes up arms, and he recaptures Corioli for the Volsci ... Coriolanus passes from space to space, ceaselessly making rectifiers function; he crosses a landscape in which the real and the imaginary, myth and history, fact and representation are never cut out with clear borders; they have fuzzy edges, in the narrative as in life, today now right here.

Point, line, space. *The principal elements of the usual theories of history are decidedly less subtle and less elaborate than those depicted or suggested by Livy in his narrative. Our logics are cruder than those implicated or unfolded by myth or legend.*

The legend of Aeneas saved from Troy in flames, the battle of Romulus against the Sabines, the grounds for war invented by Tullus against the Albans, the expulsion of the Tarquins and the death of Sextus and the rape of Lucretius, Coriolanus' very complicated and fuzzy situation, in a word, the entire meditative narrative on the rule of uncertainty which puts hospitality over against hostility, or rather the one in the place of the other, leads us by the hand to the first principal element. Here it is. Some given line is an edge or border; it separates space; it defines sets; it closes cities; it limits belonging; it designates the enemy. It is one of the elements of the ordinary, analytical or dialectical theory, Hegel or Fustel, classical or presumed revolutionary. This first element seems to me to be put into doubt from the first line of the narrative, put into doubt by Livy, put into doubt by Rome, put into doubt by me. There is no such line; there isn't only one such line. The city wall is porous, the sanctuary woods has fuzzy edges; a grey or blurry band takes shape there, so wide that it can occupy the inside of the entire set plus its complement. On the grey of this margin, no one truly distinguishes the hospitable gesture from the hostile threat, a Sabine from a Roman, a foreigner from a king, or even a god from a wolf. The principle of the excluded middle suspends its legislation. This is no longer the same violence, nor the same sacred; this is no longer analytics; this is no longer the dialectic. To do without the logic of fuzzy subsets, to erase – in the name of rigour – this band is to forget from the outset the ancient hospitality, to close everything over war, expulsion, dissection, to reduce the city to the perfect model of the three hundred and six Fabii heading out for combat in lines and columns on foot, unitary, homogeneous, as though cloned. Antenor or Aeneas would not have, in this case, been able to save their lives from the flames, and Rome would have disappeared, from the first skirmishes, at the first scattered calves in the plain. To do without mixture, without the fuzzy, to be unaware that definitions float, is to abandon time, the dispersed circumstances of contingency. The usual theories of history heavily dominating our thoughts play at recovering time by means of notions come from eternity.

Sextus' death, his traitorous person, the lynching undergone by Remus, Coriolanus' silence during his mother's sharp remarks, the heroic misadventure of Manlius Capitolinus, saving the Capitol from the Gauls and dying pushed by his own from the Tarpeian Rock, in a word, the entire meditative narrative on the king, on the length of the reign, on who reigns and how and why he reigns, leads us by the hand to the second principal element. Here it is: it's the point. The pole or the mono-pole. I should have cited it first. First the point, then the line. History laughs at order. Remus reigns for an instant, on the point of death. A point swelling up to several years in the case of his brother and his successors, who see their execution suspended, a paradoxical point in inflation, a point returning to the apex in Sextus' case. It stretches out the way the line becomes a margin. This principal element is as important as the preceding one. For the excluded middle or third suspends its legislation in this point as well. In this pole, the king reigns; the king is expelled; he is the third, excluded. Everything is shaken up, enveloped, invaginated in this limit point. Violence shoots up from it, the very potency of power, but it receives violence just as much as it produces it.[10] It must be understood that Jupiter receives onto his head all the thunderbolts he casts or hurls. In the swamp of Capra, Romulus admits into his body all the force or power of the storm he emits. He tears to pieces, he is torn to pieces. He strikes down, he is struck down. Where do you expect the power of kings comes from? It is active, it is passive at the same time. The effective power is exactly equal to the affected power. The monopoly or mono-pole of legitimate violence is in this point. In this limit point of equality. It is legitimated by this equality between the violence received and the violence hurled. The point of the mono-pole or monopoly is the site of passage, the hole, the pass, the exchanger of these two violences. In this point, the victim of everyone has the right of life and death over everyone. Whoever is on this point, in this point, on this throne or under this crown, is a murderer and a victim at the same time, absolutely guilty and sanctified, wolf and god, hated and adored, loved, feared; further, he is the point, he is identically the point where love and hate, twins, become the same. Without contradiction. As though he was himself the exclusion of the excluded third or middle. A difficult intuition, a black hole. This punctual site is Remus and Romulus together; it's the point of departure; I have placed it in the middle between the Capitol and the Rock; I should have written that it's the site where, without contradiction, the Tarpeian Rock is the Capitol itself.

The line is a margin, and the point is a hole. It is a gap in space. The usual logics do not help us to think such situations; they impose hard boxes, rigid edges, points that are not singularities; they impose stiff iron collars where space is paradoxical, singular, puzzling, where a new intuition is required.

Above all these logics assume that there is a single, homogeneous space, and this is the third principal element. Whether it's a question of analysis, of inclusion in the ordinary sense, of exclusion or dissection, whether it's a question of dialectical clashing, everything rests on the unspoken idea that everything is immersed in the same world, the same space of immersion and so of impulsion. The same space of immersion, of extension, and of impulsion. Everything is communicated from near to near and from near to far. Who gives such an assurance? Who said it was like this? God himself no doubt. For it is enough to observe the Romans from their origin, or at least what Livy says about them, or to observe, without searching so far, around oneself to laugh at this assurance. The abduction of the Sabine women during the games for Neptunus Equester, the chanson de geste of Horatius, Sextus Tarquinius or Coriolanus, the entire meditative narrative on combats and spectacles, capturings and representations leads us to think mixed places, with contingent, unexpected proximities, a heterogeneous space. The rigorous, analytical definition of a set, like the vignette of the dialectical combat of the master and slave, is quickly enclosed in a circus, a space opened by a window where a rectifier is placed. The victor doesn't reside where the battle is decided but in the site where the rectifier is located. The winner is neither the blue nor the green, but the Roman who grabs the Sabine woman; it's not the plebs on the sacred mountain, it's Menenius, it's the tribune: they've changed the stake of the battle. The struggle is lodged in a camp or in a vignette; the set is lodged in a camp or in a cartouche, an ensign, a fable. The amphitheatre in which the heroes die, the coloured cartouche representing them are both immersed in another space that only concerns them a little. The stakes are no longer where the actors are. This immersion takes place as many times as you like, as many times as is needed, as many times as a ruse wins by changing levels. In the vicinity of the battle, for example, space is no longer the same; it can be not the same from vicinity to vicinity. These are no longer the same forces or the same flows; this is no longer the same topology. Space is no longer homogeneous; it is many-coloured, it changes colour, form, properties. The sequence of places we pass through, from window to window, from rectifier to rectifier, is often unexpected, and along this sequence the general impulsion often gets lost. It is sometimes preserved, not always. This paints a landscape that seems to me to be the space of history; this draws a place that's historiated, blended, tiger-striped, streaked, damasked, the third principal element discovered. It suffices to itself; it implicates the two others: in this motley, composite and diverse space, in this system of mixtures, the lines sometimes form fuzzy margins; the points can form holes, singularities. Perhaps I've only written this book to bring to light this new transcendental place. Neither dialectical reason nor analytical reason accounts for the strong complexities of history; both for the same reason: logical poverty, simplifications, rigours.

The point, the line, space, nothing is clearer or more luminous. The point of singularity, the line of definition, the space in which forces or flows move, are born and pass. Men themselves, groups, their worlds. The point is not so simple, nor is the line so pure, nor space so unified. The point yields, the line vibrates, space is historiated. New monads, new multiplicities, time occurs, finally.

The elements merely shake. And change our ways of thinking.

6 WAR AND PLAGUE: THE MULTIPLICITY IN REPRESENTATION

Livy 7.2; 5.13.4–8; 2.26; 1.9

Before the largest lectisternium with twelve reclining gods, held in Rome amid the terror inspired by Hannibal, one or several smaller lectisternia were decided upon in order to ward off the plague. What plague brought the enemy from Africa? Conversely, what enemy is more terrifying than the epidemic? The gods – I mean the images, statues, wicker mannequins in human form, symbols – twelve gods, or six, were there immobile in the public square by twos on magnificent beds furnished with cushions to feast hieratically. Mouths closed, empty eyes, white faces. Foreign, this had to be terrifying. Did they want to invite dead Hannibal, deified?

These events are said to have been borrowed from the Greeks: this is no doubt true. The sibylline books that recommended them had just been imported into Rome. It sometimes happens that sibylline books, difficult to decipher, bring the plague some place at the same time as the rites of healing.

During the feast, in the entire city the doors of the houses open; everyone has free use of everyone's things. Those known and those unknown are received; foreigners, even enemies become guests. The conversations of everyone with everyone are benevolent and kind; quarrels call a truce; the chains are removed from the prisoners.

The books came from Greece and the lectisternium as well; later the histriones will come from Etruria and the Attelan Farces from Osci: foreigners are very welcome.

Let's speak Greek again. It's the sibylline language of deciphering. The Greek celebration is said: theoxeny. When a god is so named, its function is to protect foreigners. Everything becomes clear: on this day of feasting when anger is appeased, everyone is everyone's guest, including the enemy.

The Hellenic *xenos* designates the foreigner, but it also designates the guest. The same word says at the same time, in the same respect and in the same place he who is outside, beyond the borders, and who, invited, now finds himself inside. The same being is in two places at the same time, the same word blows double. In this point, single and fuzzy, our maternal languages have some blurriness. Just as the French language gives the same name to he who is received and he who receives him, just as *hôte* is, without any other mention, an indistinguishable doublet, just as the Greek language gives the same title for the guest and the foreigner, so the Latin language, less sharply but more strongly, plays on the almost indistinct names of guest and enemy; Latin indicates the relationship of hospitality to hostility. The proximity *hostes hospites* is not rare in Livy, I mean in his language; it's frequent in the situations.

This floating grouping was analysed fairly extensively when describing the parasitical relationship; here it is reproduced in the archaic rite. The rite is a meal. Since statues are feasting, it's an interrupted meal. As though eternally interrupted. At which deadly mouthful were they immobilized?

As I had announced, the parasite enters into history.

Theoxeny: Let the foreigner be a god; let the gods be foreign; let foreign gods be welcome here. *Hostes hospites*, let our enemies be our *hôtes*, welcoming or welcomed; our *hôtes* are our adversaries; we have abducted the Sabine women; our women are enemy women. Abruptly, by an unforeseeable leap of logic, a value passes from one excess to the opposite excess. The plague they are trying to appease by the lectisternium, which they will later try to ward off by means of the theatre and stage games, was brought about by an unwholesome summer following a harsh winter, 'whether as a result of a jump in temperature that abruptly went from one excess to the opposite excess, whether for some other reason'. Nature, like the *hôte*, blows hot and cold at the same time. A jump in weather, a jump in meaning. *Raptim mutatione in contrarium facta …*

All other reasons, in addition, are receivable as well.

Hercules and Diana, Apollo and Latona, Mercury and Neptune, statues, were feasting. Rome invited the statues of those in command to dinner. The lectisternium instituted against the plague is anterior to the stage games. Theatre, satire and Atellan Farce will be organized following the lectisternium, as perhaps more effective ceremonies than it.

Comedy at the origin is a remedy for the plague.

At the origin of comedy is the stone feast.

At the same time the statues are having a banquet and the gods are there, back home everyone is peacefully receiving everyone, saying welcome to the first comer. The first comer is not going to die today, sacrificed at the crossroads; it's the festival of the neighbour, of the passerby: foreigner, bitter enemy.

Let's be attentive to what can be called a sum; it's not every day that a group simultaneously reveals its local behaviour, I mean familial, individual, private behaviour, in each person's own place and in parallel, a global custom: in the public square is the collective integration of every-body's customs. The city receives in sum, the citizens receive apart. And this is the same action, and these are the parts of the sum. Such a harmony of public and private life, in Rome or elsewhere, is extremely rare. For it to be clear is even rarer. Here then is the global meal of local meals, the total feast of particular suppers, the integral comedy of singular comedies. I understand 'comedy' literally, that is to say, in the sense of a banquet.

Is the aim of the rite summation? Have we struck upon a figurative case, precious because of its rarity, of the passage from the local to the global and from multiplicity to unity? A constellation of suppers are unitarily ordered around the lectisternium. The multiple becomes one; it is represented in one. Is this the foundation, once again? Is this a foundation, once more, without death? Is this the represented foundation? Is this the moment when politics and history leave sacrifices for the stage of the theatre, leave corpses for mannequins, leave death for representation?

Enter everyone: take and eat. Time flows back from Friday to Thursday.[1]

The day of wrath and tears is calmed; here is the day of grace, of welcome. By day of wrath I mean the state in which everyone is hostile to everyone. Two states are to be defined. If everyone is a wolf to everyone, unleashed wolves run in Rome, and every Roman is the son of a she-wolf to every Roman. There are only wolves in the city, naked, as during the Lupercalia, or dressed in wool as every day. That is the state of nature Thomas Hobbes talks about. I don't really know how things are with nature, but it's the usual state for the city of Rome: wolves. I think we can speak here of war, so much is war order and rule. If it isn't the war of all against all it's the plague. The epidemic plague, threatening the collective body with extinction. The plague runs and threatens everyone, without known order, without foreseeable rule. No one knows any longer who is wolf. That is therefore the state of plague, frequent moments of crisis, in which even the struggle of orders is no longer sufficient to fix violence; that is the state of plague beneath the state of war, a disordered state beneath diverse ordered states, a state of plague that's so common it can be said to be natural in the most common sense. And here is its opposite, during the week of the lectisternium when the gods fixedly feast.

Everyone is no longer the enemy of everyone else; everyone is rather their plague. No one knows who carries the plague, who gives it, who receives it. The enemy is the enemy, hereditary, familial, personal; he is recognized, ordered, foreseeable. It's easy to be wary of him. When everyone is the plague of everyone else, all order has vanished, all foreseeability is erased. Everyone passing through the door is carrying contagious hatreds. Here is the opposite state, on the day of welcome. Whoever you are, whatever your hatred or your breath may be, whatever germs you are transporting, enter and be blessed. Rome was the city of unleashed wolves. Rome was the city of the invisible and unforeseeable plague. The city of wolves is still a city, and Rome has proved this; Rome has found Thomas Hobbes' mistake. Rome can't endure being the city of plague. So it reverses its customs. It doesn't reverse its behaviour due to acts of war or crimes of predatory wolves; it only reverses them due to acts of plague. So Rome is no longer in Rome; it is entirely hospitality. Everyone is everyone else's *hôte*, even though everyone might be the enemy. And the language says: it's the same person. And the language says: it's the same state. Notice the strong parallel between the local and the global, or the private and the public; the custom lets us see something simple: everyone, the *hôte* of everyone, is a god to everyone. Man is a god to man. And the wolf has become god.

Let's not listen to the philosophers; let's examine what happens. There is no state, nor any wide or long succession of rare states. There is no slow grand law ordering time. The state of plague, the state of war, the state of hostility, the state of hospitality succeed one another here quickly enough; they often come back, mixed. The pact is made, unmade; it collapses, is reconstituted. The wolf becomes god, the god becomes wolf, the god-wolf becomes plague, and the plague dies down, page after page or time after time, quickly, in a disquieting chain of crossfades.

Take a look again: the gods are public guests, the unknown people are private guests. Are the gods unknown? The gods are invited by the city; the foreigners are invited by each citizen. Are the gods foreigners? The gods are feasting in public. The enemies are feasting here in private houses. Are the gods enemies? Those who are invited by everyone are known and unknown, neighbours or foreigners, friends and enemies. Are the gods close neighbours too, who pass by and who enter, who stay, who leave, known since named Jupiter or Latona, but unknown, never seen? Are they close and distant, friendly, protective, beneficial, and thunderbolting enemies? The answer to all these questions is affirmative, and the nature of the divine begins to appear. The divine is terrifying; it is there, present at my table; it has been known to me forever, as familiar to me as myself in my solitude; it is unknowable to me, as incomprehensible as it is possible to be.

The supper of statues, or the stone feast is the collective sum in the public square of everyone's meals, with open tables. The gods are the guests of Rome; I know which ones are the guests of everyone. The gods therefore are the sum of the guests. God is therefore my neighbour and the sum of those close to me, the first comer who rings and the sum of encounters; God is the other and the sum of others; he is my enemy, the set of my enemies, at the same time the singular known and the global sum of what I don't know, the local unknown and the sum of my knowledge. God is the link of the same to the other; he is the integration of the local to the global; he hooks together the places torn apart by the excluded middle; today he hooks hostility to hospitality. Conversely: the first comer, the foreigner, the enemy, the neighbour, the person adhering to me better than I could adhere to myself, all of them, together and in their sum, are gods.[2]

The stone feast invites the gods during the week of the lectisternium when everyone invites everyone else. Who is god? Everybody. Everyone is the god of everyone else. And, through integration, man is a god to man. The single wolf, Romulus, became God, single, through the *diasparagmos*. The wolves, unleashed in the city of wolves, sons of she-wolves all of them, become gods today at the banquet: all of them.

If man is a wolf to man, only one value is thought. Friend, enemy. A value on the left and an identical value on the right, as though by symmetry. Wolf, lamb. Nothing can equal the hatred of the lamb, unless it's that of the wolf, except that the lamb's hatred in addition compensates for its lack of fangs. Everyone has one value and only one for everyone. But if man is a god to man, many values are thought at once, friend and enemy, close and distant, hôte. Or rather: friend and distant, guest and unknown, enemy and known, victim and invitee, whoever. God is not the opposite, the reverse, the converse, the contradictory of the wolf; he is the recruitment, the amalgam, the alloy of values. The amalgam or the statue, the statue cast in alloy. If you are my god you have every possible value, and you can be wolf and lamb, in particular. If you are god you are without any third. Without the third of exclusion. If you are god you are endowed with the included third.

God is not the inverse, it is not the opposite of the wolf. The opposite of the wolf is an opposite wolf. They have the same wet muzzle; they wag the same tail; they show the same fangs. The opposite of evil is an opposite evil; the opposite of violence and murderous cruelty is a symmetrical and twin horror. Rome is full of wolves, by pairs; the history of the city is ceaselessly dotted with such pairs. No, the lectisternium is not the opposite of the Lupercalia; these statues of reclining gods are not the opposite of wolves. Love is not the inverse, the opposite of hatred. If you are a god to me and if I am beginning to love you, you are at the same time my most immediate and my most distant neighbour, the most unknown of foreign beings; you are my closest guest, you are also the she-wolf, hostile. The she-wolf is in god; hatred is in love; war is in the plague, as hostility remains in hospitality. God is of every value, including the single value wolf; love is of every value, including the value hatred; the lectisternium is everything, including the Lupercalia. 'I love you' says: you are my father, my mother, my ancestor from the depths of time, my sister, my brother, my female twin, my daughter, my son, my final descendant; you are the other and the unknown woman of my family, and you are the foreign woman whose language I can't understand; you pass by and enter, unrecognizable. 'I love you' doesn't specify place; 'I love you' doesn't exclude anything, lets everything in, is ignorant of status, determination. If you are only my female twin, I recognize that I hate you; if you are only my mother, if you are only my daughter, if you are only a foreign woman, I know that I hate you. Hating is bringing the omnitude of values down to a single one; hating is reducing a god to a wolf; hating is folding every position over a single one; hating ravages the possible; hating is determining, negatively defining a single element in the inclusive possible of love. Hatred is at the heart of knowledge, which always begins with double negations. Loving contains hating in its bouquet of omnitude; loving takes the risk of hatred and place; the god is in danger of the wolf; love risks knowledge in the carillon of possibilities. Hating and knowing are perhaps coextensive; loving includes knowledge the way philosophy, well named, surrounds science. Hatred is assignation of place and site. Hatred is not merely antithesis; it is already the thesis. Love is the geometral of places and sites; it is god.

The two states, plague and war, are differentiated as follows. In war, the elements are globally ordered, and they are locally alike; war is a homogeneous state. Class struggle or the combat of orders, *certamen ordinum*, causes division to appear: the classes are in conflict; combat makes the classes. Order always appears in and through war. War produces classification; it renders everything monotonic. How, it is asked, did the plebs form? The answer is simple and clear. The plebs appear as plebs, to themselves as to their adversaries and the historians, it is constituted as a class or an order through struggle, through the war against the Fathers; combat, little by little, makes it be born, models it, forms and defines it. Rome itself in turn only knows unity through waging war ceaselessly against the Aequi or the Hernici. The city as such comes undone in peace. That is the global order; this is the singular monotony: nothing is more like a military man than another legionary; in the uniform and arms of the soldier, they are exactly the three hundred and six Fabii. The history of the *gens Fabia* is as good as a long theory; the nobiliary group departs for war like an abstraction. A multiplicity in conflict is always more or less this family, this concept. Better: combat makes a diverse multiplicity a united family; war subsumes it under conceptual unity; the fight makes it into a concept. Conversely, when you encounter a concept, look first for what violence, what war, what hatred crystallized it. It is often only some concretion of hatred. The three hundred and six armed Fabii, a patrician order, a nobiliary class, a family, a concept, have lost the multiple; they have a single name; they are Rome outside Rome; they are the example, the abstraction, the champion of the unity of war. Three Horatii twins or three hundred and six clones, cloned from hatred and squabble. Engage, and you will be monotonic. The state of war classifies; all classification comes from war; war vitrifies multiplicity; everyone suddenly resembles everyone. Noble blood is not the blood of birth; it is shed blood; this is the class. It suffices for plebeian blood to be shed for the plebs, little by little, to form. The state of war ordered the collective; it reduced the individuals to resemblance.

In the state of plague, no one knows who has the plague; no one knows how to decide who has it and who doesn't, who carries it and who gives it. In the state of war, we are all Horatius or Fabius, plebeian or Veian; we are all in uniform; in the state of plague, we no longer know the for or the against, the close or the distant, the unknown or the known. If war strengthens recognition, the plague destroys it. I encounter the enemy: if he doesn't bring me the plague, he can become my brother, while if my neighbour is an active vector for the epidemic, I stop being his friend. The enemy can be benign; I no longer know who my neighbour is. I don't know if the guest who enters under my roof is going to blow hot or cold. I don't even know if I myself carry a benevolent breath or deadly agony to the one I love and to the one who hates me. The reference points are drowned by the diluvial rise of the pandemic. Everyone is wary of everyone; even the swallows flee one another; love, carrying death, is erased.

The principle of individuation is lost. No one knows who is who; no one any longer knows what he himself is. Dionysian intoxication causes the solitary person to lose his individuation; strictly, it is only the narcosis of Narcissus. He falls asleep in a shady corner; this banquet ends in sleep. But the plague causes everyone to lose their individuation distributively in the set. It's the relations that are affected, the set of reference points and means of recognition that create the individual in the group. Intoxication puts the monads to sleep; the plague causes a network to dissolve. The plague then is more fundamental than intoxication; it precedes it in what is said about the gods Apollo and Dionysus as well as in what was lived at the origin of the theatre. Before representation, the plague, in which the multiple is lost. It's the fleeing of the people; it's the fleeing of the swallows.

The historian marvels at the fact that the plague spares neither Camillus nor the consuls. This again distinguishes the state of war from the state of plague. War spares the great leaders, who rarely die on the front line of battle. Absent from the intense engagement, positioned high in order to observe better, protected by the last square of the old guard, war surrounds them without touching them. The plague doesn't recognize them; it doesn't save them; it doesn't set them apart. Possible victims of the state of plague, the great are safe from the state of war. This is so remarkable that it can be used to define them: always spared by the state of war, the great are designated by the state of plague. They become great through the plague, and they remain so through war. And this is so remarkable that it can be used to define these states better: the leader saves himself from the plague in war; the state of plague is the one the great are wary of; the state of war is the one they take refuge in. The one who understands that he is perhaps going to die from the plague is the one who orders, prepares, directs the war. And he does so from afar so that the multiple will murder the multiple and protect the one. War is the sacrifice of the multiplicities perpetrated by the one. Or rather: when the multiple hurls itself at the one, the name of this action is sacrifice; when the one makes the multiplicity hurl themselves at the multiplicity, the name of this action is war. These are two equilibriums and two representations. The state of plague loses both the one and the multiple, every individuation; it floats between the equilibriums; it floats between the representations.

The social bond in the state of war is easily identifiable. Everywhere identity is recognized. To know who I am myself, it suffices for me to look around myself; to recognize those close to us, those distant, those unknown, it suffices to consider myself. A monotonic class, a well-ordered state, under the sole grip of hatred, a binary logic. The state of war is a limit state; the state of plague is a possible state. This is because the social bond becomes unrecognizable, and each individual takes on a thousand values in it. The collective fills with jokers. The equivalence of hostility and hospitality could be said to be the relation of uncertainty. We have lived moments of history, we know of groups today, in which war is nothing next to this hard uncertainty. In which even the mother has to be wary of her child, in which the lover is never certain of his mistress; we know of regions lastingly poisoned in this way by a political pandemic.

The state of war is a standard state; the state of plague is a non-standard state. Everything is standardized, nothing is standardized. The non-standard state is fundamental. It is so from the epistemological point of view; it is so for human groups, and it is so for the time of history. The foundation is the passage, the foundations are the passages from a non-standardized state to a standardized state. Livy describes wonderfully the great non-standard multiplicities that float, and he keenly observes the transitions between these latter and the standard multiplicities that are ordinarily the only ones marked out. Before writing history, the book of foundations must be described. This book has the many-coloured multiplicities as its object.

Satura, from which we get our 'satire', is what the ancient Romans called a dish garnished with every type of vegetable and fruit, macedoine, jardinière, pudding, stuffing [*farce*], pâté, stew, pot-pourri or hodgepodge, not forgetting the meats. The list of recipes for a mixture is never closed, nor is the list of its names since the cook is in the trade, or art, of mixing. Satire then is a mixture that isn't hidden beneath a binding. The strategy of the amalgam in political matters and the block vote on diverse laws were also called *satura*. So literary satire should be a farce, a composition of separate genres, indeed, what is condemned under the insult of mixing genres. Satire is *The Decameron* during the plague. Which is as good as saying it's rare. As rare as a serious and profound meditation which would have as its support or source a wide variety of scholarly specialities, as rare as a philosophical meditation. In the mixture of foods or laws, of texts or ideas, the elements are neither melted nor chained together.[3]

This Latin satire makes an abundance of differences be near each other. It amazes with its riches; it quickly saturates weak stomachs; they criticize its excesses or its unexpectednesses. Yet it has one merit, that of simplicity: on the plate, it presents an easy, clear and distinct model of non-standard multiplicity, the object of my meditation. It's not very often that an object of philosophy can find its counterpart in a way to prepare a dish or in the wide space of a plate. When I describe a multiple scalene set in which the discernible is best preserved, in which the either global or local unity is retained, deferred, suspended, I don't see any problem if one refers to this

Latin satire, about which the learned agree in scorning its crudeness. It is, as one tastes it, of a high rational delicacy.

It belongs, moreover, to the origin, the same learned agree. We must practise scorning nothing, not even our fathers' dishes. This satire arrives at the origin of the stage games, instituted as remedies for the plague. The state of plague is also a non-standard state. The first of these remedies was the lectisternium, a meal, a feast of reclining gods, a general invitation to every passerby to consider themselves guests. In the beginning is the supper. No one tells us what they eat there. But I know to what extent they eat in comedy; I have known this since 'The Stone Feast'. We shall have to go back over comedy. I imagine that during the lectisternia everything was offered to the gods, just as all that one had was left to all the passersby, including the enemy. The essential thing is this omnitude; it's the feast of totality: not retaining anything of one's goods, not chasing anyone away from one's kindness, not saying anything except welcome, opening the doors and windows. This omnitude is the opposite of exclusion; this opening is the opposite of cutting up, that is to say, of the temple; this latitude is the opposite of purgation. If you lift, in particular, dietary restrictions, you will produce satire in the kitchen. No element is excluded from the dish; no invitee is unwelcome in the house; non-standard multiplicity remains. It resists the excluded third. It is certain, as much as possible, that this dish was offered to the gods. Loathing the mixture of genres or the juxtaposition of thoughts or fruits is the domain of the religious gesture par excellence, of the sacred gesture, exclusion. Everything happens as though the feast at the lectisternium was the discovery of a non-sacred state, or a non-sacrificial one. Everything happens as though non-standard multiplicity too was non-sacrificial, as though standard multiplicity was a remainder of the sacred. At the lectisternium, everywhere and in every home, everyone eats with everyone every kind of vegetable, meat and fruit. In the beginning is the supper. And the supper assembles a diverse multiple; during the course of the meal, satire is served.

In the beginning is satire. In the beginning is non-standard multiplicity. It is going to deviate through sacrifice. We have time again. Exclusion or purgation can only be practised on a prior state that doesn't know them.

Hobbes only thinks the state of war; he only thinks a standard state. The state of war is already under contract; the enemy is discernible and marked out. Hobbes doesn't posit a non-standard plague that would precede war; he can't think a multiplicity of jokers with no individuation.

Hobbes wrote in the seventeenth century. The classical age, or Age of Reason, produced and made infinitesimal calculus triumph. A global system can be decomposed into very little local individuals; it's always easy to trace a path from these little localities to their sum. And this is especially possible since these places more or less resemble each other, since the differential divided parts are never irreducible. Hobbes prepares the classical age; he is its canonical expression in societal matters. The state of war vitrifies space; it renders it monotonic; war prepares the great classical rationality; it makes it possible. The state of war makes a society rational; hatred makes those it fills resemble one another; consequently integration is possible, is easy; it is done. The big animal Leviathan was created by an integral calculus before its discovery; I would like to say that it makes this discovery possible. The Leviathan is formed from standard localities; it is a definite integral. So much hate and war then were necessary for reason to occur. The Leviathan state installs reason. 'Classical' indeed means in line, armed, before meaning a cultural era.

Perhaps we have to generalize. Perhaps there exists an inescapable relationship between the easy integration inside a set and the standard character of its elements. They relate to a standard; they begin to imitate the same ensign. War, violence and hatred immediately succeed in this exploit. They laminate the multiple; consequently the elements become laminar. Let's compare Hobbes and Leibniz: the monster Leviathan is formed by the state of war; the non-standard multiplicity of monads, irreducible singularities, never manage, under harmony, to form a monadology. The path from the individual to God remains a mystery. The Republic of Minds remains peaceful; it is non-standard; it is only metaphysical. Hobbes, I mean the state of war, reduces the monads to resembling one another; the Leviathan, I mean integration, becomes possible. The modern state standardizes, makes standard, laminates the non-standardized. Founding a city consists in standardizing the non-standard.

When the collective is formed, when the city is founded, when a political state appears, a process of standardization begins.[4] I'm seeking to think a prior non-standard state. The set there is not the same; it hasn't already been grasped in categories. Can ways other than these seizings or capturings be imagined? Can society, the social be thought otherwise than in sequential terms, as the very etymology of the word seems to urge? Can we reason directly in the non-standard model, in disequilibrium and not in a state? Can we think, without war, sets that would subsist without standardization? Utopia or new reason? A more subtle and broader new reason, suppler in any case, than the repetitive and slightly stupid rationality of the standard models. Will this new reason free us from the repugnant and ancient alliance of violence and war with our old reason?

I'll return to the state of plague, to the epidemics ravaging Rome, which the Romans are trying to ward off by the feasts of the lectisternium, then by the organization of comedy. In fact, we don't know what happens in that state. I mean that if the history were reporting a recent event, we would be clear about said disease. But here, the same discourse – the narrative of uncertainty in which hospitality can abruptly turn to hostility as to an opposite excess, and reciprocally – the same remark is valid whether it's a question of a social crisis or whether it's a question of an authentic epidemic. The words say this equivalence.

The words say the law, the law of the plague, during the week of the lectisternium. It's the same law for a spy or for a germ. Here is the parasite. He is the neighbour that's been invited, or the foreigner, the guest in any case. He is *pasteurella pestis*, a contagious microbe. He is this tiny noise that's so difficult to eliminate that causes me to confuse, when I hear his name, the one who has nothing but hostility for me and the one who displays hospitality to me. The same medical, social, verbal law, the same behaviour, the same physical, hygienic, political, religious narrative, the same interruptions in logic and language, the same abrupt leaps. Whatever the cause or reason, the phenomenon is the same. A strange bridge thrown from nature to culture, from an unhealthy and harsh temperature, from the appearance of a virus, to practices at the table or altar, to private or public manners. A strange passage from knowledge to a very archaic age, from usages proper for healing to hospitable mores. This passage from the hotel to the hospital is the one I have named the Northwest Passage.[5] Here the archaeology of the passage from objective knowledge to the social sciences and vice versa is said.

I don't know if the plague took place, I mean the epidemic, the coming of the microbe, its multiplication, the buboes and the dead. The great mass of corpses that year isn't enough to decide if there had been a real plague. A crisis is enough, one of those that spreads in the social body like a plague epidemic, by analogous laws, to get the same result.

At least if the plague did take place, they didn't cure it by the lectisternium. Or the stage games. But yes, they did cure it. So the plague was the state of plague, the one I have described in relation to the state of war. So the rite was enough; we will call it general hospitality.

I don't see how the state of war might stop; I don't see any reason for it to stop. Nor does it stop. It has redundancy for it, the power of repetition.

History, as everyone has said, is simply coextensive with the state of war. This is true; it's enough to make you sick.

I see how the state of plague stops. I see it clearly in the description of the state. I don't see how the contract would descend into the middle of war. I don't see who would draw it up; I don't see who would be the subject of the general will, whether it be the sum or not of particular wills. It is true that it is easy to arrive at a sum if all the singular wills want the same thing without distinction. This is rarely the case. The question of the sum is the question of their differences. In a standard model, the question of the sum is trivial. In brief. The state of plague stops by perpetuating itself. General hostility is close, infinitely close to general hospitality. In our ignorance of who is who, friend or hostile, including ourselves, we might as well open the doors wide. Might as well open our doors when we know that the doors no longer protect us. When defence is no longer possible, what good is defence? When we no longer know how to wage war nor who to wage it against, what good is war? When theory itself doesn't know what the general will is, practice quickly knows how general hospitality is made. Here the day has come; here the week of the lectisternium has begun. The gods are at the feast; they form the symbolic sum of particular feasts; the gods are invited by the city; they form the abstract sum of singular hospitalities. All that is mine belongs to all. And the contract is the meal.

On this day, the sum and the different elements, the gods and the dwellings are seen at once; it's the day of general hospitality, when the social contract, the social meal can be seen.

I don't know if the real plague really took place. We are beginning a make out a little of the history of epidemics, the importance of sources of infection, the large movements of vectors and microbes. Rome was founded on a swamp; the environment for a long time was fairly unhealthy; Rome knew how to build sewers as its cloacas; the Gauls who held Rome succumbed above all to pestilence. They didn't succumb to war, but they did succumb to the plague. What plague are you talking about? Perhaps one day we will be told what the Roman armies owed to pernicious germs for their victories, their conquests and the immense number of dead before their advance. Power spreads pandemically: this can be a figure of speech, this can be true. This Italian site was surrounded by swamps; its inhabitants were accustomed to microbes. So, under some consul or other, a plague rages. What is it? Is it a variety of some epidemic? Did the Romans die covered with buboes, vomiting white secretions and burning with malignant fever? Is it an indication of a recurring return to a social state of exasperated crisis? To a societal disequilibrium?

These two states require two thoughts; these thoughts demand in their turn to be thought together. One is from physiology, the other is political; one is medical, the other is social; one seems turned toward the object, the other seems entirely immersed in relations. Let's return a little to religion. It reveals the same gap; it seems to want to hold both ends of the chain. For religion is natural; at stake are atmospheric phenomena, rain, thunder, earthquakes, daylight; it has to do with human conduct, crises and lynchings, sacrifice, *diasparagmos*; it also says my relation to the father. The peasant prodigies, the devotion in the forum, the name of the Capitoline god together show this hook fastener, this brooch, this fibula that attaches as best as possible two separate panels of cloth, that attempts to hook together two elements that don't fit well together. Religion connects the tatters of an open rag.

The plague is a disease of the body; it's an accurate image for a certain social state. Either it refers to an object that's fairly independent of us, a germ or a virus, or it refers to the remarkable relations in which hospitality mixes with hostility, welcome with death. In both cases, everyone can die; for these two reasons, the group runs the risk of extinction. This identity, this confusion of names and dangers, causes and effects, requires a bit of reflection. Yes, the wolf accuses the lamb of having poisoned the river upstream to better devour him, juridically; it remains that the lamb could be suffering from sheep pox. There is an object, a boil, in the epizootic, as well as an object, a microbe, in the epidemic.

Never does the object appear as long as the collective is fascinated only with itself. It is most often fascinated in this way; it's not a question of time, date, culture or history, it's its equilibrium and its attraction. The group delights in the group; it isn't capable of observing the world. Or the world is never anything for it but a projection of its relations. So the gods are only of the city. So the city is only sick from the breaking down relationships Romans maintain with Romans. So history doesn't take the world into account. So history only says plague for crisis, germ for hatred, earthquake for insurrection, and rain of flesh for the rapid dismemberment of a seized victim. The object doesn't exist. This archaic idealism is a terrible equilibrium, a permanent, recurring equilibrium, I was going to say an animal one, but I don't know anything about beasts. Man, they say, is a political animal; this simply signifies that the exclusively political man is bestial, I mean to say attached, tied, bound without recourse or any other horizon to the internal relations of the group. He is a pure idealist, the one for whom an object is nothing other than social representation. I think – but I could be wrong – I think that this is why animals, even the superior ones, even the ones living in a strong collectivity, never have an object. When the object appears, another man appears.

It was no doubt necessary that certain people had to go far, very far from the clutches of the collective, very severely detaching themselves from the relational servitude, breaking their political equilibrium with an inexpressible heroism in order to find the object. The group is nothing but closed. There is no open society. Those who step over the limit go toward what is not the group. This voyage is so difficult it passes for incomprehensible, so difficult many moralists say it's impracticable and blameworthy, so difficult that those who make this journey are often put to death. These voyagers go to the object; they are born to and in the world. Then the groups open to reabsorb them as well as the objects. These objects don't stay independent of relations for long. The time that they are so is the time of discovery. Suddenly the plague has a virus for its cause, a virus having few relations to our relations. This objective knowledge is hidden by the knowledge that the collective tries to learn about itself. Knowledge of our relations implies ignorance of the world, and knowledge of the world implies ignorance of our relations. Since the world is nothing but an aggregate or projection of our relations for the first knowledge, since the second knowledge has to detach itself from them to reach the world. The worldly social world covers over the worldwide objective world with its noise, and the latter world is only discovered in the desert. In other words, idealism is the rule; realism is only a fairly rare singularity. But only realism is hominid. We never become human except by means of objects. We remain animals through our representations. Humans are animals who have found the object.

So under one consul or another, the plague rages. It's reasonable to think that Rome is in a state of crisis. It's not excluded that there might be an epidemic. Likewise for the prodigies: an earthquake is an insurrection, but it's not excluded that the earth might quake. This link poses a problem that I'll resolve a little further on.

The name Jupiter contains the name for daylight and the name for father.

I'm looking for the Northwest Passage; I'm looking to connect the exact sciences and the social sciences; I'm looking for the passage between theories of the object, the systems of the world, and theories of the subject, the systems of relations between people. I'm probing the ford between nature and history. It isn't possible that there is no world; it isn't possible that there is nothing but world.

Jupiter is a name; he is an image; he is a person, a symbol, a concept, and I know not what else. Jupiter is a god.

Jupiter, first of all, is the daylight. That means a time, a light, a beauty, a set of phenomena that take place without us. This day is not one of wrath; it is one of nature, and it is objective.[6] *There have been, there will be days without me; there have been, perhaps there will be days without any of us. Jupiter is a god of the world, Greatest. Light, lightning, time.*

Jupiter, next, is the father. Perhaps he's the father of the gods and men, perhaps he is their prince and king, perhaps he is so for me. We, of this group or of this city, of Rome, of the family, we, perhaps, of humanity, we call Jupiter – a god – by the ancient name of father. That means our relationships, our relations of society, of engendering, of authority, of majestic dignity. Jupiter is a god of men, Best.[7]

Jupiter is a god, religious. What is a god here? What is religion?

Every religion, it was said, comes from the feeling of being overwhelmed humans have in front of nature. The gods are the intentions of the lightning, the subject who holds the thunderbolt, the power of germination, the irresistible surging of spring, the dark and cold terrifying entrails of the earth. The gods are astronomy, atmospheric phenomena, genetics, agrarian and pastoral activities, the elements. In other words, religion is physics in its nascent state, archaic. Invent the hard sciences, and you will no longer have religion. In other words, Jupiter vanishes into an electrostatic short-circuit. And so on. No god stands behind lightning, nor in the middle of the daylight. Our enlightenment erased the daylight god.

And yet, the father remains. The entire secular effort of the natural sciences will not prevent me from kneeling in front of the father my father worshiped or in front of the prince of the city. We have to begin again. The physicalist explanation of our religions has been declining for a century; the text of the Flood no longer poses many questions to the physicists of the globe, but it does pose some to theorists of collective violence; we no longer look for its truth in geological strata, but rather in social crises. And so on. Consequently, religions are the social sciences in their nascent state, archaic. And the gods are no longer anthropomorphisms of the rain, the lightning and the four seasons, but rather condensations of familial, tribal, social relations, Best Jupiter, father and king. Invent the social sciences, and you will no longer have religion. In other words, Jupiter vanishes behind the image of the father, behind the schema of the social organization or of cultural history, before the violence of those who thus engender the sacred.

I'll begin again. The name Jupiter contains the name for daylight and the name for father.

I now know enough physics to no longer be afraid beneath the lightning bolt. I have learned or created too much social science to let myself go with the collective pathos any longer. Jupiter is no longer the daylight; Jupiter is no longer the father. It sometimes happens that he is the father for those who know the light of day with exactitude; it sometimes happens that he is the daylight for those who know the hidden workings and forces of symbols. Those who are saturated with relationships worship nature, those who master nature sometimes worship relationships. Everyone carries the myth of his complementary ignorance. Does the educated third no longer have gods? Will he no longer have gods? God is no longer nature; God is no longer history either.

Perhaps Jupiter was not the god of daylight, perhaps Jupiter was not the father, perhaps he was god in order to be both. The troubling question is not that of light or lightning, is not merely knowing how we are together, the question remains of understanding that our relations take place in the bright clarity of the day. We are immersed in the collective as in a black box; our group is immersed in the world, and it's this double immersion that poses the third question. Jupiter is the daylight, a phenomenon of the world; Jupiter is the father, the princely relation of the collective; Jupiter is at the same time daylight and father, god of nature and god of society, god for putting together what no doubt has no relation.

We are seeking to resolve one or the other of the first questions; we are blind and clear-sighted at the same time: learned in the order of the world and unconscious of our relations, or very enlightened in regard to our relations and forgetful of every object. Even assuming that, wise, we were advancing with an even step in the third knowledge of nature and history, it would remain to master their relation. Religion is the knowledge in its nascent state, archaic, of this link. Jupiter is the father, and he is the daylight; he is the god of the link of culture to nature, the god of the connection between the human world and the inert forces. Religion is the very link, the very relation, the black connection between the two seas and the two continents; it is the Northwest Passage to the first state, ancestral; it is the matrix or womb of the third education, as it was the mother of the first two. Jupiter is the hook fastener of the father to the light; he is this incomprehensible connection. Religion is this ancient alliance.

Once again, we have to understand an ancient black knowledge.

Jupiter, daylight. Religion is first of all the set of natural sciences in their nascent state. The emergence of said sciences causes it to disappear. Conversely, they have an interest in interpreting it as being their archaism. Jupiter, father. Religion is second of all the set of social sciences in their nascent state. The *emergence of said sciences causes it to disappear. Conversely, they have an interest in interpreting it as their archaism. The first case is that of the Enlightenment; it continued during all of the 19th century, while the second one, starting last century, occupies this one.*

Jupiter, daylight and father. Religion is third of all the passage between the set of the objects of the world and the set of relations between men, from nature to culture, from the world to history, from the natural sciences to the social sciences, in their nascent state. This passage is in two directions; it also opens from our histories to nature. From the daylight to the father and from the father to the daylight. Religion is the first hook fastener, the archaic fibula, which creates one vague coat from these two rags. Will recognizing this passage between said sciences cause the religions to disappear again? Are we going toward new interpretations? The relation of the daylight to the father and of the father to the daylight is what I've called the Northwest Passage, or the third education. Jupiter is third between the father and the daylight; he is their copula.

Jupiter, daylight and father, again and lastly. Religion is fourthly the knowledge of knowledge, in its nascent state, and that is one of this book's outcomes. We have separated logic and myth for so long that it seems to us that only logic explains myth. But myth is logic in its nascent state: lucidity, the light of day or genealogy, on the father's side. But logic is too poor a word. Epistemology is too ugly a word; gnoseology is too rare a word. Myth, religion – dense with physical knowledge and interpretable by it, dense with social knowledge and interpretable by it, dense with relations between the one and the other and interpretable by them – are fourthly dense with knowledge in its nascent state of the functioning of knowledge. We never cease, in this book, to recognize its constellations, from the constitution of the object to the strategies of the associated ignorance, to the principal elements of composite spaces. Jupiter, still there, is the father of a certain daylight.

Religion never ceases to resurrect, after the announcements of its death.

The reclining gods at the feast unite, link the social plague and the physical plague, blindly.

The week during which the gods feast on the public beds was invented to ward off the state of plague, whether microbial or societal; a single religious act speaks about it in two voices. It doesn't always appear to be effective; the plague continues; general hospitality is a refined state, in disequilibrium. So Rome passes on to stage games. The bed of the lectisternium is the first scene.

The origin of the spectacles follows a sequence that's marvelous in its simplicity. Before some game is seen on the stage, the god lies on his bed, an immobile mannequin. And the game will begin when the statue stands up. When the corpse dances. Before the stage game, the lectisternium; before general hospitality, the plague. In the beginning is the plague. The plague is a non-standard state. I have imagined that at the stone feast and the private suppers satire was eaten, with a non-standardized recipe. General hospitality doesn't chase anyone away; it's the feast without any excluded third; it's the omnitude fair; it's the non-standard week.

This state is delicate. The standard state is one of equilibrium. An irresistible slope leads to standardization. Here is the beginning of the scene, the pantomime. The young people imitate the dancer. Through gestures and grimaces, dance, without language, the mimicry communicates. But who is the dancer, the first dancer, who has just stood up? I'm going to tell; I'm going to devote myself to thinking how the dance begins. Here, in the original theatre that is not yet a theatre, is the moiré, many-coloured multiplicity, the irreducible crowd of the state of plague during the seven days of omnitude. Pantomime is an operation of standardization. It is powerful, fast, effective; it causes the passage from the non-standardized state to a more unitary state. Yes, it's a foundation. The origin of the games is one foundation of Rome. The origin of the spectacle, of the representation, is a political foundation. The foundation amounts to equilibrium, standardization.

Who is the dancer? He is called the *ludio*. He has a Greek name; he comes from Etruria. At the origin, everything comes from foreign lands. We suspected so. During the seven days of general hospitality, we must assume that foreigners are travelling all over the city. Whoever you are, enemy or friend, enter and be blessed. The *ludio* is one of the jokers the city is full of. An example: during the games of Neptunus Equester, under king Romulus, the city is crisscrossed with Sabin men and women. An example: during the games that took place at the time of Coriolanus' exile, the city is crisscrossed with Volsci. The hospitality offered to the Sabines turns against the Sabine women; the Sabine men become enemies. The Volsci leave Rome in a pitiful file, quasi-driven out; they will return to lay siege to it under the orders of Coriolanus. The *ludio*, come from Etruria, has been invited, like a Sabine or a Volsci. The games follow the lectisternium; the foreigners are there. What's going to happen to them?

Who is the dancer? He's called the *ludio*. The ancient form of *ludus* – game, ludic activity – seems to be *lœdus*, which was used at least once by Cicero. The corresponding Greek seems to be λοιδορία [loidoria], a harsh reproach, a hurtful term of abuse. The game, whether word or practice, is one of making fun of the *ludio*, of laughing while ridiculing him. The *ludio* becomes the plaything of the surrounding crowd. I am almost certain that the learned will reproach me for evoking the word λοιμός [loimos], the plague, quite close to λοιδορία. The games in which the *ludio* is on the stage begin in order to ward off the plague.

In the beginning is the plague. The *ludio* dances on the stage; derision is hurled at him, it is said, imitating him all the while. He is covered with verbal abuse. Only with verbal abuse. Should words become stones, he is no longer the *ludio*; he is Tarpeia. He falls. He has fallen. Stiff. So, the statue, immobile, on the stage, on the bed, is invited to feast. It's the stone feast. Hospitality ceases, it becomes hostility; hostility ceases, and it's hospitality.

Who is the dancer? The statue of the commander has just stood up. Who is the dancer? A resurrected god. Apollo returning, Dionysus returned. Gods of plague. Apollo rises, Neptune rises, on horseback; Apollo and Neptune lie down, statues.

Who is the dancer? A Volscian, a Sabine? No. When the Sabines return, it's war; when the Volsci turn around commanded by Coriolanus, it's a crushing. Hospitality again becomes hostility: return to the state of war.

The invention of the stage games is a new solution for a warlike people, who previously had only ever had circus games.

We need to go back a little. To war and the circus.

Georges Dumezil, following Vegetius or others, contrasts the Roman legion, lined up, coherent, tightly-knit, monotonic, in lines and columns, with the Celtic hero hurling his singular challenge in a state of fury. This is speaking of gesture before speaking of war; this is above all speaking of the spectacle and representation, of the theatre of operations. Is it speaking of dance? Perhaps. The Celtic schema in which the multiple comes toward the one can be called a star, and the Roman drawing in which the multiple becomes unitary via order is a grid. The analysis opposes the star to the grid; we are on the stage assuredly.[8]

The hero moves forward at the challenge, drunk with ire. A space is left for him. All eyes watch, fascinated. He is going to kill, he is going to die. He becomes intoxicated, they say, with a vengeful wrath to kill. His eyes flash like lightning: with fury or fright? His body trembles and seems to dance: with fury or anxiety? I don't know. All I know comes from the word *furor*, fury. Its Greek root is θύω [thuó], to sacrifice. *Furor* is the pre-sacrificial state. The hero has the choice either to kill or to die, but for the spectators, the enjoyment is equivalent; it's death in both cases. For him, the terror is equivalent. Enjoying terror, this is tragedy.

A space is left for the hero, drunk with ire. This space in which he is seen is the first theatre. All eyes turn, fascinated, toward this vertiginous well of attraction. Nothing is as interesting as a combat; nothing impassions like death. Let's make no mistake, the first spectacle is murder. Here the first circus is depicted, before the Romans and the Albans come to blows: everyone watches Horatius and the Curiatii bleed on the duelling grounds. Murder attracts men the way a nauseating odour attracts flies. I say men in this situation, all men universally. I don't know if there is a human nature; I'm not the master of concepts, but I do know that sometimes we can speak of men, of all men together. This is now the case. The combat and the putting to death attract mimicry. So the collective is standardized. It becomes monotonic like the Roman legion. Unanimous. If you don't have anything interesting to say, attack or say that you're being attacked. If you don't have anything interesting to write, kill or say that you're being killed. Everyone will surround you to look at you. This is the theatre of success. For men love to see killing. You'll be a hero. A victim or a murder, Curiatius or Horatius. Desire is nothing next to this attraction. Should a naked woman as beautiful as Venus appear, eyes would hardly turn aside; should a common brawl break out, all business ceasing, the crowd comes a-running. This is how things are. Human worms feast on this. No, the gladiators don't reveal a declining Rome; no, from the beginning Horatius and the Curiatii are already gladiators; no, the gladiators endlessly repeat the origin of the spectacle, the atrocious origin of tragedy, its ordinary, everyday origin. The proud hero, fuming, sparkling, braided out, decked out, green with fear, red with anger, yellow with fright, ignoble, terrifying, terrified, faces his peer hero; he kills, he shows, he presents the slaughter, and he represents it by killing again, again and again, twice, three times, Horatius and the Curiatii. The space of combat is the first stage; the companions-in-arms, panting, in suspense, moved by fear and terror and pity are the first audience.

The origin of the theatre is not always in the places the theorist says it is; it resides in the places the narrative involuntarily recounts. Narrative is often complete theory, and theory is often a thinned-down narrative. Tragedy and representation are so formidably present in Livy that his narrative is a treasure trove for tragedians. Corneille and Shakespeare didn't have much trouble cutting their poems out from it; they were already there, living and entire. The hero, on the other hand, is the representative of the army; for proof just look at how it flees if its actor gets the worst of it. The hero of the Roman legion has the virtue of being just anyone; he is so unexceptional that he is substitutable; each of them can come out of the ranks if need be. The legionary is the first comer. Each of them is thus representative. The Roman is more representative than the Gaul, again. More indifferently substitutable. More mimetic. More twin. So more theatrical. The one of the multiple is the exact definition of representation. The staging is much better in the legion.

And now open your eyes. Every Celt, stirred, follows his unique champion with his gaze. The multiple-one relation is polar; around the hero a star is drawn. Each Roman, squeezed in the compactness of the lines and columns, is at the centre of a star passing through the columns, lines and diagonals. This is the same schema, more complete. Each point of the legion, each element of the grid is a star; each Roman is a Celtic hero. That which was to be demonstrated.

I doubt that the real work of force, de facto military exercise, can be seen here. It's a staging. This soldier people was gifted at theatre. Already. Nevertheless I don't doubt that staging is the essential thing in the military profession. The show of force in the theatre of operations is most often the entire battle. If you want peace, prepare for war. This means: if you're terrified of fighting, show your teeth. Are they chattering? Show that you bite. Are you only Matamore? Play El Cid. If you're afraid of fighting, say that you're going to, shout it out, show that you want to. Grimace, roar. May your hatred exhaust itself, with your fear, in representation. Conversely, representation is entirely hatred and fear. The Romans did this better than anyone, and visibly they knew that the distance from the actor to the warrior is nil, that El Cid and Matamore are twins to the point that you can't tell them apart, that the difference between the military man or the militant and the stage producer is undeterminable.

Someone said it much better than all of us historians or philosophers or abstractors of quintessence; someone recounted it in a scene en abyme in which the concepts are dressed in a long white robe slowly moving forward on a bent over old man or in bright leather breeches running under a sharp and cutting profile.[9] The observer, hidden behind a curtain streaming with imperial bees, puts himself into the scene. And the scene, like every successful comedy, like every perfect tragedy, is the origin of the theatre. Nothing is ever recounted on the stage but the beginning of the stage. A soldier, violent, must be there. Mars must be there. Violence must change into the sacred there, Jupiter. A *ludio*, dancing, must be there. A white statue, immobile, must be there. Everything speeds up. And here is Jupiter, god himself, the pope. And here is Mars, Mars in person, Bonaparte. And Bonaparte dances around Jupiter – sorry, Pius VII – immobile with his hands clutching the eagles of his armchair. The pope lets out a word that causes the fury of Mars to explode, drunk with ire. Lightning thunders, the hurricane rages, all the furies of the great military man are released. A new word. These two words passing in the short-circuit of Jupiter and Mars, of violence and the sacred, of the dancing *ludio* and the divine immobile statue are the instauration words of the stage games: *commediante, tragediante*.

Why did Vigny, in his profound and withdrawn, unknown and scorned philosopher's genius, leave the all too beautiful part to the sacred statue? Why didn't martial violence, in deflating its outward show of anger, itself let out a little noise too, the meaning of Jupiter's game? The hidden observer shows us Mars as comic, then tragic, El Cid as Matamore – there is no war any longer; but he only shows us tragic Jupiter, with a tear running down the statue of this dying Christianity leaving the world to chance: *tragediante*. These two bodies, Pius VII, Bonaparte, these two bodies, Mars and Jupiter, these two bodies, the warrior, the histrione, these two bodies, the statue, the *ludio*, these two bodies form only a single body in the chain of crossfades of time. Violence becomes sacred. It passes on to the theatre.

This theatre was new for this warlike people, who had until then only known circus games. Everything happens as though, seeking an archaeology of the law of arms or of the education of the martial class, Georges Dumezil had struck upon the beginning of the stage games, on the beginning of the circus, on the origin of tragedy, on its current foundation. Current, percurrent, all the way to decline, current, and ordinary, and come all the way down to us.[10] The historian had forgotten Corneille.

The star coming from the one, the hero, *ludio* or legionary, to the multiple, or running in the ordering of the network or the disorder of the crowd toward the one, risen, dancing, furious or combatant, is a simple and powerful operator of standardization. Below the law of arms lies representation. And in representation, pantomime, the work of the mime plays on satire, the work of the standard plays on the non-standard. This is again the foundation.

Let's resume: the plague breaks out; the lectisternium is instituted to treat it; the general hospitality isn't sufficient; stage games are instituted.

Hospitality has just fallen back into hostility. I mean: before the stage games, the circus games sufficed for this warlike people. This is falling back into the state of war. And into its staging. This is where we come from.

Let's return to the lectisternium and its hospitality. The foreigners have returned: Sabines, Volsci or Etruscan. Even Oscans for the Atellan Farces. In brief. The *ludio* has returned; he dances. In the beginning is the dance.

I'll begin again. Who is the dancer?

We are at the beginning, the true beginning. Everything begins with the dance; I must learn how the dance begins.

Rome was precisely making preparations to begin the great games again. They had taken place; Rome begins them again. Why? A sin, a religious sin was committed. It is necessary to start again before the games. As though they hadn't taken place. It is necessary to begin again, or start everything again at the origin. Here we are. What was the sin? It happened before. Before. Before the games took place. It was morning. Early in the morning. Before the start of the spectacle. A procession passes by. A file passes by. In front of the procession is a slave, in front. In front a master driving him on, and punishing him with blows from stirrup straps. The slave is bent over, his head in front. His neck in the middle of a forked yoke.

Rome begins again; it starts again upstream. Before the games, early in the morning, before the start of the spectacle, in front of the procession, with the slave in front, a sin occurred. When you start again, when you want to start off again on the right foot or on the right path, you return beyond the point at which the wrong path was taken. From this upstream, the best method appears. The design of this crossroads appears. The design of the fork appears.

It's the forked yoke the slave wears around his neck.[11] We have gone back far enough to discover the bifurcation point. The problem of origins is a question of bifurcation.

Everything begins with the dance; I must learn how the dance begins.

A prodigy, a rare dream, a divine word comes without necessity at the beginning of Coriolanus' chanson de geste. Here, the narrative turns its back on every theory about the origin of the theatre; it's a question there of instauration. Of instauration, that is to say, of origin, and also of the games, that is to say, of representation. It's a matter, as I've said several times in introduction, it's a matter of a recommencement for a failed beginning; this happens in the morning, early in the morning, before the spectacle's opening, in the circus itself, almost without witnesses. A father, a master, passing through the circus, is driving a slave in front, a forked yoke around his neck, with lashes of stirrup straps. The first procession, in the dawn, in the empty circus, with the victim in front. The first file. The slave being tortured is in the centre of the space; he is at the beginning of this time. He is the bearer of the sin, of the sin denounced by Jupiter. This is the point where everything bifurcates.

In a dream, Jupiter says that he didn't like this first dancer. The god even calls him a dancer, the god even puts him at the head; the god is right; the dream explains the thing itself. Everything begins with the dance, and the dance begins with gestures of horror, of suffering, of instinctive pain; stiff, abrupt, disordered gestures of defence made by the victim during the instant his body is dying, an indescribable epilepsy, spasms, fits, shaking, convulsions, contractions.

Everything begins with the dance; a few people are going to speechlessly imitate the disordered sequence of these horrible contortions. It's the god who is right; he saw that the dying body dances under the whip. This is how the dance begins.

Livy farther on teaches us the origin of the stage games. He treats this question by talking about this question. Five books earlier, he is talking about something else, but he turns to the games and religion. So without thinking, he brings us to the circus, not to the circus seen, but to the circus dreamed, not to the merely human spectacles, but to the representations such as can be seen through the intermediary of dream by the master of the gods. This procession, this climb to the divine word is every bit as good as a theory, abstract or historical; it is its equivalent. We discover there the origin and its covering over; we see the beginning and the veils, now transparent, of its ignorance.

Everything begins with the dance; the gods themselves have shown this to us. Jupiter appears in a dream.

Is it more reasonable to explain the dreams than to take them as explanations? We have to look where it is clearest, listen to what is most audible, move away from what makes the most noise. The wars of interpreters are so noisy and confused that the dream seems simpler in comparison.

If the mêlée of theories forms an immense nightmare that's difficult to decipher, some dream might one day permit us to see clearly about it. If the mêlée of the sciences brings back ignorance, what waking dream will inform us?

Titus Latinius, a simple man, a man as ordinary as his quasi-common name indicates, Titus Latinius, a plebeian, had a dream. He saw or thought he saw Jupiter in a dream. Jupiter, the first of the gods, told me to go tell the consuls, the Senate, the first of the city, that the first dancer, at the head of the procession, had danced so poorly he was displeased.

The Ancients had no need for the intermediary of dreams. The other world could appear during the lucidity of the day. The groves were populated with nymphs and the springs with hamadryads; the clearness of the air let them be seen. It was enough to observe, it was enough to listen. I mean: another world exists.

Does another world exist? We laugh at the gods of the world; we laugh at the serious or premonitory dreams that instilled fear in our ancestors. The forests are empty, the willows are alone, space is homogeneous, science is possible.

How is this science possible? It can only be built if some phenomenon of the world is put into relation with some ideality stemming from mathematics. All bodies fall, all bodies have weight: this is not science. They fall according to the parabolic law: that is science. So I say: there exists another world. For the law is not of this world; it is said in another language, not spoken by men.

We have never forgotten the other world. There exists a back-world; it is always there, present and absent. We have need of it; we have changed it; we have kept it: always different, surely, but always the same, perhaps. Is it really us who speak with numbers?

Here are two worlds without any relation, the space of the gods and that of men. Intelligibility is only gained during the moments of tangency between the two spaces. Everything becomes clear in this point through the manifestation; everything is explained by it. And reasonable action can only be undertaken in its light. A man sees a god, a god speaks to a man, apparition, epiphany, intuition or discovery; then and then only is something intelligible; a matter is possible.

Jupiter appears. He could have appeared in the light of waking. But he descends the steps of the dream, the way the plebeian will have to climb the steps of the Senate. Jupiter speaks: a dance has displeased him. That dance of the slave with the forked yoke around his neck, whipped to death, driven by his executioners across the circus. The body of the unfortunate, mad from pain under this torture, was so shot through with agitations, with movements, with contortions of every type, that the excess of suffering brought about disgrace. The sacred has an aesthetic for putting to death.

Everything becomes clear. The dancer is the slave being executed. The man that the god calls a member of the chorus, men call a victim. What the god calls a dance, men call lynching. What Jupiter says is an enigma; what the master did or causes to be done to his slaves is a sin; the putting into relation of the word and the thing is an explanation.

Explanation occurs in and through the short-circuit of this world and the other. Explanation comes in the dream that is this putting into relation.

Everything becomes clear. Jupiter's dancer is the slave put to death. Everything becomes clear; that is to say, we see clarity occur, but where is it going and how, and about what?

After great misfortunes – the death of his son, paralysis – the dreamer understands that he must obey; he goes to the Senate to tell his experience. The consuls and Fathers in turn understand that they have to instaurate the games, to begin them again, the rite having been faulty. Beginning again means going beyond the point, beyond the instant when the sin happened; then departing in a new direction from this point. This sketches the bifurcation. To the right, the wrong road, the old one along which they returned; to the left, the correct one; at the confluence, the crossroads where the paths hesitate. This forms a bifurcation, that is to say, a fork. The fork that, quite precisely, the dying slave wears around his neck.

Everything becomes clear. It's a question of instauration. The body of the victim shows the exact design of the thing to be done; his execution lets it be seen. Instauration in Greek signifies a cross. The design of the cross, the fork, the bifurcation, the point to which one must return, the point from which one must depart again. The schema of the cross, the execution of the cross. This is an image of beginning – in the beginning is the cross. We are going back to the foundations; we are going back to the foundations of Rome. This story, this dream, this paralysis for Latinius, his limbs suddenly free when the recommencement is decided upon – so many variations of the narrative of foundations. So in the beginning is the bifurcation. Rome is never founded enough, solidly enough, deeply enough, in its rules, in its rites, in the right gesture and right rubric. This is how the Roman legend must be read. The city was founded. By whom? How? History? Legend? We don't know very well. So let's begin again. Let's go back a bit to before the crossroads, and take the route again, differently and better. The history is thus swarming with instaurations, with recommencements. It is paralysed, blocked; it departs again after having returned back the way it came. I do believe that the history of Rome is that of its foundations. It's the narrative of foundations. The fork is the simple stitch of its spiralling, looping course, advancing through returns to the beginning. Here the first god, the first citizens of the city, here the first dancer, the start of the games lead back to the forked schema of the beginning, to the bifurcation. Before the origin is that point of hesitation, that undecided point of doubt, from which two paths depart at least and at most, all possible paths. Everything becomes clear. Let's start the games again at the commencement. Let's start the history again at the recommencement. Let's return to the cross, a bit before the cross, that cross the slave put to death is wearing around his neck.

Is everything really clear? It's a process of clarification in any case. What had departed in the wrong direction is being rectified, in return. The rite masters time; it ceaselessly reforms it, through revolutions.

Is everything truly clear? Everything happens as though the consuls, the augurs, the Fathers had deciphered Titus Latinius' dream, a plebeian. The latter went to consult the learned, as has been done for six thousand years. He went to see the masters of language, lying on his pallet, on his litter or divan, and he paid dearly for his experience. Everything happens as though history, that of the master and the slave, had brought its clarity to the god's enigma. It is understood that this enigma is dark and incomprehensible; it is of dream and the night, hidden; it is the son's death and the father's paralysis; it is clear that history is clear; it is of the real and the day. The clarification can only go in one direction. From theoretical knowledge to the vision, from the day to the night, from history to the enigma.

We will have ended up making an entire generation believe that all this furious madness of fighting to the death, of wars with millions of deaths, of fierce competition, blood and tears, that all this madness of slaughter, collective or familial, is the real, is the depths of the real. And what if on the contrary history, and the imbecilic hierarchies, and the absurd race for power, and the accounts of the economy, and the murders were only nightmares next to which Latinius' dream, yours and mine, would be ordinary and simple realities? And what if, for once, the dream explained what is prejudged to be real? And what if we reversed the direction of clarification?

Let's listen to the divine word of night. The dance displeased the first of the gods. Ever since king Numa, the gods have taken pleasure in dance; the ancient religion even instituted dancer priests, the Salii, the leapers. Which dance then caused displeasure? The atrocious contortions the body displays at the point of death. But that's not a dance; Jupiter speaks in enigmas, in symbols; his discourse has to be deciphered. A hypothesis: he speaks clearly. A hypothesis: we speak in metaphor. He says: the slave danced poorly. If he is pleased with the leaps of the Salius, perhaps he might say: a beautiful torture, in truth. From Jupiter's point of view, the stiffening body, in the grips of the convulsions of an intense suffering, dances. For the sacred, for the divine, for the religious, the victim is a member of the chorus; the dance is the body's flight before the death throes. For the sacred, for the divine and for the entire history in which everything brings us to the instauration, to the beginning, in which everything leads us to the foundations, to the origin, Jupiter clearly says the birth of dance. The complicated gestures, the fierce, painful semaphore of the dancer are rituals first, are, before the rite itself, the abominable repertory of gestures of the victim during sacrifice. Madness of pain, excess of suffering, dance. Everything becomes clear.

But the plebeian, like the augurs, pontifices, consuls and senators, remained in the dark. Yet nothing is as luminous as the divine word, because it's divine. It says that the divine confuses execution and dance. It says that the divine exists from confusing this art and this pain, this perfect beauty and the final agony, that the divine exists from confusing this act of culture and this barbarous act; it says that our culture is the logical result of barbarism, the hidden result of abomination. Neither the pontifices nor the consuls would withstand such a revelation. Nor perhaps history. It says that history consists in seeing a distance where the sacred sees an identity. Jupiter sees that the tortured man dances; men don't see this, they see, right after dawn, a dying slave pass through the middle of the circus; they see, in the morning, an artist dancing before the procession for the games. Time separates their passage, it's the time of history. It's the time of appearance and lie. Jupiter sees quite well that it's the same man. Men want to see two men. To listen to the myth, to read history. But the myth clearly admits to being myth; Jupiter remains in the dream and the night. But history, which claims to be clear, is only myth itself, and what is more, hidden myth. It is mythic twice over and a lie twice over. History hides the fact that it is mythical; its effect of being real is simply produced by the double appearance.

Here is the stiff body of the dead son. Here is the stiff body of the father in the grips of paralysis. Here is the agitated body of the dancer on the stage. Here is the body of the whipped slave twisting in pain. These four bodies are only one body. The body of the *ludio* and the statue of the reclining god, these two bodies again only form one. Jupiter, highest, greatest, best, does not make any distinction. The dancer dances. Complete the vision; see around him the one whipping and beating him. Complete the vision and continue it; see him fall motionless and paralysed with suffering. Complete the vision and see him dead. The feast of the gods. Now return back toward the origin or the instauration. The stiff statute rises; the paralysed one throws his crutches away. Risen, he twists with pain under the thousand rods and hundred thousand blows. Remove the criminals. Here, free, is the dance. You only see a fragment of it; Jupiter sees the fragments of places, times and persons, at once.

All the games, and their mimicry, ensue from this.

The dance is the contortion of the body in the vicinity of death; the body trembles and recoils at its sudden attacks, its bites; it tries get out of reach. The dance is death pangs, and death pangs are a struggle. Jacob, fighting the angel, dances; no one ever saw the angel; the angel passes by and isn't seen. The sole dancer is dancing a pas de deux, and his invisible partner, clinging to his body, is death. The slave, a cross around his neck and driven, under the whip, into the middle of the circus, the usual place for the spectacle, is the seat and prey of every last shuddering. He dances. The divine father sees him well in the morning light. How is it possible for the god Jupiter, whose name is daylight, to appear in the dream and at night? The consuls' discourse, the entire web of interpretation conceals the dance, blocks off the dance, pushes it into the dark, says that it must be explained whereas it is what does the explaining. Let's silence words, let's see the things.

The dreamer sees his son dead. The dreamer is stricken with paralysis. In the same house, the house of the dream, the light of day shows us two motionless bodies, stiffened, one of which is lifeless. A body frozen in the vicinity of death. The thing explains the word. Words play hide-and-seek, words play a game of hiding things. Thus things can't be seen. And yet: the stiff body of the father in the vicinity of the filial corpse is a perfect epiphany of the dream. The thing as such opens the words; here it is, totally clear. The dreamer's body does what the dream dictates. The body, opaque, plays the role of the unconscious, but I don't know such words. An opaque and present yet motionless body, this is the son's mortal remains; a body mobile from having spoken, throwing away its crutches and getting off the litter before the eyes of the terrified senators, a body slowly and over a long drawn-out time imitating what the victim did quickly in the fast spasms while being flogged. Two bodies stiffened before death, the one explaining the other, and the one unfolding the time of the first one in a more than slow repertory of gestures. I see here a first ballet, another ballet of origin, and the advantage of dance here would be that no one speaks, so much do words of explanation hide the thing to be explained: in the theatre, in the middle of the circus, in the miming, pantomime, the thing is bathed in full light, silent.

Livy and Plutarch and Macrobius and even Cicero tell, without being aware of it, the birth of dance. One would seek it in vain in the works that seek it out. They don't tell it; they let slip that Jupiter told it. This is a good source since it's involuntary. It's a source; the source is divine.

The gods, reclining, have risen.

PART FOUR

CROWDS

7 IN THE CITY: THE AGITATED MULTIPLICITY

Let's return to the exact and first hour in which Rome, they say, was founded. A little before, in the kingdom of Alba, enemy brothers are killing each other again. Numitor, aided by Remus, has just killed his emulator, Amulius. He immediately assembles the people. Pay attention from here on to the subtle movement of the words and things, pay attention from here on to the recurring movement: the multiple hardens. The murder took place: the assembly holds a council. In the middle of the council, the twins enter with their band; their band is far from being a council. The two groups intervene in a united set; they hail Numitor with the title of king. So unanimously, so with a single voice, the multitude creates the king. The two bands accelerated the movement of union. The multitude was a concourse right after the murder; it is so again around the king; the concourse opens before the two diverse bands; the multitude again consents with a single voice. The multitude becomes an assembly through the lynching, through the king, through the suffrages.

The same movement begins again. From concourse, Alba becomes a multitude again: the population grows. We are transported to the sites where the twins were abandoned in order to found the new city. Visibly, each of them still has his band, his group, has his clique, has his multitude. Two multiplicities do not make one city; six and twelve vultures aren't equal to a single flock. This is the true question: each twin is surrounded by his vultures, and these vultures, carrion-eaters, want a corpse. Yes, the auguries tell true; yes, the inauguration clearly precedes the foundation. The two teams come to blows; they form, by their indistinct sum, mixed together, a mob. A crowd becomes a mob, and the mob kills – the vultures finally form one flock. So, we are told, the city is founded.

Foundation happens when multiplicity becomes unity. The multiple hardens around the unity of the corpse, around the place of dead man.

This is the concept of Rome, this is the concept and its name.

The narrative relates the murder, its true and false reasons. And it abruptly jumps to after the foundation. We didn't see the foundation. We have to believe that it's the murder itself. If moreover we see the names given to the groups, the foundation appears: the collective is first named the multitude; it is called the mob; it is a city.

The same movement starts up again, recurring everywhere. The city grows: Romulus populates it via the sanctuary woods. Who comes to this dark woods? The multitude. The multitude there again becomes an indistinct mob of free men and slaves. The king enframes it via council.

In every case, the dynamic goes from a multiple set to an indistinct collective, and from there, via a circumstance, comes to unity. This circumstance is the murder of Amulius; it is the murder of Remus by his brother or rather his lynching in the middle of the mob; it is the shade of the sanctuary woods. Here obscure people, in an enclosure between two woods, conceal their origins. Rome conceals what it has seen in Romulus since its birth. The sanctuary site conceals; it is closed; it is protected by two woods; it is guarded by the sacred. The narrative also conceals: one might think that the foundation there is something entirely different from what is said.

The passage from multiplicity to concourse, via the mixture of the mob and the lightning flash of the lynching, is a description of the social contract. This is not a contract; words have to melt into the cries and noise of the brawl; meaning returns to rumbling, relations to quarrel, and the total set to noise; no, this is not a contract, but it is nevertheless how the collective is founded, how a society begins. Society is never done beginning in this way.

Livy shows in addition a conceptual fairness that the philosopher forgets to practise. The sanctuary site or the dark woods in which people of obscure birth gather, Cacus' black cave in which the cattle low, the difficult, symbolic addition of six and twelve vultures, the dark grotto where, in secret, Numa receives counsel from Egeria and from which an inexhaustible spring flows, these are better scenes than that of the contract. The philosophical concepts of origin are presented clearly, even though they are obscure. Livy's objects bring their shadows with them: they are black boxes, a cave, a woods, figures; they let our ignorance be seen. They make us think without concepts. They show at the same time the thing, the dynamic of the thing and the ignorance in which our knowledge of the thing is immersed. The clear and bright that doesn't admit its shadow is a deceit; the chiaroscuro that shows it is more honest and exact.[1] We don't know our origins; an irreducible shadow prevents us from seeing them; something is behind our backs toward which we don't turn around. We don't convert. The social sciences include this shadow. Legend lets it be seen; myth is accompanied by it, but the concept suppresses it; positive science eliminates it. A good theory of knowledge subtly negotiates its associated ignorance; a good theory of science knows what it can know; it knows the functioning of the secret; it knows the strict limits where knowledge turns around into the unknown. Livy is sharper, suppler and subtler in the epistemology implied by his narrative than a philosophy or a theory that would play at clear ideas. He makes us see the thing and its shadow at the same time: the origin, the murder, and its covering over.

Livy 2.23–24

We haven't meditated enough on the flight of the people and on its concourse on the day of the Poplifugia. We have seen the Fathers up close, their dense and bloody ring around the royal corpse's scattered limbs, but the fuzzy set of those calling one another or throwing stones at each other was abandoned a little. I'll return to it: much time has passed; the Republic has been instaurated; twin consuls, often rivals, replace the expelled kings; the battle of Lake Regillus permitted the usual carnage; debts are posing a problem for the first time. The people, irritated, agitated, enter the scene. You might say that this scene slowly details the death of the king and the flight of the people: a multitude, which will have to be named, at least, first surrounds a fantastical old man, a figure without a name stemming from who knows where only to disappear who knows where; it then surrounds the senators in discord. The people form a dense ring; the Fathers scatter – inversion.

I'm going to try to name the crowd. It is first of all the multitude, it is multiplicity. Ever since the adventure of this book began, ever since the adventure of our culture started, I've found nothing but multiplicity. A set of termites and balls of clay, the inaccessible geometral of myth under the marks of the hooves, the herd of cattle, the two flights of vultures on the day of the inauguration, the white surface of the Albula, the growth of the innumerable to the point of the incandescent in the kingdom of Alba, the set of the parts of the empire and the members of the carved up body, the volleys of stones, the bursts of voices, the rain of coins, a sixth of an *as* per head, onto the head of the hero on the day of his funeral; the band, the groups, the sanctuary woods, assemblies, the mob, the army. Multiplicities. It's time to name them, it's time to recognize them and write their history. It's time to recognize that history is a processing of sets. That the sets produce the time of history. Hence this book, whose stable object is multiplicity. But Livy's book has the same object. Or rather: the same subject. The effort always begun again consists in capturing multiplicity. Multiplicity is sometimes so torrential, so turbulent that even the concept can't stop it, can't cover it over, can't subjugate it.

The multitude abruptly occupies the scene. It spreads in the city like the blaze of a fire. Which smoulders for a long time in silence and without anyone thinking about it, and then breaks out all at once. War is imminent; the Volsci are at the gates of Rome. Also imminent is civil war, that of the creditors against the debtors: revolt is brewing, plebeian against Father. Those in debt are tied, immobilized, captured, chained up. The enemies are less fearsome than those who, inside, reduce to slavery. It's a second generation war, I mean the war of foreign war against civil war. Mixed violences that break chains and become unleashed, free.

Mars engenders violence: war. Quirinus engenders violence: debts. Jupiter engenders violence: justice and sovereignty. Everyone is right at the same time and says the same thing. All the final authorities engender violence. Yet it calms down at the end of the scene in the order of the camps. Mars holds back the violence; the war against the Volsci wins out over revolution, at least temporarily. Quirinus calms the violence; the question of bonds, debts and slavery is deferred a bit. The sovereignty, Jupiter, calms the violence; everyone turns toward the Senate; the consul decrees a law that calms the crowd. Money, as we knew, freezes violence; the sacred, as we have learned, also freezes it; alas, we are learning here that a good war also freezes it. The alignment of the camps is a peaceful order. The alignment of the front, classical order, prohibits outbursts. If you want peace, make war. In a legion.

Each pole, each authority, each institution engenders and curbs violence, seems to produce it and channel it, holds it back, captures it with the participation of each of the others, with the help of the two other gods.[2] And this is no doubt how each institution, each authority, each pole is founded and instituted. De facto and de jure. De facto, for the army as such, for justice and the circulation of money, and de jure for theory. Each god, each social class is also a class of theory, a class of interpretation.

Livy recounts a story, real or legendary, scene, representation, no matter. You can take a common philosophy of history from it, through economy and class struggle, *certamen ordinum*. You can take lessons of power from it, Machiavellianism or Realpolitik, a strategy for the prince. You can detect the traces of the three gods in it. Each of them is right, and the story or the scene includes its interpretations. And this is perhaps simply another foundation of Rome. It's the geometral of our philosophies.

Money and the economy envelop war and religion. Religion envelops war and economy; and law, and sovereignty. War envelops the economy and religion. Each term envelops or implicates the others, and can be implicated by each of the others. De facto, I repeat, in the hard wall of the temple, of the camp, of the tribunal or the Senate; de facto and in language, in the explanation said to be theoretical, when he who speaks rises and he means to be right. He is always right. He commands. And he is content.

No doubt there are boxes rigid enough so you cannot cheat about their size or form. Little hard boxes can go into the big one; the opposite is not true. It isn't possible to put a big rigid and hard one into any of the little ones. This is how things are. If there's a logic of boxes perhaps there exists a logic of sacks. A canvas or jute sack doesn't only contain wheat, flour or some kind of cement. It can contain sacks as well. It is fuzzy enough to be able to be folded in a sack at the same time as all the folded sacks, including the one that formerly contained it. I believe that there are box thoughts, said to be rigorous, hard and rigid boxes; I believe that there are sack thoughts, fabric systems. In philosophy we lack a good organon of fabrics; I often dream of this. If we had one, many forms of cheating would no longer be possible, but also reason would be saved much stiffness. There are conditions that are prior to implication, which prohibit it from turning around. They aren't always fulfilled. Elasticity isn't always a sin against straight reason. It only is if it's hidden. Our multiplicities are like gases; they can invade Rome, the forum, the streets and plazas; they can become denser in camps. The concepts that capture them are as fuzzy as they are; the concepts mutually implicate each other – what a scandal. Let's learn to negotiate soft logics. They're only crazy when they're misunderstood. Let's finally laugh at those who called their precisely soft discourses rigorous. And let's no longer scorn the soft: the fuzzy sets.

The question of the geometral is immediately settled. We haven't wasted our time establishing it. Here the certainty has come that all interpretations succeed each other as scenographies before the multitude. It remains to consider the multitude as such.

It forms a fluctuating field tossed between these three poles, which are only poles in appearance, or rather according to the violence. It forms through these forces, and this is exactly what Livy's narrative says. Our theories lack this fluctuating field, this moving set, and first and foremost, the multiple that moves or rushes in it. It is always captured. The multiple is captured. It's captured by the one, and this is the concept and this is synthesis; it's captured by one or some individuals, and this is power, and this is also representation, tragedy, political assembly. All of Livy's narratives recount the capture of the multiple by the one. This history is the history of capture; this capture is our very history. The multiple rushes; it's trapped by the one. Whether called theory or practice, power or representation, it boils down to this primary and constant operation. So we must seek the one, king, hero, master, slave, this one or that one, authority or final authority onto which this operation projects the multiple. Theoretical representation or social practice or political astuteness or historical narrative, and so on, project the set as such onto a singleton. So we must, first and foremost, pay attention to this set.

Question: what does the author in the narrative call the crowd? A series of names is all by itself worth many theories. Livy is crafty about the multiplicity. He names it multiply.

The Volsci, the plebs, the Fathers. The sets are there, united separately, and disjoint. The forces are in opposition, it is said. As usual, they are in the number of three, Saint George, the Dragon, the pile of corpses. Fire can break out, is going to break out; war is imminent, external or internal, lance against breastplate or cutting up into little pieces.

For violence to flame high, there must be a spark; let's pay attention to this singularity.

The singleton, extracted from order or projected outside of order, is up to his eyes in fury. He burns, he flames. No, he isn't merely a warrior. No, the question doesn't reduce to the beginnings of combat, to the initiations of societies of soldiers; it plunges into the deepest foundations of social order, of group conflict, and all the way to the very foundations of Rome.

An occasion is needed; a spark is needed. Let's pay attention, I was saying, to this singularity. Perhaps the hero is going to be born, and perhaps we're going to witness the origin of tragedy. Witness the origin of the concept, the capture of the multiple.

Insignis unius calamitas, the remarkable misfortune of a single man sparked the hatred. I'll specify that this hatred is said in Latin as malevolence, *invidia*, what is seen with an evil eye, or what we look upon with an evil eye. We shall have to specify what 'division' means from the same point of view. What causes violence to flame up is the remarkable misfortune of a single man. *Insignis*, that is to say, marked, remarkable; this singular person bears distinctive marks, signs. Here they are.

These are signs of old age, of suffering, of exhaustion, of illness, of combat, of torture. There isn't one mark on his crushed body that doesn't speak of the vicinity of death, age, scars and the fresh traces of blows from a rod. He arouses horror, and anger, and pity; this isn't a mediocre tragic hero; he bears the motivations of tragedy. He bears the signs of battle, the chest scars of the brilliant centurion he once was, marks of Mars; he bears the signs of the plebeians' combat against the Fathers, vestiges of rods, bonds, tortures for debts; his filth and thinness are traces of prison, poverty, of servitude; a victim of the sovereignty, Jupiter, a miserable victim of fortune, Quirinus. Yet his age and his air are those of command. Who is the singleton? You have recognized him although he is unknown; the Romans recognized him in a flash. He bears the totality of signs of a victim. He is the intersection of the opposing sets. He is the intersection of the enemies, the Volsci, the Fathers, prison, the plebs, poverty. He is the intersection of the three functions: a centurion with a brilliant service record, a peasant, a stock-breeder ruined by debts and taxes, an imposing old man due to his beard and hair, a strange and charismatic apparition, an authority emanates from him. His body covered with signs has already been cut up: part for the soldiers, part for the farmers, part for the tribunal. He is the joker, quite exactly, he bears every sign, he bears every value. A sum of signs and their union, an intersection of groups and their conjunction in one divided individual. A union and intersection of the opposing subsets.

He is alone and the separated sets touch at this point, like tangents. In this great emaciated old man, contingency appears. And the geometry or the logic of contingency is not insignificant. We're in the habit of scorning it quite a bit. It's not the absence of law; it's the local accumulation of subtle little laws. The joker, placed along a sequence, neighbours one value upstream and another value downstream; it therefore makes the sequence bifurcate. Through it, the sequence jumps, from war to debts for example, or conversely; through it, the sequence jumps, as is said, from power to act; without it, the sequence does not jump from one state to another. At this point of contingency, two unrelated varieties are tangent; this is the role of the old man, it's the role of the joker. Here, through it, in it, depending on the circumstance, I mean what is locally around it, history will hesitate: it will take, it could take such-and-such a direction or meaning. Contingency, exactly, is the site of bifurcation. The singleton old man is a singularity, like Cleopatra's nose; he is the projection of the given multiplicities. I'm assuming that the famous nose of the Egyptian queen was a sign that's just as legible by the multiple as the signs of the joker's body are visible.

The singularity old man, bearer of traces and marks, is capable, capable in the geometric sense, in the sense whereby a segment is capable of the thousand angles by which it is seen, is capable of the sets that look at it. The soldiers see him as centurion, those in debt see him as whipped or bound, and thus those in debt conspire with the former soldiers. This capacity has the same name as potency – it is potentiality. This potency is power. He who has power is capable of the angles, the views, the sets; for this, he can only be a many-coloured joker or a white-haired man, white with the sum of possible colours. He bears all signs. He is already totally cut up. The joker old man bears on himself, in himself, the vestiges of possible violences. Thus he is read, he is seen by the *invidia*, the hatred that sees with its evil eye. He is cut up, torn up, divided. He is seen by the mixed gazes of the divided multiplicities. The *invidia* of the *divisio*.

A strange mathematics or a strange chemistry. The body is well marked with a precise, decomposed, legible formula. Yet it enters into mixture. It drowns in contingency. It's absorbed by the crowd, by the text; it will no longer come out; it will no longer be mentioned. Annihilated, dissolved. Like the king Tiberinus in the waters of the white river. Expelled. It is expelled from the text like a king.

On the contrary: will it reappear?

Around him, the crowd. Now pay attention to the denominations of the crowd. They form an impressive series that's as good as every theory, as I said. With every fluctuation, with every transformation, it changes name. With every reaction, it changes formula.

Turba circumfusa, first: the crowd spreads, liquid, in fusion. It surrounds the old man like a vortex [*tourbillon*]. *Turba, turbo*. The crowd flows, and it comes around him; you would almost think it a popular assembly, *contio*, a convention. He speaks and it speaks, and the crowd says among themselves that it recognizes this singleton. It rushes around him; it reads him.

So in the middle of the *turba*, in the middle of the turbulence, an old man – quite close to death, his body covered with scars, a hero who had come a hairsbreadth away from death, a stock-breeder, a peasant, ruined, in debt, ploughed with sticks, whipped to death, thin, gaunt, dying of hunger, with long hair, wild-looking – is there, like an abstract operator. Nameless, substitutable. At death's door.

Everyone looks at him, interrogates him; everyone recognizes him. A joker, he has every value. A catalyst, he precipitates, he makes the entire process possible; he is its condition.

He recounts. He recounts the populations. No, it's not a question of the usual population, but of the pillaging of pillagers. *Populari* signifies ravage, devastate, depopulate. The population passes over this singleton, pillaging his farm, stealing his harvest, taking away his cattle. And again the state, another population, demands taxes, forcing him to borrow, passing over the land of his father, over the land of his grandfather; the old man is subject, subject, subject. It doesn't matter if it's the Sabines that are at issue. Why not the Volsci? Why not the *turba*? The latter is for the moment a population. This is how it occupies space. The crowd listening to him can become a population.

How is a space occupied? How is it held?

A solid can't invade an expanse; it remains local. Determined, defined, decided, it is restricted; it has limits, rigidity, a cut out, catastrophes.[3] Liquid doesn't have any; it spills, it pours, it spreads. Vapour flies in the volume; it turns there sometimes, turbulent. Fluids fill the possible with their inundation; they abound. The crowd is fluid. An institution, stable, is solid. The foundation solidifies the crowd. Cools it, freezes it, restricts it in space. Defined, it has limits: it becomes reasonable, it becomes rational. Thus Romulus' trench belongs to a decided society; thus Remus' leap belongs to a labile crowd. The multitude, liquid, passes limits. The trench functions to evacuate water. In Rome, it is the cloaca, it is the sewer. The usual history, solid via gold or bronze or polished stone, defines the liquid histories or the ages of water. It stops them. Foundation. It evacuates them.

The destruction and the ravaging occupy space; the devastation advances over the vast plain, without limitation. The conqueror spreads through the fire that propagates, through the iron that reduces everything to light dust – this is the population. The population pillages. Occupies the world by destroying it. Violence invades the expanse, without constraint. Violence invades the pillagers as well. Violence stops violence. Foundation. It limits it. Trench. The sacred according to violence, Girard, makes the sacred according to the boundary, Eliade; this is indeed the foundation of civil society, Rousseau: delimiting a field. But Rousseau, intelligent, only asked for foolish people. That isn't sufficient.

The disease, the contagion invades space; the germs spread; the plague contaminates the expanse; the former occupants are no more than vectors for the epidemic, for the epizootic, for the pandemic. The pandemic kills the vectors. Stop. The dynamic of conquest is that of its limitation.

The clamour and the noise invade space; the tumult occupies the expanse. There is flood, deluge. There are destructions, violences and wars. There are the diseases, tabes or plague. Here now is the hubbub. These are the images of the multitude. These are the avatars or the apparitions of the population. These are its performances as well. So foundation is the passage from the waters to stone, a phase transition; let's not forget the primal waters. It is the passage or transformation from violence to the sacred; let's not forget the populations. The passage from the plague to its own destruction; the group is mithridatized, vaccinated. It's now the passage, the same passage, phase transition or transformation, from senseless clamours to language, from barbarous language to human language, from noise to the voice, from cacophony to meaning, from sea noise to harmony, from background noise to music, from white noise to informed messages, from hubbub to contract. The clamour of the multiple rumbles; it suddenly forms, hope or disappointment; it comes into accord, and this accord is the contract. Before this unanimous cry, noise.

We forget the nature of the phenomenon preceding the foundation. Be it fluid or flood, violence or pillage, plague or clamour, it's always a process that spreads, that propagates into space and occupies the volume. The pure multiple expands. It pours, it propagates, it invades the expanse and holds it, it grows.[4] It pillages, it scatters. The multiple multiplies, or perseveres in its being. And this is the essential thing, and this is the secret of its namings.

Before the contract, in the exact or figurative sense, noise holds space.

Here first is the plague, *tabes*, rot and contagion. War grows, debts increase, flood and violence, the plague grows. The old man is exceeded by growth: no more farm, no more land, no more personal property, no more family; he is bound – no more body. Violence on Jupiter's side, via justice and power; violence on Mars side, via the Sabine war; violence on Quirinus' side, via exchanges and debts. The disease spreads; it goes everywhere.

Facing the mob in the forum, the old man recounts the population. Crowd here, crowd there. This is representation: the present relation of the one to the multiple is expressed by recalling a relation of the multiple to the one.

So, *clamor ingens, tumultus*, noise is born in the plaza; the noise grows; it rises, fills the forum, slips into everywhere, occupies the city. It accompanies the multiple, and it is the multiple.

The sedition clamours. The noise is causing quite an uproar.

Sedition indicates a coming-and-going, a fluctuation. *Itus et reditus*, *itio et seditio*, goings, returns, to-ings, fro-ings. The *turba circumfusa* of just now, the diffuse mob is rather the cloud chaos and the turning chaos; we hear its hubbub; sedition, through goings, through comings, local, separated, through Brownian motion, is the Poplifugia, that flight of the people where the people encounter and call each other. The flight of the people is its sedition; they are going to withdraw to the Sacred Mount.

Howling bands run to the forum: *multus agminibus per omnes vias cum clamore in forum curritur*, a stampede of the multiple in little packs through every street toward the centre, amid the clamours. The howling, the shouts and the noise have seized the city: there's no longer a single place in Rome where some volunteer isn't joining the rioting. There's no longer an anechoic box; this is the law of propagation. Plague: they won't all die, but all were stricken. Clamour: not everybody approves, not everybody participates, yet everybody, even if they aren't repeating, hears. Phenomena of expansion that have no obstacle, whose law knows no exception. The multiplicity rises to totality through the capture of space. Rome is seized, Rome is captured, Rome is Rome. All the streets are invaded: all of them. All of them then run toward the forum. The centred schema of the star – fuzzy in the case of the crowd, stony in the schema of lapidation: Tarpeia, or the women of the poplifugia – is here constructed in dirt or stone, drawn in the geometral of urban architecture. Does the constructed city harden the drawings of the hot and fuzzy multiplicities? Does it on the contrary channel them? Does a river dig its valley, or does it choose it?

Everything hinges on the question of bonds. The debtors, bound, knotted, imprisoned, are free, unbound, when they are solvent. A multiplicity, unbound, moves and rushes; this is the flight of the people. We remember that atoms bind or not in the vortex that attaches and constructs things, and that they become unbound and detach from one another in the same vortex that erodes and destroys. Are you talking about the world? Are you talking about men? The parallel is merely using an ancient image from physics. Certainly, but why do we say free energy or bound energy? The language of energy was often, is always a simple or complicated balance sheet of exchanges and debts. Thus the question of indebtedness freezes or liberates a tremendous social energy.

The economy freezes or liberates violence. The accounts of gifts are companions of the accounts of damages. Quirinus has weapons of the same type as Mars. Quirinus has subtle weapons, subtler than those of Mars. The economic violence is going to quickly end at war. The bonds of debts will be removed so the debtors can gird their swords. Violence, whether war or civil violence, ends – elsewhere – at the sacred. The three gods are not on the same level. Quirinus is deeper, more concealed, more powerful, more recent than the two others. The economy is a strategy, a stratagem, that are lower than those of Mars. More refined. It is a theology, a jurisdiction, that are lower than those of Jupiter. More refined. More implacable. Economic tyranny succeeds the previous two; it has preserved their lessons. Money procures weapons or monstrances; the economist is a master plus a soldier; he capitalizes the other functions. History is not forgetful. Tarquinius knows how to wage war; he stands up to the soothsayers. Money strikes lower than fetishes and weapons; it digs a greater slope; it recruits more.

Yes, we are going to be very unhappy. Our ancestors experienced sacred tyranny. Those following them suffered from military fasces. We experience the oppression of calculation and currency. This oppression is more implacable than the two others. It more easily passes to the universal, leaving no gaps and having no opposite. The tyranny of information follows it, more terrible still. To such a point that, like Roman plebeians, our contemporaries are seeking refuge in war. Mars seems less fearsome to them. Jupiter, the sacred, seems amiable, old-fashioned.

The freed energy is, again, the *turba* of origin. And great was the danger for those senators who found themselves in the forum. The crowd floats; it seems now that the old man is no longer there, and that he has been absorbed by, in the pure multitude. The assembly comes undone; the energy bound around its singleton becomes unbound; the crowd floats, it goes, it comes, *seditio*, from senator to senator without becoming fixed.

Is the senator who is in danger here the selfsame old man who has just lit the fire?

Suddenly the multitude turns.[5] It turns, veers, inflects its course, is converted, *multitudo versa*, toward the two consuls. It travels the exact history of Rome: it has left the victim; the narrative forgets him; Rome has excluded the king; the crowd is around the consuls; it is around the curia. The rotating chaos, liquid or cloudlike, versatile, turns. The cloud becomes a vortex, for it is centred. Social physics. The crowd turns from the old man toward the senators, then toward the consuls. A play of substitutions. The joker begins to be identified. He had no name; he was bearing signs. They had no name; they were bearing titles. They have names, and they are two: Claudius and Servilius, the slave and the lame man. The old man, by means of the signs, was a full intersection. The consuls are so by means of their names; the one is on the side of the plebs and the other on the side of inequality.[6] In any case, both are marked, as is fitting, marked with the old man's signs, marked with some victimary sign, marked enough to substitute for the first joker. The intersection old man becomes double; by substitution, he becomes two opposed consuls, the one on the side of the slave plebs, the other on the side of the nobles, opposed like classes or parties, twins all the same through their function; here are Romulus and Remus; we are indeed in a primitive scene, I mean of foundation. And history progresses by means of substitutions. This is how, by means of the joker, it bifurcates.

Around the curia, the people are rumbling angrily; Livy now says *iras hominum*, the ires of men. The senate is divided, like Rome itself, into partisans of each of the consuls: each twin has his own flock of vultures, every little leader has its pressure group. The multiple – men, the burning multiple, angry men – surrounds in a ring a curious place that's quasi-empty. The senators are few in number, fairly disordered; most are absent. Attention: the plebs is close to power; it approaches the empty place, as the Fathers, long ago, approached the throne of apotheosis. Servilius wants to bend this powerful movement; he doesn't want to break it: *concitatos animos flecti quam frangi*. This bending is an inclination – we always hear Lucretius' physics – but the consul fears the fracture, the fragments, the fracas; he's afraid of the suffrages. Insofar as, for the first time, the uprising is called communitarian, insofar as the movement, the motion is under the prefix of accord: the multiple is no longer named by separation and disorder.[7] It is necessary to decide between liquid and solid. What is liquid can't be cut up, nor can it be broken or decided: it bends.

We're at the summit. So, during the tumult, the thick cloud of Volsci enters at a gallop into this form in formation. Only another multiplicity can undo what's being done here or what's being born from a first multiplicity, only another multiplicity can make it bend.

I'll resume: around the curia, the people are rumbling angrily, and the Senate is divided. Around the city, the enemy is rumbling, and Rome is divided. These images are fundamental. Around the stage, the public rumbles, and Curiatius clashes with Horatius. Around the theatre of war, weapons rumble; the king is going to meet the dictator. The crowd in fusion, as though chaotic, surrounds the rivalry of classes, of people, of individuals, of kings, of heroes, of nations. Everything is played out, and always, in this relation of the multiple as a fuzzy crowd to the one, to the combat between two, in this relation of the great number to rarity. History, philosophy, the philosophy of history – in a word theory – and narrative only mark out the stage, that is, the hero, the twins, the fight, the rivals, and rarely the energy cloud of chaos bordering around them. As though the author of the text or the concept, taking a place on the stage, always brought back the stage, as though the concept, through capture of the multiple, always brought back unity. What to say then about the multiplicities? They float, they change names. Horatius will have the name Horatius, and Servilius Servilius, but the cloudy mass that couldn't be a concept will have a name: mob, pillaging population, plague, noise, clamour, tumult, multitude; since it escapes unity, it is without representation and without concept. Like chaos, like heat.

The figure is what I've called the star or the relation of the one to the multiple. On the side of the one can be seen: the aspect of the concept, the aspect of science, the aspect of the actor and of representation; the side of the multiple must also be seen, and this turning around isn't common. It's useful to put the persons, masks, heroes, prosopopoeia into sets and crowds, into a set theory logic. The important thing here is the population, in the categorical sense as well as in the concrete sense; it fluctuates, it evolves; the energy there moves; the singleton is only there to stop, freeze, bind that energy and make the set be seen as stable. It captures the force of the multiple. This is how the sharp concept acts. Romulus kills Remus in the first version, but in the second version, Remus falls struck to death in the middle of the crowd. The second version goes a little beyond the stage. It's useful to introduce set theory schemas into political theory, into history. Beneath concepts, the beach; beneath the conceptual pavement, the beach in sandy myriads.[8] The crowd is absent in the traditional duel of the twin brothers. I now hear better the clamours around the combat of Horatius and Curiatius, the noises that are silent in history, since Abel, since Cain.

It's not only those one has wanted to reduce to silence, by force, by exploitation, by elimination, who are silent. Silence is the zone that surrounds concepts, theories, orders in general because they are theories, classes or concepts. History, by the very fact that it is said, stated or recounted, produces of itself this deafness. The multiple shouts out its noise; the capture of the multiple is silent.

So the thick cloud of Volsci enter at a gallop into the narrative. Listen to the clacking noise of the hooves; Latin horsemen announce the enemy. The schema doesn't change form; it only changes place. The two rivals, Remus and Romulus, no, Servilius and Claudius are surrounded by the feverish mob, and now the two subsets are surrounded by feverish enemies. No, it's never the work of the negative that transforms things, it's the work of multiplicities.

Suddenly, the bonds change, the knots change; the energy moves from Quirinus to Mars; the debts are remitted for the duration of the fighting. The logic of gifts lets itself be perceived under its profile of being a logic of damages. The plebeian set, multiply named, passes from prison, which it came out of, to the military role, which it enters, from chains to oath, from *concitatos animos* to *concursus*. It is now in concourse in the public square to take the oath.

Servilius, the consul, presents himself before the people, alone; the people are assembled; it is an assembly, *contio*. The consul discourses by classes and subsets. Concepts form quickly when danger presses. The set becomes assembly; assembly becomes concourse under enemy fire, under the pressure of another crowd, under the new work of another multiplicity.

The Senate likewise decides quickly under the pressure of the people shouting around the curia. The plebs was in the process of bringing off its unity, its union, its totalization; the narrative was ending by saying the men and binding their community. Hardly had this accord occurred than the concourse was displaced by the Volsci all around. From politics to the military, from civil war to external war, from class struggle to armed conflict. Out of breath, the narrative moves faster; it piles up new names for the multitude finally penned up, finally reduced to unity: the men, enlisted, form one body, *manus*; but why say one body since they form one hand? The consul controls these forces, *copias*; he encloses them in a camp, *castra*. The end of the narrative, one thing is not dared to be said: its goal. The public tumult is silent in the concentration of the camp. War captures violence; Mars calms violence, even though he appears to launch it. Mars – to talk theology – or struggle, war, combat, duel and strategy, dialectic – to talk about history – transforms the work of the multiple into the work of the negative; they transform the real into representation.

Lost effort after won effort, the Roman people, after the victory, seceded on the Sacred Mount. War orders violence; it seems to liberate it; it negotiates it; it domesticates it. Either the mad clamour of the multiple is projected onto the hero who accumulates its furores – this is the solution of the barbarians, or it's concentrated in the camp, a squared construction, or in formation by lines and columns, and this is the Roman solution. They aren't so opposed. The multiple is ordered on the one in the first case; it is unified by order in the second. The multiple is reduced to unity, to order, either by a star or by a grid, by polar space or by Cartesian space, but it's always an order. And it's always a representation. Are there not centurions, generals, and Masters of the Horse in the camps? The essential thing is to erase multiplicity. And this is how Mars tames violence, by seeming to unleash it.

The multiple takes refuge on the Sacred Mount. The sacred then will be the site where violence becomes civilized again. In the same way, this negotiation will see the passage from the multiple to the one. We're going to say it soon.

A quick inventory of these multiple names of the multiple. *Turba*, first of all, the turbulent crowd. *Prope in contionis modum*, as though in a quasi-assembly. *Populatio*, the pillaging band. It's not uninteresting that a given space is peopled by sacking; the multiple rushes; it forms, in a place, that tabula rasa I elsewhere called a white domino. Turbulence passes like a devastating storm. *Tabes*, plague or contagious disease. The whirlwind passes in the city of Athens; it leaves piles of dead. *Clamor*, *tumultus*, noise and clamours. The crowd passes; it whirls about shouting. The swarm passes buzzing. *Seditio*, this is the riot, the multiple movement of the multiple, and its non-unitary fluctuations; everyone runs in every direction, every element going its own way, separately. Sedition is not at first the negative, the rising of a mass against a force; sedition is at first the almost Brownian motion of the elements in a set; it is *Poplifugia*, the flight of the multiple. Sedition considered as uprising is the work of the negative, but sedition, in its radical sense – fluctuating movements – is definitely the work of the multiple, that is to say, the motion of each force in the multiplicity, a force that's different in every point, a movement that's different for every difference. The work of the multiple has not been thought, has not been directly assessed; yet everything happens as though it were primitive. Is it really assessable? *Agminibus cum clamore*, shouting bands run through every street toward the forum. Sedition is channelled through the roads of urban planning, through the topography of places. Little formed packs converge toward the unity of an assembly. Subsets appear in the midst of the clamours. In the noise, *sens* emerges: first in the directional sense. The mechanism described here is the polarization of the sedition, its inclination. The groups are each on their sides: suddenly, they all go toward a one and same point. *Multitudo versa*, so the crowd turns. It does seem that the crowd has reached a point here, a threshold of crystallization, of coagulation, for the movements are directed, are inflected together toward the forum, around the senator, in the direction of some person or other who was passing there, posed there; it's the polarized space I was talking about. We don't really know how to say these phenomena; we only have abstract names, physical images for them – in all, metaphors. Why does this lone man, an old man, a consul, hero, soldier, orator, supplicant, actor, dictator or victim cause the multitude to turn? Does it suffice to say that he bears the marks of the set on his body? What is this process of identification? What is this unleashed fury? Why does this singleton cause the multiple to veer, to rotate, to turn? Why, how does he make the turbulent *turba* twirl around? How does he make the vortex turn, bend, move? Why, how does he sow revolt or revolution? Why these well-aggregated words, these well-formed phenomena? Let's admit that we know nothing on this score. All that we do know is that the language says a turning motion that suddenly appears immediately after the disorder. After the chaos of sedition, little packs form, and the multitude turns. Revolt, revolution, considered as uprising, do the work of the negative; but, in the radical sense, in the sense of birth, revolt is the turning motion of the crowd, of the turbulent crowd, its first ordered movement, the first global result of the work of the multiple. So the multiple moves in its mass, compact. The Brownian sedition makes turbulent revolt. The first is scattered, and the second one turns. The integrating force is born here; we don't know very well how. Synthesis is born there, the synthesis of the multiple. What is this unity, mobile and floating?

The impressive thing here is the fidelity to the physical model. The impressive thing would be that our physics models – hardening, cooled liquids, crystallization, cell formations, spiral formations – might be inferred as well by what we know of social processes. I don't know how to decide. Who knows how to? We're even less able to do so since this is also the idea we create of the formation of ideas, or of representation: through synthesis of the multiple. As though we had a representation of representation. Suddenly stripped of the means for thinking, we're going to lose heart. A sign no doubt that there is something here to think about.

The multiple is primitive. It is everywhere differentiated, floating, fluctuating, chaotic. Yes, the chaos is primitive, and our myths have always said so. The mass is irreducible to the state: this sentence has a physical meaning, this sentence has a social meaning. The multiple is anterior to every formation and every synthesis, and every formation and every synthesis are a derivation, a declination from it. In Rome, when the multitude became concourse, it was deviated, led astray, toward the troop, the army corps, the camp. The force of the camp, the force of order in the hands of the consul against the enemy, tomorrow in the hands of the tribune against the consul, stemmed from the sudden integration of the multiple. The troop is a crowd that has lost its difference, its seditious motley colours. The big problem is this loss or this forgetfulness. The mixed set becomes homogeneous. How, once more, does the multiple become one? How does the entire crowd let itself go toward the singleton? Livy's old man already bore, it is true, everyone's sorrows.

The multiple becomes one by a change in phase. We have to be attentive to the intermediary states; it is true that our knowledge of the collective often stops at states, I mean at equilibriums, at institutions, at classes, at subclasses, in short at a statics, even and above all when this knowledge hides this statics by means of a dynamized discourse. However, the collective changes phase; it experiences intermediary states, turbulent states that don't merit the name of states. No, I'm not projecting one language onto another, a physics onto history, an exact science onto a social science; I'm merely trying to speak in several voices. I'm trying to think multiplicity in its difference and its fluctuations. I'm lost, without place, right in the very middle of the Northwest Passage, in an intermediary state between the sciences, in the fractal and multiple distribution of land, water, scattered ice and ice floe. I mean that I'm trying to be without speciality, in the fairly wide desert between the exact sciences and the social sciences, outside the very exactly divided space of classification. I believe that this place is one of the sites of philosophy today. I'm trying to think the intermediary state here whatever it may be, wherever it may be, in the upstream vicinity of formation, before synthesis, as close as possible to integration. I'm trying to think nature in the sense of birth, when newness happens, is going to happen, appears, unexpected. I'm trying to think the margin that separates the multiple and the ordered, the moment when the solid is on the verge of hardening into pressed crystals, when the turbulence is screwing its whirlwind [*tourbillon*], when life is becoming linked, freed, woken, organized, when the message is saying a meaning in the clamouring tide of the hullabaloo, when the music is raising its voice above the scattering of the noise, when the first hallelujah is arising amid the stuttering, when the concept is cutting an exactitude out from the rich sowing that precedes the intuitive dawn. Everything is first in the work of multiplicities. It's still not easy to think; it is as though suppressed; it's negatively named nonsense, chance, disorder. Take heart, the multiple is arriving, from all sides and from every knowledge.

A word about this place without place, intermediary, where I am. It's a place for collection, I mean by this that in this place I collect the voices issuing from elsewhere, almost equal in intensity. The intense division of knowledge defines the sites, the places from which to speak. Above all we speak about the site itself there. The places impose speech; they are spokespersons. An inhabitant speaks his language and defends his culture. Have you ever heard some specialist praise the speciality next door? Such speech, outside, would be unheard of. The division of the sciences creates the conflict of the faculties; conversely this war creates this division. Newness would be – the truth? – outside speech: I will no longer believe anything but citations outside the pressure group. All the rest is only publicity; all the rest is only war and competition. If philosophy adopts the language or metalanguage of a selected place, it merely adds to the conflict of the faculties, a redundancy of redundancy. Thus we often see discourses be constituted with the sole aim of showing the nonvalidity of the discourse next door. This is literally a political discourse, the discourse of the plaster dog about the plaster dog facing him.[9] Such sayings are empty, alas, of saying; they no longer say anything but the place and the hatred nourished there toward the neighbouring places. The space echoes with squabble and noisy quarrels; nothing moves, for this is the most deeply rooted conservatism since the dawn of time;

knowledge – and newness – dissolves. The work of the negative always freezes a state into a state; it is conservative. So the philosopher must lend all his strength to not be from a place, whether physical, social or ideal, must put all his care into trying to avoid every speciality, must put his passion into not being from a group. He avoids redundancy; he avoids the discourse that duplicates the place; he avoids freezing into polemic's statue of salt. He puts all his strength into hearing the specialities. Of course he loses in this, and seriously, he loses his listening post and a few amenities; he accumulates every inconvenience, but he gains in mobility, he gains in truth, through detachment. He listens with what I've called equality of intensity; he can try to speak a multiple-voiced language. He is the man of the multiple; he tries to think the multiple. He leaves the one to its command. He sees it enclose the multiple into the concentrated camp, between four trenches. Divide the multiple from inside, divide it up into sites. A military discipline into which the plebs falls, a scientific discipline into which thought can collapse, technical languages traversed with bonds.

Livy 2.32

The military solution is worn out. The people retire; they have distanced themselves, in the literal sense; they have fled. And it is rightly said that the people fled calling to one another. However they are following the customs given to them: on Aventine Hill or the Sacred Mount – it's of no matter, I'm opting for the Sacred Mount – on the hillock where they have withdrawn, they establish a camp, stakes, trenches, stockade. A camp without enemy. A camp for civil war? There, peaceful, in the midst of their provisions, they eat and they wait. And they know that they form a body. A military body in their camp, made up of maniples, members, hands.

So Menenius, Valerius – no matter – comes to talk to them about the body. About the body and eating, about the stomach. He tells the old apologue of the body, the members and the stomach. The noble Patrician is speaking to the illiterate people in a language they can understand: so this scornful stupidity was already being said. That matters; so does this: he speaks alone in front of the full plebs. May the members understand, he says, that the stomach is a member.

In the middle of the scattered members, does one of them form a band apart? Let's redraw the archaic biological model of the group in that good old Latin we had lost. Menenius, the popular orator, speaks.

Today the body forms a harmony, he says. The Latin says: *omnia in unum*, which I read as: all in one. Traditions and translations readily write here that all the organs, all the members consent, *consentiant*, in a harmonious whole. All, distributively, move together to a global accord, *omnia in totum*, all, separated, toward a unitary whole. That is not written, Livy does write: *omnia in unum*, all in one. I'm not sure about this one, I'm not sure about this *in*. All consent in a single one; that's how it's written, and I can't do anything about it.

That's how it is today. But there was a time when each of the organs, singularly, had its counsel and its own discourse. Each had its *consilium*, whereas now everyone reaches *consensus*. So at that time each deliberated. Separately and for itself, *cuique*. Indignation suddenly. Which organs were made indignant? Precisely the rest, *reliquas partes*. Which rest? Those that were left out in the count and left out of account. Which count? Precisely all of them except one. This one is well placed, *in medio*, the stomach is in the middle. Quiet, in repose, without labour or care, a luxurious sinecure, he enjoys the work and ministry of the others, the rest. And the rest becomes indignant at working for it, at working, each and everyone, for it alone, in the middle. I like the word 'indignation': dignity is decency; one becomes indignant then at what is not befitting. Because it's the opposite of harmony.

Horror. Hypocrisy. Is Meninius kidding?

Hypocrisy: the rest, all except one, work for the one in the middle. Precisely: *omnia in unum*. Now this is how the orator defined harmony. So the problem has already been solved; it was solved even before it was posed; the gap is nil between those fabulous times and the accord of this very day. All do consent, in some way, since each one – separately forming this all except one, that is to say, this rest – is or are toiling for the one, located right in the middle. The *omnia in unum* is invariable across time, whatever the catastrophes may be.

Hypocrisy. Each does his work, takes care, carries out his ministry. I quite like the word 'ministry', even if I hate administration. A master, *magister*, a master, that is to say, a great one, *major*, is surrounded by ministers, little ones, *minus*. All these little ones around the great one work for the great one like the anthill Lilliputians around the lying Gulliver's mountainous belly: cables, ladders, cranes. All these minims are ministers.

I'm inventing along the way, since we have the time, another apologue, for another time. Look at the hypocrisy: the master with the round belly, wanting to make his greatness and the smallness of his minims be forgotten, subtly takes their name. The great is going to call himself minister. Or secretary, or servant. The great names himself little. The strong one takes everything from the weak, even their name. Gulliver comes to the land of the giants, and he becomes a minister there. The wolf has itself called lamb, the minister, nonetheless a master and grand personage; the master takes the slave's name; the *major* plays *minus*, and the famous large dialectic is thwarted. Everyone then sees that the minister does his ministry, that he, small, carries out his servitude. Hypocrisy.

I've finished the demonstration; I've finished my work and ministry; the proof of it is that I'm amusing myself talking about the little minister. The demonstration has been closed since the origin. If the aim is *omnia in unum*, then the rest works for one, and the problem is resolved. Strictly speaking, for this rest to truly be all, it suffices to minimize the one, it suffices to make it minister. The remaining gap is no longer seen; it is only barely seen. No, I no longer see the fabulous difference between that time and now; no, the time and the history, the time and the evolution from state to state is nullified and crushed; the comparison disappears, just like the narrative, just like the apologue; the model vanishes, whether organic or other; what remains is the dismal repetition of the relation of several to one, of the silent plebs and Valerius holding forth in the middle, *in medio*; what remains are the converging lines of the multiple and of the one, *omnia in unum*, the star. I'm not very sure about this *in*. But the one, long ago, now, recently or yesteryear, is Valerius, is the stomach; what does it matter whether it's this one or that one; the essential thing is its site, at the intersection. At the bottom or on top, in the periphery, in the centre, in the middle, *in medio*, the essential thing is not the quality of the site, but that the intersection takes place in this place.

Hence the giant and minimal cheat, the cheat during revolution, the cheat during the time of illusion, I mean the cheat during that illusory time in which people think they change. The apologue repeats, the apologue varies, the way what we learn under the category of history varies and repeats. The dismal iteration of the star, of the all-one diagram. It is changed, and it is still the same. Horatius alone and the Curiatii. Or: the combatant heroes and the army watching them.

Hence the conspiracy. *Conspirasse.* Now *consensus*, long ago *consilium*, in between times, *conspiratio*. That's all very well. But perhaps we need to see here primitive and hidden organic models: feeling, sensing. As though an organic model was exposed by means of hidden organic models. Before eating, together or separately, it is necessary to breathe or sense. Or think. Just as the star is invariable across apparent changes, so the harmonious body is invariant across variation of functions. The proof by digestion presupposes that other proofs by respiration or sensation are acquired.

If they conspired it's because they were in accord, still. They were in accord against. All against one. All against the stomach, all against Valerius. Understand now the value of the *in*: *omnia in unum*. The genius of the Latin language is to say the for and the against in one word. Only our geometry has the same capacity: the bouquet of the star goes entirely toward the intersection, toward the fixed and central point of the sheaf – or of the cone or of the circle, it makes no difference – and this doesn't prejudge what moves along the lines. Working for, conspiring against, is always to repeat *omnia in unum*, the multiple-one star, the schema of power, of representation, of the concept. The plebs served Valerius; they conspired against him. But what does it matter to Valerius? He hasn't changed site. Victim or despot, sacrificial king or oriental tyrant, beheaded Louis, guillotined Robespierre, Napoleon at Saint Helena or elected president, the invariant remains from being the centre of the star. The fine-talking Valerius occupies the place of power. Or Menenius or another orator. The apologue endlessly repeats the scene it institutes and plays.

The conspiracy, it is said, turns out badly. The body falls ill. *Tabes*, putrefaction, epidemic, contagious disease. The plague, they all have the plague. *Una*, each one, *totumque corpus*, the entire body, it doesn't stop. They are always in accord, let's say, through contagion. They won't all die, but all were stricken: all. In accord through counsel, in accord through conspiracy, in accord through contagion, in accord through consensus. Nothing new under the sun except this star.

Of course the plague is violence, as the conspiracy was one of violence, as the work of all for a single person was through violence. How does one get out of this plague? The apologue gets out of it, because it doesn't budge.

Apparuisse. It appears. It becomes manifest. One gets out of it by understanding. The sole solution to this problem is to understand. To understand well what is happening and not to hide it. At the very moment he is showing the plebs what is to be understood, Valerius, the patrician, is hiding it. He's hiding the *divisum pariter*, the redistribution.

It appears to all of them that they are all working for one, the belly, and that the belly, a member, is working for all of them. The schema hasn't budged an inch, *omnia in unum*, whatever the meaning of this *in* may be, for, toward, against, in the direction of the centre or of the periphery; and what does what transits along these paths matter: nourishment, hatred, words, plague, blood? The veins go to the stomach, they depart from it. A flood of blood flows from the crowd to unity, or from unity to the crowd;

we have known this since the death of Romulus. An organic model, violent, religious? A flood of blood, a flood of noise, of words, of meanings, a flood of hatred, of quarrel, of plague germs, a flood of harmony, it's precisely the flood that changes along a set of converging lines that itself doesn't change. The apologue of the stomach takes the schema, folds it over, takes it again, inside out, outside in, tucks it over itself, as the baker does to the dough. You believe you're feeding me; it's me who's feeding you.

Hence I read, stupefied, for the first time in my life, the word 'division': *divisum pariter*. Division is precisely the vision from the starred centre. The vision that the one can have of the multiple is called division. And the division of labour is this very vision. Divide in order to rule,[10] a tautology, a dismal iteration of the same schema; ruling consists in occupying the place from which one sees by division. I, Valerius, the stomach, am talking to you, and I see you according to the thousand veins of my gazes; I distribute words and nourishment to you; I distribute blood. This is my blood. He who distributes, who portions out, who divides is the master, *magisterium*, *ministerium*; he is the central point of the star, on the exchanger, on the turntable; all alone, he relates to all. A minister due to the smallness of his site, a magister due to its capacity. *Omnia in unum*, this could be said in elementary arithmetic: do long division.[11] This can be said just as well in Greek: *diasparagmos*, eucharist. Because this can be read in one direction or in the other.

Indeed, all this historical misfortune and this entire trap can be understood. We don't know how things are with all. *Omnia* and *totus* escape us. Society and the group are black boxes. Our general will remains black; our contracts remain black. What remains black is the act of uniting us. Union is the black operation. Difficult to think, difficult to direct, difficult to bring about.

The hypocrisy consists in thinking, in putting intersection in union's place, in practising the one in substitution for the other, in constructing the former and never the latter. But maybe I'm being severe, maybe this hypocrisy is only impotence. The intersection appears to be clear, distinct, immediately distinguished; it is thinkable, it functions conveniently. The union appears to be black, chaotic, dangerous, and the crowd rushes. It is what rushes toward the *diasparagmos*, toward the intersection. Intersection is the set theory operation named by the name of *diasparagmos*.

Fear seems to choose between tyranny and the crowd in fusion. Between intersection and union, our culture and our history seem to choose, while often hiding this, the first one over the other.

Unions. I'll sum up the story. Each person, long ago, had his *consilium*. They then proceeded to *conspiratio*. The crisis spread the *contagio* over them. And the end of the evil was the *consensus*. So much for the body. Stability replaces history.

The father's discourse was comparison, *comparando*. Then comes *concordia*, concord. For good measure, Livy gives: *de concordia coeptum, concessumque in conditiones*. He accumulates these words of union. We remark in passing that foundation is one of these words. *Ab urbe condita*. Foundation is condition. Condition is union: what's placed, put together, what's put in stock, put in reserve, as in a safe place, densely packed, therefore what's hidden, sheltered from sight, from knowledge.

Everything I've said since the beginning has been nothing but the explanation of the foundation itself. *Ab urbe condita*, from the union of the city. This condition is buried, is hidden. This union is hidden. Yes, we don't know what union is. We thus never cease founding the city, founding Rome here. All these words of concord and conspiracy, of contagion and counsel, are terms of condition and infinitely vary the very act of founding. We vary from not knowing.

Alas, everything begins again. The concord only brings the same schema again. The intersection. Tribunes of the people were thus named. In the very place of Valerius or Menenius, consuls or patricians, are Gaius Licinius and Lucius Albinus, tribunes. A new multiple-one relation, that is to say, the same one. And the star returns. What do leaders or the leaders of the non-leaders matter to me since it's always a question of leaders? Masters of masters or masters of slaves, what's the difference? What's the difference for the union of slaves? The law of history is substitution.

Union produces intersection. Can such a thing be said? It founds it, I do believe, at least the language claims it does.

In any case, I'm content that the first in the tribunal bears the same name as the man with the cart, the vestals' rescuer when Rome was in the hands of the barbarous Gauls, the man of the black jar and the white jar, divine vision: Lucius Albinos, white light.

Apparuisse. They had understood. Perhaps the simple and dismal law of history has to be understood. Since everything is in the comprehension, since the one explains to the all, who begin to understand, to change for having understood the comparison. So the consuls go to fight against the tribunes, delegates against delegates; the little leaders, outside their class, away from the line of battle, go to make a spectacle for the masses united to see them. Intersection, the all-one diagram begins again. And it is called politics. Horatius, with or without his brothers, comes out of the ranks;

Curiatius comes out of the facing one; they fight each other with equal sabres on the stage; the union is nullified since everyone, united, watches. They don't watch their contract, rather they blind it in bringing it about. Horatius or consul, tribune or Curiatius, what's the difference?

Leibniz said it very well: representation is the one-multiple diagram itself.

I'll stop for a moment.

The plebs withdraws to the Sacred Mount; they mark out their camp; they entrench themselves. They dig a trench; they put up a stockade. They dig a trench: why didn't they found a new city? Answer: they neglected to kill Valerius, leaping over the trench to enter and talk to them.

If they had put Valerius to death they would have, through the *diasparagmos*, in blood, drawn the schema of intersection anew. That didn't take place; we were on the Sacred Mount. They wanted to massacre; they didn't do so; they were bound under oath or under sacrament. They withdrew to the Sacred Mount.

They dig a trench. They draw a closed curve. They unite inside. Set. Union.

Valerius arrives; he speaks. Each of them, in revolt against him, looks toward him, holds his listening out toward him; each of them will later delegate a tribune of the plebs. All of them hold one of the converging lines running toward him, which runs toward one. Intersection.

All of them? Not all, says the apologue, but *reliquas partes*, the rest, all minus one. Singleton, remainder, subtraction.

Seen from the singleton, the rest is divided. Valerius, the stomach, the tribune, the consul, no matter, see the union according to the lines of convergence, of the cone of vision. Division. I'll stop.

The entire process simply adopts, at each stage, an elementary operation of set theory or of arithmetic. Better, the process lets us understand them better. It's true that I had never understood the word 'union' so well: counsel, conspiracy, contagion, consensus or concord. Never understood so well the operation of intersection, never understood at all the term 'division'. In other words, exact knowledge awakens the apologue, and the fable of the members and the history that stages it receive an undeniable clarity from it. But reciprocally, the social and political process awakens exact knowledge and lets us better grasp its first steps, perhaps. Add to this inclusion, exclusion, the excluded middle, belonging, charged with hatred, all of them.

We will be asked to decide here, but decision is absurd. Is this a genesis of knowledge, a genealogy of operations, a famous episode in the prehistory of science: might there have been, at the origin, a social set theory? Perhaps. Is this an explanation of social processes by an operational method: is the mathematical model indeed the best for understanding? They understood, and we have finally understood they they didn't understand and were letting themselves be deceived. Paradox: the apparent organic model, the latent organic model both vanish, and they give way to the arithmetic or set theory model, valid at the same time for the body and the social body. And, indeed, we need to think *totus*, the whole, and *omnia*, the distributive whole. Perhaps. Is this some isomorphism between an event stemming from the fabulous depths of our cultural history and the categories of reason taught today in class to children: the blind mathematical education of the Roman people, the blind Roman education of the calculus class? Perhaps.

The first hypothesis is evolutionary. But the operations of calculus can be engendered by means of little pebbles. And Rome never invented what the Hellenes invented. The second hypothesis is from epistemology, via the theory of models. Yes, models are convenient, and we change models every day, for convenience. The last hypothesis is structural, adventurous. Why choose? And what if we had crossed the Northwest Passage three times in one? We have simply understood a little better. Every theory would like to hold the facts, all the facts, in its hand, in its own hand, unique: *omnia in unum*. Not here. Here we remain with multiplicities.

But why didn't they found the second city? The stockades were high, the trenches were dug; the other Rome was ready to be born. Soldiers, they only built a kind of camp.

They had understood, we are told. They had first of all understood that they had to fight. They had understood the relations of force. In fighting, they failed to found. To found elsewhere, it's necessary to leave; one mustn't remain next door: not to one's brother, not to one's city, not to one's enemies, not to one's discipline, not to one's familiar and customary thought. In fighting, they didn't see the singleton capture their forces. They were trapped by class struggle. The only trap is war; the only true trap is polemic; the only trap is hatred.

They understood, white light. They understood, and they didn't kill. Murder was transformed into spectacle. The thing was transformed into apologue. Into words.

Romulus left. Romulus is excluded. Runs through the woods. Doesn't understand. Romulus buries his thought at the bottom of the trench. They understood. And they did not found. They form a non-founded city in the founded city.

8 IN THE FIELD: THE MULTIPLICITY IN PEACE

Livy 2.5.2–5

Rome has just driven out its last king, Superbus. It is said that liberty took place. He left his possessions in the city; they were given to the people to pillage.

The domain of the Tarquins, located between the city and the Tiber, was consecrated to Mars; it was from then on called the Campus Martius. It bore, precisely, a ripe harvest. But consuming wheat from the Campus Martius would have been sacrilege. So the assembled crowd came to harvest the field of wheat. It was summer; the river was low, and the waters few; it could have been crossed by fording. The crowd, with full baskets, without separating the grain from the straw, poured the wheat into the bed of the Tiber, onto the sandy and muddy banks. This pile, this heap, caught in the mud and sand, adding to the loads the Tiber was by chance carrying, formed, little by little, an island. They then built an embankment from the island to the shore. Thus a place high enough and firm enough to support temples and porticoes came about.

A place solid enough to serve as a foundation emerged.

The foundation of Rome was not one event. It was an event, assuredly, but this was only the first variation of a theme to be taken up again in a current fashion. The foundation is recurrent. It returns, like a refrain. Rome never ceases being founded; the gesture of origin or taking root is endlessly taken up again. This is what Rome owes its long survival to. But this cannot be seen if one remains blind to the variation. The variation makes use of several languages. Or rather, we are accustomed to classing in different places forms of narrative that always say the same thing in another way.

Time moves forward by returning, like a helix, along a line of origin. This latter is not a point; it is a generatrix; it is a long sequence of founding circumstances. Time doesn't return. How could that happen? Time never ceases to move forward, but it sometimes passes – when, how, why, I don't know – it passes along the line of origin, geodesic, generating, I know not what else. I only know that there is no regularity. I let a helix be seen to give a fuzzier idea; I like the word generatrix more for its common meaning than for its geometric definition.[1] So the foundation is, again, a foundation; it happens, is said, is carried out, is described, is recounted through other acts, other gestures, other words, other circumstances. We clearly see the repeated course; we clearly see the current foundation. The irregular star drawn a little while ago is the plan view trace of this long movement.

So Rome starts itself again. It has just, from what has been said, expelled the Etruscan kings. This banishment is a purification. And what if liberty was only the flight of the kings? And what if a king was only a king through this suspended banishment? But, in addition, the personal possessions of the excluded kings are at issue. A certain plot uncovered just in time, the plebs fought over the personal effects, a field remained. How can one plunder a place or pull a space to pieces?

The field ran between the city and the Tiber. It bore wheat that was ready to harvest. It was, the history says, consecrated to Mars. And suddenly it was the field of violence.

Who can drive out a field? Who can drive out a field of wheat? Who can clean, purify, the space of violence?

This space is sacred. We must try to understand. Consuming the grain of this field would have been sacrilege. Neither the grain nor the straw of violence can be destroyed, can be eaten, can be exhausted, can be used, can be exchanged, or received, or taken. I'll explain the word 'consumption'. It is said: you shall consume neither the grain nor the straw of violence. Don't eat the grain of Mars; don't drink the field of blood. Who can it be sold to, for example, and what can be done with that money except to throw it away? But where can we throw it away? We are, it might be said, in religion, and yet we're in pure logic. He who uses violence never exhausts it; he who eats violence never destroys it; he who receives it and he who launches it are indiscernible; giving it and accepting it are equivalent; this is perpetual exchange, and this is perpetual motion. Whoever says history has violence as its motor has an easy time of it; he has found, like every religion, the perpetual motion. He who holds the sword will die by the sword, but the sword that kills him is held by he who ... He who eats the grain of the field of Mars will never destroy the field of violence: how to destroy the very power of destruction? Violence has no antithesis, seeking to destroy is still violent. What then is to be done with violence? What then is to be done with the field of Mars? What is to be done with the straw and the grain of this non-consumable harvest? This never stops.

Religion perhaps, wisdom no doubt, logic certainly, demand that the wheat of the field of Mars not be eaten. He who eats from it enters into its perpetual logic, until the consummation of the centuries.[2] Whoever eats from it enters into history. History exists from having one day eaten from it.

This wheat returns irrepressibly, like couch grass. Ineradicable. Its grain gives straw, and its straw gives grain. Perpetually. This is how the men of history are perpetuated.

The hot summer days were there; it was the month for harvest. The watercourse, due to its low waters, was revealing its sandy banks; it could have been crossed by fording. The large assembled crowd came to cut the wheat; it came, with full baskets, to pour it into the silty water. The straw, in piles, and the grain, in heaps – no one had separated the straw from the wheat – drowning in the silt, covered with mud, remained attached to the sandy beaches. The Tiber was continuing to carry its loads; by chance and by circumstance, they joined this pile. An island, hardening out, formed from these attachments and contingencies.

I believe that an embankment was added to it; it's probable that hands, will, technology or labour came to the aid of what was done, and the area went up; it was firm enough to support temples, to bear porticoes. A part of Rome is founded, if this verb has any meaning. Is all of Rome founded in this simple sense?

The Tiber, during low water, reveals the deposits of its turbulence. The sand banks are arrested whirlpools, a little congealed in a longer time. The sandglass, as though viscous, slows the flowing time. Rivers and turbulences, liquids and sands. Each laminar layer of water carries a grain, an atom of sand along with it. The Tiber flows with time, it flows with water, it flows with sand; the atoms fall. Lucretius has returned; Livy reveals liquid history and the ages of water. The assembled Roman crowd in the wheat field, pouring the wheat into the low water, is one of its tributaries.

What the silty water is carrying along makes the water a little viscous; the river is no longer merely a time-counter. It carries along sand, it carries along wheat, straw and grain. The river is peasant; the river is bargeman. It flows with grains in the water, of sand or wheat. The atom enters the clepsydra. If you make water glide along, make sand glide along, make grains of wheat glide along, a clock will happen. The Tiber is a clepsydra; the river is an hourglass; the Roman crowd pouring wheat at the Tiber's edge is also a clock. If you let sand flow in the water, pour wheat grain into that silty water, everything changes, through mixture. The clock, the clepsydra, the hourglass don't merely count time. The water is stopped by the sand, and the sand is stopped by the water; the grain slows down the water that slows down the grain and straw. All of time is transformed; it doesn't flow as before. We're going to see, at the bottom of the scanty waters, something like a deposit of time. An immobility? A zero point? The congealed whirlpool of an origin? Can time stop?

The atoms of sand or grain descend the white fall. In the beginning was the Albula, the white river. Only the Albula flows, the ideal laminar clepsydra without mixture. A clock is posited there, ideal, before the city is founded, at the edge of the city, a city founded at the edge of the water. Newborns, the founders are deposited on a dormant sheet of water; a whirlpool of the Tiber in spate was stagnating in this deserted place. The crowd, with full baskets, pours wheat into the low waters, in which the straw and wheat stop. Some carriers deposit the twin's cradle basket on the high waters in this vast solitude. The time-counter immobilizes into a dead whirlpool. The crowd pours out, with full decanting baskets, the grain and straw of violence. The clepsydra immobilizes in the middle of the sand bank to which the hourglass of wheat is attached. Deposit, return to zero. The old king Tiberinus, the prince of Alba the White and the first grain of sand, drowned swimming across the Albula. He must have flowed downward quickly. He rests at the bottom of the river, the first sand bank or the first deposit, so tenuous that he was only a name. Tiberinus, drowned, fixed by the passage of the white waters, the almost drowned twins, fixed by the passage of the high waters, the attached poured harvest, fixed by the passage of the low waters: dating. The king of Alba codes the clock; the twins code the city, and the wheat founds the island, all of them in a stoppage of the time-counter.

Tiberius, Romulus and Remus, the harvest of hatred. A man and a name, two brothers and a murder, multiplicity lastly: growth in the middle of the waters, the city grows.

The first inclination around which the atoms, grains of sand or grains of wheat, fix themselves. Sand banks or knots of straw, an island is born from this, an island of the real, a fragment of the world. Lucretius founds his objects in the fluvial diffusion of the atoms, in the white cataract screwed with whirlpooling stoppages, in the sand banks and knots of wheat. The natural world is founded on the waters. Livy, a historian, following Lucretius, a physicist, founds the social world on the waters.

Physics and history are founded in the same time.

The crowd, at the edge of the water, pours the straw into the water, pours it by the basketful, in cataracts. It was the month of oppressive heat; the river's waters remained low; they disappeared, scarce, into the sand banks; one could have crossed by fording. The wheat flowed like cascades from the baskets; the water hardly flowed at all in the middle of the layers of mud. The principal pouring falls from the men and women; nature held back.

Nature poured the waters, the mud and sand long ago and continually; tomorrow and continually it will carry its loads of sand and mud, but that day, in that month of sultry heat, at the edge of this ford, the new flow issued from human hands. A tributary of sand, a tributary of wheat, two pourings, here are two time-counters and two clocks, two clepsydras or two sandglasses – what is the word for a clock using wheat grains? – here are two times mixing, the time of the Tiber and the time of harvests, the time of the river and the time of violence, the time of sand and lustral time; here are two times at the confluence, knots of time, of mud and of straw. It's human time's turn to be the principal flow; the summer month suspends the world's time a bit. You could have crossed by fording during that time of nil flow during the sultry heat. Physical science, the philosophy of nature, on the Tiber; social sciences on the bank.

History is a knot of different times.

The straw and wheat flowed in a crowd from the baskets and panniers. The crowd poured, spread the wheat, the way blood, pitch and tears pour or are shed.[3] The crowd dispersed the wheat; it disseminated it in the ford; the wheat escaped and became distributed on the muddy and sandy banks. The crowd was throwing the sacrilegious wheat away; it was driving it out from the field belonging to the excluded kings; it was expelling it, as an enemy is dispersed. It let the wheat go; it let it spread; the wheat covered the sand. This wheat produced in abundance in the field of violence abounded in the river's meagre waves. The crowd poured out knots of silt, straw, sand and wheat, as it would have poured bronze. And it saw the bottom of the baskets and panniers.

I'm slowly translating Livy's narrative. The crowd cuts the harvest, he says; it throws it away. The crowd pours it out. I have just used verbs that only translate one verb. Without omission or repetition. The crowd pours.[4] Livy says: *fundo*.[5] And I say: poured, spread, dispersed … all terms of distribution. All terms of liquidity. All terms of abundance, of waters, of purification. But in which, at some moment, metals are poured. The liquids harden; the sowing forms a body.

Livy does not say: *fundo*. Otherwise I would have translated: sit solidly, consolidate on a base, to build. This will only be said after, for the porticoes and temples. But the text doesn't say it; it prefers the word 'support'. For: if only a portico were at issue, then it would only be a question of supporting. If a city were at issue, perhaps it would go differently.

History is founded in time. We now know how.

The crowd founds Rome through the sowing of time.

On that summer day when the great heat made the water fordable, women and men were sowing Rome in the silt.

They founded the solid city through fusion and diffusion.

The flow of the crowd sows the waves, and the Roman *turba* sows the turbulence. The people become the Tiber; during those ages of water, the people mix with the Tiber.

The crowd, martial, expels the harvest from the martial field. One set excludes a set from another set. As a tide can drive away the sand. And the crowd pours a crowd onto another crowd, in the banks of numerous sand.

The crowd didn't separate the straw from the grain; it didn't sort one set from another; it didn't disjoin this crowd from the other. Kill them all; God will recognize his own.

Magna vis hominum, a great crowd, a great force, a great energy, a great violence. Crowds of violence spread in the field of Mars.

Spaces of forces, fields of forces, fields of energy. The sets, the flows and forces are distributed in space. This is the material or the base of history: distribution of energies, of multiplicities. From these distributions, through a certain labour, scattered, islands emerge.

Then the consul, the king, the hero, the historian make history starting from these islands. But they have nothing to do with their constitution.

The foundation is beneath history. Perhaps it laughs at it?

Uncovered here, like a sand bank during low water, is a reality covered over by history, lower than it. A motionless moment during the dog days of summer where he who is fascinated by history no longer pays attention. Nothing notable happens in the annals; this is simply a rite, some ceremonial. Almost some symbol. The precise moment, nevertheless, when the king goes into exile, when his fortune flees. Yes, politics calls a truce; the foreign war and the struggle of the orders are absent on that day; that day doesn't interest the historian. The big actors have disappeared: no consul, no hero, no tribune yet, no more king. Profoundly, no unity. No concept, no unitary idea to recount by, to relate by, no character to stage. And therefore, and suddenly, no illusion. What disappears is the theatre.

The one has vanished; the one has disappeared in the swaths; multi-plicity remains. The crowd pours the king's small change into the river. It drove out the one, named Tarquinius Superbus; it's now throwing away the multiple of the one. The one unites, the one intersects the multiple so that the representation called history might take place. On that hot day, the one drowned in the cataract of wheat. History is in parentheses; the Tiber holds back from flowing, as though time has called a truce, amid the silty banks and the sandy ford.

Multiplicity remains. The field is a set, and the harvest is a set. It won't be threshed; the straw and the grain will be left together. The crowd is a set, and the sand and the mud, by banks, are also sets in the multiplicity river.

The one is no longer there to represent them. Expressly, it was expelled. The one isn't there for history to represent them to us. History is no longer there.

The work on that hot day when the river could have been crossed by fording didn't consist in sorting out one grain of wheat to say and conceive the entire pouring of wheat, didn't consist in extracting one straw to represent the harvest, in pulling one mask out of the crowd to hide the multitude; the work didn't consist in the sorting or in the threshing either; the threshing didn't take place. On that summer day, in this field said to be of violence, the crowd didn't use flails; it left the straw and wheat together; it left behind the flails of threshing and of sorting, of distinction, the flails of work and of history. All those who take up the flail will die by the flail. They didn't have to sort; they could have crossed by fording.

The straw remains in the grain; the grain remains in the straw, subset in subset; the undistinguished crowd scatters in the harvest; the harvest dispersed in the field is spread by the crowd in the sand, in which the mud and sand mix, subset in subset, amid the bogs and the backwaters. And the water is low enough for it to, far from passing on, mix with the sand. The sets here are flows. Mixed.

Intersected by the one or united by the one, the sets are only categories. Fixed, static, they are only classes. If by chance, if by miracle the one is excluded or put in parentheses, this fixed class will become a set again, it will become a flow again; it will count its own time. The one will no longer steal its time. This is no longer the time of *fasti consulares*, nor the time of *annales maximi*, nor the time of annuities, this is no longer the time of the plebs, the time of a formed category; it's the time of the crowd that pours, it's the time of the multitude scattered amid the harvest, and it's the time of the population ravaging the field of Mars in which the harvest is ripe, it's the time of the mob, the pourer of wheat into sandy waters. The plebs is no longer the order at the orders of the tribune, or at the counter orders of the patricians; it is no longer squeezed like sardines in its class; it takes on all its other names, the names it takes on when it moves, alone, in the clamours;

it becomes dynamic again; it is force, it is energy: what enters in the wheat of the field of Mars on that summer's day is not a category; it's a great power, *magna vis hominum*, a great force of men or the great force of men together. Everything happens as though the set were frozen by the one, solidified by the one, as though it were immobilized by it. But Tarquinius Superbus has fled, and the consuls didn't enter the harvest – no heroes on the horizon. On this hot day, the categories thaw, the plebs liquifies; the sets become flows again. Representation is closed: separation, immobility, theatre and theory, illusion, and the unities. Livy's narrative stops, a bit like the Tiber's waters; it uncovers its time-counters, the mixture of the banks of sand, mud and straw. The narrative comes untied.

The sets are flows.[6] The crowd flows in the middle of the undone sheaves. The poured harvest isn't taken into account in the economy; as we are told, it is sacrificed. The crowd, pouring, pours the harvest into the pouring river. A human cataract, a cataract of wheat, a cataract of sand and silt, in the middle of the withheld water of the reservoirs. The flows mix together. The water mixes with its own loads; the harvest mixes with what the river carries and its sediments; I imagine men falling, as though swept away, in the middle of the banks. The flows fasten together; they form a sheaf, an exchanger, a knot. Adhesions in the bog water, a numerous bouquet of several times.

A certain time must be stopped for several times to be as though liberated. Quite as though the time of history was freezing, covering over several other times, as though it was living off them, a parasite. As though political time was imprisoning, in its representation, all the others. The time of kings has stopped; the time of the *fasti consulares* has barely begun, so the immense sheaf, the immense knot happens: the time of the waters of the old Albula slowed by the dog days of summer – the rhythm of the world – under Canis Major come back again, the natural time of bringings, of carryings of sand and silt, bogs, backwaters, dead arms in the nearly empty river bed, the living time of the harvest, straw and grain, the living time of men and women, crimson and sweating in the field, plant time, animal time, mixed together, during the great heat of summer, the time of technicity, scythes and sickles to cut what was sown, the embankment soon built between the sand bank and the shore, between the island and the city, the time of collectivity, the crowd, mob or population dispersed in the harvest, the time of religion, the expulsion of said harvest in cataracts into the river, the rite to the god Mars of violence, this is the time knotted with seven different times, the time that mixes and exchanges beneath the single time representation of history, beneath the abduction by unicity.

In this point, beneath the island that came about, in this point and forming, in this knot of time, the island itself, are squeezed together all the levels of being or the real. Together they form the foundation. The world, the sun, the waters. The inert: liquid, fluid, viscous, solidified, firm, lastly compact. The living: vegetal in its straw, animal in the arms of men and the strength of women. The crowds of the collective and the technologies of work, agriculture, craft industry, civil engineering. Finally Mars above the heads and in the heads. The entire ladder of the real, without omitting anything, without repeating anything, plunges down into the banks of the Tiber here as soon as the king leaves, when the consul is silent. With the one erased, the real returns, as though irrepressible. The one weighs on it, and sits on it, and covers it with its shadow and cruelty. Let the one get up and leave, and the foundation suddenly appears. A complex, knotted, multiple, rich, powerful beauty.

Nothing happened. For the historian, certainly, nothing happened. No archaeologist will be found to go look for the straw beneath the island; the straw must have left with the current as soon as Orion replaced Canis Major. Some circumstantial lamina of water must have even carried off the pollen, that stubborn pollen that remains a thousand years. Nothing happened that can be found again. There is no remainder, there is no monument. And yet it's this fusion that founds. These levels of the real melt together in order to found the city and history.[7] There is no remainder and yet everything flows from here. No monument remains, and every monument comes to us from that day, from that summer's day when one could have crossed by fording.

Nothing happened worthy of historical attention. A rite, some ceremonial. Positively, it isn't possible, it isn't probable that a pile of grain and straw forming a hurdle dam left a beach of sand continued by an embankment on which some day some well-founded portico could be put up. Islands are not sown like this; a city is not sown like this. Certainly, nothing happened; what is told here moreover is not probable.

It was a question of a rite. It's a question in the text that recounts it of an image, of a symbol, of three words of literature. Beautiful. Three lines of beauty amid the carnage and oppressive hatred, amid a text without a single word of love. No, it's not love that causes hatred to call a truce; it's an abrupt rending by beauty. The high sun of a summer's day, the ford opened amid the sand, the large harvest to be expended in the low water, the tanned multitude with slow gestures on the raised banks, a pouring of wheat. Fascination of the knots of straw in the mud, the wheat forms fascines for the embankment. What interrupts the hateful and repeated representation – bloody and imaginary, insane – is a reality strike, as one says a lightning strike: this sudden confluence of several pourings, this knot dense with different times. Nothing historical happens; it seems nothing but an empty symbol happens.

And yet this is where, like lightning, the real comes. History is in parentheses; the usual masks – pride and arrogance – are absent; here is pure evocation. The sun, the harvest, the sand. The unities being dissolved, the multitudes appear. The characters, the proper names, the unitary concepts capture the multitudes, repressing them; the multitudes disappear. The crowd is repressed. It is repressed by the unities; this is its function, and its habit is its erasure. Redouble attention when the narrative says: multitude. The crowd returns. It returns at hot moments. The harvest returns. The sand returns when the water is low. The real returns, multiple and numerous. The real is sand; it is a bank; it is a set. Its concept is nothing but its capture and its repression. The multiple returns – river, silt, crowd, harvest. Who ever speaks of such things in the Senate? Who harangues the front lines in the field like this? What tribune, ever, used this eloquence? Historical hatred of the world, historical hatred of number, historical hatred of the real.

The narrative plunges to the bottom of the Tiber, to the bottom of the world, to the bottom of the Roman crowd's number, to the bottom of the harvest, to the very – sandy – bottom of the foundation. Seeking the natural world, it finds rite, symbol and the ceremonial. The narrative plunges to the bottom of the rite; it is the myth of foundation; it goes from Mars, the god of violence, to the liturgies of purification; it ends with porticoes and temples. Seeking the cultural world, seeking the cultual world, it finds the river, the ford, the harvest and the sand. As though the real, natural, was at the end of the rite, as though the symbolic was at the end of the natural world. The confluence of the world and the other world, of the world and the back-worlds, of the real and the imagined, behind the fine screen of historical representation, a bright and dark alliance, deep and suddenly there, of nature and fascinations, behind the time of hatred and power, behind the time of history itself, perhaps imaginary for having excluded the world and the rite.

The real: when the rational can't go there, may the rite go there. The knot of nature and culture. The passage, ford, the passage finally where the ice thaws during the heat of summer.

Contrary to the literature and experience, contrary to all good sense and all good philosophy, the crowd on that day didn't found on the solid. Doesn't a good foundation dig into rock or stone? It's not on a rock that the Church will be built, but on a man of flesh named Peter, on a decomposed body, on a metaphor, on a transport, a bringing, a carrying.[8] The crowd therefore on that summer's day didn't found its temples on rock; it didn't found them on stone; it founded them on what melts.[9] A good foundation occurs on what moves. The crowd founds the island on liquid, on the viscous, on the sandy, on the muddy banks. The crowd founds the island; it founds it, as in a crucible, that hot day. One only founds on what flows; one only founds on time. Time always avenges itself on what happens without it. The crowd, wise, takes time into account. The crowd founds, but the river, afterward, will found.

Look at the river's shore, look at those jagged edges, look at the alluvia depart from the graphite, the marble and the ophite; the solid is not solid; it erodes and it flees. The sand in the bank is the small change of what appears to be hard. Look at the water scatter in droplets, depart in steam or evaporate, run through the clouds, the waves, the spindrifts; not one atom of it has gone missing since the world was the world; liquid is not liquid; it's the most solid, the most resistant, the most permanent of the beings of the world. Founding must be done on the liquid, not on the solid; founding must be done on time. Or on sand, the sandglass of time.

Rome is first founded on the Albula, the white river, in which amid the *turba* and the whirlpools the old father Tiberinus drowned.[10] Rome is first founded on the Tiber, in the dead arms of the flood in which the basket of the two twins whirls around itself for a long time. Rome is founded on the island; porticoes and temples are built on the island and embankment; we all come from an island between two arms, between two rivers, between two times.

Foundation is a thought, a practice of the moving. Of fusion and mixture. Of the multiplicity of times.

In the literal sense, yes, all foundation is current.

The embankment was built from nature to culture. From there, one could easily return.

Mars is the father of the twins by the vestal. Mars is the father of the harvest by the field that was consecrated to him. Mars is the father of the city, and murder is the father of Rome. Romulus kills Remus, or Remus was killed by the mob of nascent Rome. And Romulus was carried off to the heavens, or he was cut into pieces by the group of first Fathers. Mars is always there, since the dawn.

No. Mars goes absent that day; his harvest is not ordinary. That day of harvest, when the Tiber could be crossed by fording during the immense motionless heat of summer, that day was the only one when no one was killed. History kills; history never ceases to kill. From the day Tiberinus, the king of Alba, drowned in the middle of the first *turba* of the Tiber up until the day when the city of Rome fell into the hands of the barbarians, from the founded city to the captured city, history has feasted on murders; it is ceaselessly reborn from this fury for slaughter.

Our senses no longer tolerate this immense sewage field. The education of my youth, the education of the youth of the fathers of our fathers were entrusted to Livy and Virgil, renowned for their piety, their gentleness, their wisdom, their austerity, and to Plutarch, for his examples. Who to cite as an example? The repugnant Brutus who enjoys killing his sons, the repugnant Virginius who enjoys killing Virginia, the repugnant old Horatius who regrets that the last of his sons wasn't killed? Barbarians, all of them, by a bloody pen. Here, Aequi, Volsci, Sabines, Etruscans, Gauls, Carthaginians are dispatched by the thousands; on their bodies is built the greatness of Rome. What greatness? What culture makes us believe that this is greatness? A history to make you vomit blood, a culture to make you vomit with disgust. Philosophers, historians and moralists with sturdy stomachs who give us assassins and murders to see, admire and imitate. Culture has never been born; education has not begun; philosophy and history are the continuation of barbarism by other means, by the same means.

We no longer have such a good stomach. The piles of corpses that delighted our fathers' competitive morality, that made history appetizing to them, those mass graves have grown all the way to the universal. Our old culture, our old morality, our old science, our archaic history now have the means to superslaughter humanity. A different sensibility has since grown. Many exploits that commanded the admiration of our ancestors today fill us with horror. If this is how history is made, we only have one goal: to change histories. Not to transform it; repetition always reappears in falsely new forms. To change histories. To go elsewhere. If this is how culture is made, we have never experienced anything in regard to it except repugnance and disgust. To go elsewhere. To invent something else. Or another time.

On that summer's day when the ford opened beneath one's feet, as though the river of blood had stopped or its pools dried up, it was only wheat being delivered up by the crowd to the time of historicity. It wasn't the king that it tore apart. The flail didn't beat upon a body in pieces, falling, rolling, from the top of the water's edge, dispersed, consumed, spread, poured into the waves of the Tiber. It was a day of peace on the sand banks, in the wheat field. This day was another day; this place was another place;

nothing like this has ever happened in all of history. How did our old history retain the memory of this?

From the lynched twin, a king is born; Rome is founded, we are told. From a dead king torn limb from limb, an interrex is born. From a raped daughter, the Republic is born, another foundation. From a virgin killed by her father or by a decemvir, liberty is reborn. This is the law, the sole law. From a corpse, always, some unity is born: group, class, city, reign, a new era, another false newness. This recurrent corpse in current history is its current foundation. Those who discover a head while digging the foundations of the Capitol supposed, I think, that their ancestors deposited it there. Death is the perpetual motor of this repetition, precisely its eternal return.

But on that summer's day, during the scorching dog days, it's a torrent of wheat that descends the bank, it's a cataract of mixed straw and grain, poured by the basketful by the crowd from high on the shores, that tumbles down into the Tiber. This cascade rips apart the eternal return. The assembled crowd in the swamp of Capra tears the king's corpse limb from limb; the mob around Remus slaughters him beneath its blows; the star of horses' quarters, distracted, the dictator of Alba; Tarpeia disappears beneath the bracelets or under the shields, which didn't fall from the sky; Turnus suffocates in the Ferentina spring beneath a hurdle loaded with lapidary stones. Piles, scattered limbs, precious stones, the crowd has beaten bodies with the flail. The crowd here is pouring wheat, unbeaten wheat, wheat not separated from its straw stalk. What then is this wheat, this harvest, what then is this that's flowing toward the Tiber?

This. What is it that the crowd is showing in silence in raising their baskets, in elevating the bottom of the panniers, in revealing their wicker bottoms?

This is the body.

The body of all the dead and all the murdered.

On that day, under the great summer sun, no one takes the place in the centre of the crowd; no one rolls, bleeding, in the field of violence; no torn apart victim descends down the bank, in tatters. On that day, the multitude only harvested wheat.

Today the multitude has contented itself with the harvest. It didn't sort it, it didn't beat it, it didn't grind it, it didn't crush it into flour, nor did mix it with a leaven or make bread. The harvest has deviated from its end, mixed with sand and mud, for a non-bleeding dough.

This is the body.

The poured body, the spilled blood. Poured in the sand, spilled in the silt, mixed into the low waters.

This is no one's body today, no one's blood; this is only wheat, this is only straw.

Peace.

Magna vis hominum simul fudere in Tiberim, a great multitude of men poured wheat together into the Tiber for the foundation of the city. *Qui pro multis effundetur*, this blood will be poured out for a multitude.[11] By it, for it, before it.

The multitude pours or unity pours for it.

There wasn't, on that summer's day, any Friday after the speculative Holy Thursday. No body, no dead man, no tomb beneath the island. There is no horror beneath the Tiberine island. No decapitated head, no ignoble reliquary.

History goes in the other direction; it suddenly turns back along the eternal return's dismal path. No dead man, no Friday, no bread, without ground flour, no Thursday. Is this Holy Wednesday? The multitude goes no further than the wheat; it goes no further than the multitude. It holds back from flowing, like the waters of the Tiber. Time goes back up from the body to the bread and from the bread to the wheat; it has left the wheat mixed with its straw. It goes back up toward Palm Sunday.

That day of sun and low waters on which not one man suffered or was put to death, that day of full harvest and crossing by fording suddenly unveils the tragic to us. *Coriolanus* is a tragedy; *Horace* is a tragedy. Here are two heroes; they kill; they are about to be put to death; the crowd follows them, the soldiers, the people, the women. Rome is the source of the tragic.

But that day of sun, before the held-back waters, there was no tragedy. That day: there was no day. Perhaps one day the crowd poured a harvest of straw and wheat onto the banks of sand and silt, but above all hundreds of days were needed for the alluvium and sediments to come and fill up these knots of wheat; thousands of days were needed for the fusion to harden. No day, no place. Here the silt is deposited; the sand and the straw are carried there, whirlpools and circumstances, turbulences, and no one has ever said who the temple was consecrated to, and we would no longer be able to find the porticoes. There was no place. And above all, there was nobody. The crowd enters into the wheat; it scatters; it disperses the harvest; it spreads; it spreads the wheat in the scattered silt. So who was there that day? Everybody, nobody. Each person lost like a straw in a haystack, like a grain of wheat in a wheat pile, like a grain of sand in a sand bank or like an atom in the river of atoms, the Albula. Nothing notable happened in the annals that day.

How does the multiple change into unity? Via the tragic. Via the tragic, the here occurs, amid the dubious and uncertain places, the now occurs, amid the moving duration, the this that passes and is represented occurs, and the proper name to be retained. Via the tragic, the *hic et nunc*, the *ecce homo* occurs. Via the tragic, the spatial, temporal, nominal capture of the multiple occurs. Via the tragic, the concept occurs.

Poets had misgivings during the French seventeenth century about respecting in tragedy the rule said to be of unities. It was said to be superfluous; they asked: by what aberration does one submit to such a constraint? No. This rule is not supererogatory; it is essential. Better, tragedy is made for it. Better still, tragedy is made only for it. I mean by this that it is the crucible in which the unities are forged.

We could claim all this endlessly and put it forward without proof. We wouldn't know it without a counterproof. Now on that summer's day that lasted several summers, on the edge of that ford that no doubt often fluctuated, what occurred has no name, word, genre or category; what occurred has no concept: nor time, nor place, nor event; this is the non-tragic, or that soil on which the tragic comes or doesn't come, or that soil on which history will be written.

Let the multiple graze in peace; tragedy vanishes.

And consequently, history is erased.

I know what I'm writing, finally, and in what genre I'm writing it.

Time descends the days along the sand banks; the place where a temple is built is uncertain; an uncreated hero is distributed in the anonymous crowd. No flail comes to separate, right in the middle of the population, the king's grain from the common straw; the hero neither dies nor fructifies, the grain neither dies nor gives fruit. During those non-dated times, the heroes come to nothing. And this is how that crowd intends it. Flails hadn't yet been invented.

These examples fluctuate. Like the river. Like the sand banks. Like the crowd. Like the harvest.

No, this isn't history. Is it prehistory? Maybe. But all the same, it's not the time of before since the foundation requires the river's carryings, that is to say, the course of its time. It is not prehistory: it's what history discovers when its representation calls a truce. It's what shoots like a geyser out of a fissure when the king is no longer there, or the consul or the hero or the concept, or any unity: pure multiplicity. The material of history, its conditions, its reality before.

It's what history discovers before its instituting tragedies. It's history's reality before or beneath the tragedies of its beginnings. This thing is so conditional that through it I comprehend how things are with tragedy;

those inaugural or percurrent moments of our history in which the unities are forged that allow it to be said, represented and thought: the places, the times, the murders and the masks. In short, the work, yes, the work of unification.

On that hot day, the work didn't happen. The harvest was thrown into the water. History was thrown into the Tiber. A Sunday of rest.

Shakespeare and Corneille read Livy admirably. They indeed marked out the recommencements of time, the fires in which the elements are forged. Historians read Livy admirably; they detail the time represented down to the atom. They thus rejoin a cloud of multiplicities, which is perhaps the bottom. The tragedians go beyond representations; they go and are behind the décor, in the places where the action itself is produced.

On that harvest day, there was no action. No history or tragedy. Through the dense massif of history, burst into a crazy myriad of doubts, through this massif and its strong, constitutive times of tragedy, a path sometimes runs, a rare one, by which another world is reached: philosophy.

Behind the historiated, behind the tragic – the distribution of multiplicities. Sand banks, turbulences, mob, crowd, harvest – lost to our accounts.

These are the low waters; the Tiber uncovers its banks; we can cross by fording, descend to the age of the low water level. The foundation of sand caught in the knots of straw, the moving foundation, the current foundation, a confluent whirlpool of the time of nature and the time of humans deposited at the bottom, can be seen. Fluctuating, soft multiplicities emerge. A space of distributions and flows is uncovered, in which forces pass, in which energies are consumed, peacefully.

The water now rises above the low water level. We can no longer cross by fording. It's the flood waters of the river Albula; Tiberinus, the king of Alba, drowns in them. It's the flood waters of the river Tiber; the straw basket in which the twins are deposited becomes motionless and turns about itself. Tragedy, when the water rises, is the machine that constructs the unities, time, places, action and characters. A given person was a victim, at that time, of the monstrous vortex, others on the contrary escaped from it at a given moment. The tragic transforms the multiplicities into unities. The water rises again; this is current history. We recount what goes on and what goes by; we recount what is written on the old white river.

Beneath history is tragedy. Beneath Livy, in him, Corneille and Shakespeare write and read. But even lower, beneath tragedy itself, is the foundation of sand and straw, the peaceful multiplicities, without murder, without putting to death, beneath the motionless summer sun.

Here lies the foundation; I hardly dare to say reality.

NOTES

The Greatness of the Romans: the Fable of the Termites

1   Sets=*prend*. This word will periodically pop up in the text. I'll translate it for the most part as some form of harden since the word 'set' will mostly be too vague to convey this precise sense.

2   **Serres' footnotes** will be so designated. All the rest belong to the translator. On a general note, to understand Serres' *Rome*, it is essential to read the indicated passages. It is also highly recommended to consult a bilingual Latin/English edition of Livy's *Ab urbe condita*. The Loeb Classical Library version is the standard text.

BLACK BOX: The Trampled Multiplicity

1   Serres himself switches between the Latin Hercules and the Greek Heracles, here and elsewhere.

2   Direction=*sens*, which can mean both 'meaning' and 'direction'. I will use whichever seems more appropriate given the context. But bear in mind when reading 'meaning' that it might also mean 'direction', and vice versa. I will occasionally use 'direction or meaning' when either or both may be meant or merely write the French *sens*.

3   Nonsense=*contresens*, which can also mean the wrong direction. So the misleading direction of the tracks blocks meaning. *Contresens* has already been translated as 'wrong direction' in the previous paragraph. I will sometimes translate this term as 'counter-direction'. It can also mean nonsense or misinterpretation.

4   Mob=*tourbe*, which derives from the Latin *turba*.

5   History=*l'histoire*, which in French can either refer to a definite history, in this case Livy's, or history in general. I've done my best to sort this out, but do keep in mind when you read 'history' that it might just be referring to Livy's – the – history and vice versa.

6   By reversing the direction into the wrong direction, or meaning into nonsense=*en inversant le sens en contresens*.

7   Corneille's *Horace*, Act 3, Scene 5. The phrase of the old Horatius is often called one of the most sublime in French literature. 'What did you wish that he should do?' Old Horatius: 'That he die.'

8   Cattle=*bœufs*. *Bœufs* can also be translated as oxen. Hence the paradox.

9   Serres is now discussing La Fontaine's 'The Sick Lion and the Fox' and 'The Lion Grown Old'.

10   **Serres' footnote**: *Genesis*, University of Michigan Press, 1997. Chapter 1.

11   Master=*chef*. Masterwork=*chef d'œuvre*. Head=*chef*.

12   'Geometral' is a term from Leibniz. 'Scenography represents objects in perspective, and ichnography is the elevation, that is to say, the horizontal plane or geometral.' (Michel Serres, *Le Système de Leibniz et ses modèles mathématiques*, PUF, Paris: 1968), 153.

13   Ignores=*méconnaît*; to know=*connaître*.

14   Untangled=*demêlé*. 'Mêlée' comes from a French verb for mixing or mingling.

15   **Serres' footnote**: *The Parasite*, 155–64, Theory of the Joker. [Translator's note: the previous translator saw fit to translate *blanc* as 'blank' here. While *blanc* can indeed mean 'blank', I do not think such a translation is warranted. White is the sum of all colours, pure potentiality, for Serres. It is not empty or blank.]

16   Agency=*instance*, which can mean the agencies of the psyche in Freud's psychology or an authority that has the power of decision. In a linguistic context, it can also mean an instance of discourse. Serres may sometimes be using it in its etymological sense of *instare*, standing near or in, being present. When it clearly doesn't mean some kind of decision-making body or Freudian-style agency, I'll write it as 'in-stance' to differentiate it from the common English meaning of the term. All occurrences of 'authority' translate *instance*, except on pages 176 and 199, where it translates *authorité*.

CITY OF ALBA: The White Multiplicity

1   This is a reference to the French idiom *se regarder en chiens de faïence* [looking at each other like crockery dogs] meaning to stand and glare at one another.

2   Wooden tongue=*langue de bois*, which means cant.

3   Whitened=*blanchis*, which can also mean absolved.

4   Eddies=*tourbillon*; *turba=tourbe*, which suggests turbulence, but would normally be translated as mob. All instances of *turba* in this book that occur in the context of a river translate *tourbe*.

5   Tracks=*traces*, which can also mean traces.

6   Undecided or incised=*indécise ou incise*. The connection to cutting in 'undecided' is clearer in the French.

7   Riverbank is *rive* here and in the next paragraph. It was simply rendered as 'bank' in the previous paragraph.

8   *Lame* could also be translated as lamina or sheet here.

9   A reference to a line from Corneille's *Horace*: Rome, the sole object of my resentment. Act 4, Scene 5.

10 Software=*logiciel*, which also evokes the logos. Just below this, 'hardware' is *matériel*, which also evokes material or the material world.

11 Clarity=*clarté*, which can also mean light and has already been translated that way in this paragraph. Keep this in mind whenever you come across this word. It will also sometimes be translated as brightness.

12 Galileo is well-named because his name in French, *Galilée*, is the same as the name for the region of Galilee, *Galilée*.

13 Shoot out=*fusent*; diffuse=*se diffusent*.

14 Brook Taylor (1685–1731), English mathematician; Helge von Koch (1870–1924), Swedish mathematician.

15 Unfolding=*dépliage*; implicated=*impliquées*, both of which are based on *pli*, fold. I have sometimes translated the various forms of *impliquées* as the relevant form of imply.

16 A running end is the end of a line used to tie a knot. A standing end is the end not so used.

17 Mixed sets=*ensembles à mélange*, which in *Genesis* (trans. Geneviève

James and James Nielson, Ann Arbor: University of Michigan Press, 1995, 111) is translated as a 'mixed aggregate'.

18 Serres is making a reference to an old children's song: *La boulangère a des écus*. It continues *qui ne lui coûte guère*. The baker has money, that doesn't cost her much. *Ecu* can mean either a kind of money or an escutcheon.

19 Layering=*feuilletage*, which means the layered dough of a puff pastry. In the preceding clause, 'partitions' is *partitions*, which was translated earlier in the paragraph as 'divisions of the field.' In general it means divisions.

20 'Now' in French is *maintenant*, whose root means holding in one's hand.

21 Adelos=*adèle*, a word that doesn't appear in any dictionary I can find. My assumption is that it is a negative for the Greek *delos*, visible or clear.

22 Paul Verlaine, *Sagesse* 3.3. My translation, one aiming more at accuracy than poetry.

EMPIRE: The Fragmented Multiplicity

1 Peter's rock=*La pierre de Pierre*. In French and Latin, the word for a rock or stone and the equivalent name for Peter are the same.

2 Parasitic interference=*parasites*, which has all the meanings the English 'parasite' has except one: *parasites* can also mean static, atmospherics, interference.

3 The name *Caesar* comes from *caesus*, to cut.

4 Glue=*colle*.

5 Mob=*tourbe*; vortex=*tourbillon*. Noise and quarrel=*noise*. *Noise* usually means quarrel. In Serres, it usually means noise.

6 Passes here and goes through this=*passe là et passe par là*.

7 'Superbus' means proud or arrogant in Latin.

8 Returning ghosts=*revenants*, which derives from *revenir*, to return. It normally means ghosts.

SUFFRAGE: The Assembled Multiplicity

1   Cut stones=*pierre taillée*; cutting=*taille*. 'Detail' derives from a French verb for cutting into pieces.

2   Monopoly or mono-pole=*monopole*. The French word for monopoly suggests the notion of a mono-pole more than the English does. I will mostly translate this term as 'mono-pole' but will occasionally use both or 'monopoly' depending on the context.

3   Power=*puissance*, a term which, beyond the usual meanings, is also used to translate Aristotle's *dunamis*. In English, Aristotle's term can be translated as potential, capacity, potency or power.

4   Unfortunately, this sense of 'capable' does not exist in English, and I haven't been able to discover an equivalent English term. Here's the best definition I could find: 'a segment capable of an angle is a segment of a circle such that every angle inscribed in it is equal to this first angle.' It is related in some way to the inscribed angle theorem.

5   Suffrage derives from the Latin *sub fragor*, under the *fragor*.

6   'Candidate' derives from *candidus*, white. Candidates would dress in white.

7   'Metaphor' derives from a Greek word for transfer or transport.

8   Here lies=*ci-gît*, which is mainly used for gravestones.

AENEAS, SABINES, TARQUINS, CORIOLANUS: The Composite Multiplicity

1   Guest=*hôte*, which can equally mean 'host', both of which derive from the Latin word *hospes*, from which the term 'hospitality' also comes. I will translate *hôte* as 'guest' or 'host' depending on the context, and sometimes simply as the French *hôte* when it's not clear from the context or both senses may be meant.

2   Evil=*mal*, which can also mean disease. I will mainly translate it as 'evil', but will occasionally use 'disease'.

3   A reference to Flaubert's short story 'The Legend of St. Julian, the Hospitaller'.

4   The excluded third or middle=*le tiers exclu*, which usually means the excluded middle, but Serres also reads it literally as the excluded third. I will translate it as one or the other using whichever seems to be the more predominant sense given the context. Sometimes, as here, I will combine them as 'the excluded middle or third' when both seem to be meant or the context isn't clear, but when I don't, do remember that the other sense may also be present.

5   Merged=*confondus*; melted together=*fondus*.

6   Master=*maître*, which could also mean teacher.

7   Peasant=*paysan*; landscape=*paysage*; land=*pays*.

8   To right history=*arraisonner l'histoire*, which usually means 'reason with'. Are right=*ont raison*. Two sentences below 'have rights over' is *ont raison de*, which normally means 'get the better of'. Serres seems to be playing with words more than using exact meanings.

9   A reference to Hegel's famous master–slave dialectic in *The Phenomenology of Spirit*.

10 Potency=*puissance*; power=*pouvoir*.

WAR AND PLAGUE: The Multiplicity in Representation

1   Serres capitalizes these days, which evokes Good Friday and Maundy Thursday.

2   The 'first comer' and 'the person adhering to me' are both female.

3   Neither melted nor chained together=*pas fondus ni enchaînés*, which refers back to Serres' previous use of *fondu enchaîné*, or 'chain of crossfades', as I translated it above.

4   To prevent a possible misunderstanding, I should point out that none of the instances of 'state' that follow refer to a political state.

5   Hotel=*hôtel*, which can also mean a kind of private residence akin to a mansion.

6   In French, the word for daylight and the word for day are the same, *jour*.

7 To understand the use of 'Greatest' and 'Best' in the last two paragraphs, I refer you to the inscription of the Temple of Jupiter Optimus Maximus.

8 Star=*étoile*, which evokes a lead dancer, but not a movie star; grid=*quadrillage*, which also evokes dance, the quadrille.

9 See Alfred de Vigny's *Servitude et grandeur militaires*.

10 Serres uses the adjective *courant* here, which can mean 'ordinary', 'common', but also 'current' in the sense of happening now. It is based on the verb *courir*, to run, and so could possibly mean 'running' or maybe even 'flowing'. 'Ordinary' is *ordinaire*.

11 Forked yoke=*fourche*, which is simply called a fork in French; *furca* in Latin.

IN THE CITY: The Agitated Multiplicity

1 Clear and bright=*clair*.

2 Authority=*instance*, which also has the same etymology as 'institution'. Regarding the use of *instance*, in this passage Serres evokes poles, suggesting 'in-stance'; functions, suggesting Freudian-style 'agency'; and uses a phrase, *instance dernière*, suggesting 'authority' be used. Thinking 'agency' to be too active and 'in-stance' to be a neologism to be used only when absolutely necessary, I went with 'authority'.

3 The word 'catastrophe' for Serres refers to limits on the unlimited.

4 To prevent misunderstanding, expanse=*étendue*. 'Expands' in the previous sentence is *s'expanse*.

5 Turns=*verse*, which might normally mean to pour, but Serres is using it in its Latin etymological sense of turning or revolving. It will be translated here as some form of 'turn' or 'rotate'. 'Turn' in the following sentence is a different verb, *tourne*. 'Toward', in this passage, is *vers*.

6 The name Claudius comes from a Latin word for lame. The 'inequality' may also refer to his uneven legs.

7 Serres is referring to *concitatos*, which literally reads as *con* or with, hence accord, and *citatos* or to move.

8 A reference to a slogan from May 1968: *sous les pavés, la plage* [Under the paving stones, the beach].

9 See the first footnote for the chapter 'City of Alba'.

10 This would normally be translated as 'divide in order to conquer'.

11 Do long division=*poser une division*, which literally reads as to put or place a division.

IN THE FIELD: The Multiplicity in Peace

1 Generatrix=*génératrice*. The common meaning would be a female generator.

2 Consummation=*consommation*, which can also mean consumption.

3 Pour or are shed=*verse*. The verb *verser* can mean both pouring, and shedding tears or blood. Keep this in mind from here on out whenever you read the word 'shed'.

4 Pours=*coule*. *Couler* can mean flowing, pouring, and casting a metal, among other things. I've translated it as 'pour' or 'flow' depending on the context.

5 This Latin verb can have two meanings: pour or found.

6 Flows=*flux*. In the following sentence, 'flows' is *se coule*.

7 Melt together=*se fondent*; to found=*fonder*.

8 Rock=*pierre*; Peter=*Pierre*.

9 What melts=*du fondant*. All instances of 'melt' translate some form of *fonder* from here on.

10 The *turba* and the whirlpools=*la tourbe et les tourbillons*. 'Whirls' in the next sentence is *tourbillonne*.

11 See Matthew 26.28. Or 'the blood will be shed for a multitude.'